LIFE'S DOMINION

AN ARGUMENT ABOUT ABORTION AND EUTHANASIA

Ronald Dworkin

HarperCollins*Publishers*

HarperCollins*Publishers*
77–85 Fulham Palace Road,
Hammersmith, London W6 8JB

Published by HarperCollins*Publishers* 1993

1 3 5 7 9 8 6 4 2

First published in the United States by
Alfred A. Knopf 1993

A catalogue record for this book
is available from the British Library

ISBN 0 00 215934 1

Set in Janson

Printed in Great Britain by
Butler & Tanner Ltd, Frome and London

Ronald Dworkin is Professor of Jurisprudence at the University of Oxford and Professor of Law at New York University. His books include *Taking Rights Seriously*, *A Matter of Principle* and *Law's Empire* (available in Fontana Press).

Also by Ronald Dworkin

LAW'S EMPIRE
A MATTER OF PRINCIPLE
TAKING RIGHTS SERIOUSLY

For Anthony and Jennifer

CONTENTS

LIFE'S DOMINION

1

THE
EDGES OF
LIFE

Abortion, which means deliberately killing a developing human embryo, and euthanasia, which means deliberately killing a person out of kindness, are both choices for death. The first chooses death before life in earnest has begun, the second after it has ended. Each choice has been condemned and defended for millennia. But never have the arguments been so passionate, so open, and so evenly divided, and never has controversy about each one been so closely connected to controversy about the other, as in the United States and Europe now.

The argument over euthanasia has suddenly exploded into front-page news. Doctors are now beginning openly to admit what the profession once kept secret: that doctors sometimes kill patients who ask to die, or help such patients to kill themselves. No Western country formally permits doctors to kill patients, but the Dutch parliament has declared that doctors who do so will not be punished if they follow statutory guidelines. Euthanasia now accounts for 2 percent of deaths in that country, and the Dutch practice has provoked intense controversy not only there but in America and elsewhere. In 1991, a New York doctor disclosed that he had prescribed lethal pills for a leukemia patient and had told her how many she should take to die. The patient had followed his instructions, and a grand jury was asked to decide whether he should be prosecuted for assisting suicide, a crime punishable by a jail term. It decided that he should not. In 1992, in England, a doctor injected potassium chloride into a rheumatoid arthritis patient dying in horrible pain and begging to be killed; the doctor reported the injection in hospital records and he was prosecuted and convicted of attempted murder. (The charge would have been murder if the body had not been cremated, and an autopsy had shown that the injection had actually killed her.) In two American states the question of whether euthanasia should be treated as an act of mercy or an act of murder has been fought out in politics. In 1991, the voters of Washington State narrowly defeated a referendum bill that would have legalized euthanasia there, and in 1992 similar legislation was defeated in California. In both cases it was expected, well before the election, that the bill would pass, but groups opposing euthanasia, including the Catholic church, waged bitter and effective campaigns, spending far more than the groups supporting it. Two days after the California election, however, the prestigious *New England Journal of Medicine* published two articles, one supporting physician-assisted suicide and the other direct euthanasia. No one thinks that the issue has yet been resolved in the United States—*Newsday* said that it "will be at the front of the 'rights' agenda for some time to come."[1]

But almost everywhere the battle over abortion is even fiercer and politically more important than the argument over euthanasia. The war between anti-abortion groups and their opponents is America's new version of the terrible seventeenth-century European civil wars of religion. Opposing armies march down streets or pack themselves into protests at abortion clinics, courthouses, and the White House, screaming at and spitting on and loathing one another. Abortion is tearing America apart. It is also distorting its politics, and confounding its constitutional law.

The dispute racks other nations as well. Battles between "pro-choice" and anti-abortion groups erupt periodically throughout Europe, and Germany's struggle to adopt a national abortion law illustrates the depth of the divisions. Before the reunification of West and East Germany in 1989, the abortion laws of the two countries differed dramatically. Though the formerly very strict West German law had been liberalized in the 1970s, it still required a doctor's certificate of necessity even in early pregnancy. East Germany, however, like other Communist countries, permitted abortion on demand, and many people there regarded it as a normal method of birth control. Even in the heady days of reunification, the two former nations could not agree on a unified law for the new country, and they decided to leave the old East German law in force in its former territory, as a transitional measure. That glaring exception to reunification was necessary because the issue was too emotional and too politically sensitive for any other solution to be reached. In 1992, after an agonized debate that split the governing Christian Democrat party, the unified parliament finally adopted a compromise law for the whole nation—it permitted pregnant women to decide for themselves whether they need an abortion during the first three months of pregnancy—but opponents claimed that the new law was unconstitutional and appealed to the German Constitutional Court, which has yet to announce its decision. In Poland—another former Communist country in which abortion was available virtually on demand, but which, unlike East Germany, is predominantly Catholic—political change has produced a very different result. In 1993, Poland adopted a new abortion law more restrictive than that of any European nation except Ireland.

Italy and Spain have recently adopted more liberal abortion laws, but over the fierce opposition of the Catholic church, which is politically powerful in those countries and continues to press for a return to a stricter régime. Britain liberalized its law in 1967, but the argument over abortion did not stop, and "pro-life" groups have waged a strenuous, to some extent successful battle to make it stricter. Ireland is once again convulsed over abortion, despite the church's great political power there. In 1983, after an emotional political battle, the Irish constitution had been amended to acknowledge the right of an "unborn child" to life. It became common for Irishwomen who wanted abortions, and could afford the trip, to have them in Britain, and some Irish priests, who disapproved of their church's flat condemnation, even helped make the arrangements.[2] But in 1992, the parents of a fourteen-year-old pregnant rape victim about to travel to London for an abortion contacted the Irish police to ask them whether a chromosome test on the fetus* would be

---

*Though biologists use distinct terms (including "zygote," "pre-embryo," "embryo," and "fetus") to distinguish different stages of human pre-natal life, I use "fetus" (and sometimes "embryo") to refer indiscriminately to all stages because most of the contemporary moral and legal discussion of abortion uses those terms in that way, even though it does sometimes attend to the distinctions the more technical vocabulary marks.

helpful in finding the rapist. The police, thus put on official notice of the girl's intention to do something they believed they could not ignore, obtained an injunction prohibiting the abortion. The furor that decision created—protests broke out not only in Ireland but in London and New York as well—made the Irish Supreme Court eager to find some way to lift the injunction, which it did. That decision created great outrage in turn, and a new Irish prime minister, just beginning his term, was forced to schedule another national referendum, in November 1992, in which the Irish voters declined to amend the constitutional provision to allow terminating a pregnancy to protect "the life, as distinct from the health, of the mother," but in which they did amend it to declare that women may travel abroad for an abortion, and that information about foreign abortion services may be distributed within Ireland.[3]

A FAMOUS CASE

But the war over abortion seems fiercer and more violent in America than anywhere else. Why? Part of the reason lies in the peculiar paradox of America's ambivalence toward religion. Though American law insists on a sharp formal separation between church and state, and though the Supreme Court has forbade even nondenominational prayer in public schools, the United States is nevertheless among the most religious of modern Western countries and, in the tone of some of its most powerful religious groups, by far the most fundamentalist.[4] That religiosity mixes explosively with progressive women's movements, which aim to emancipate women from traditional religious conceptions of their responsibilities and sexuality. Women's movements are also more powerful in the United States than anywhere else.[5]

Many commentators insist, however, that the major cause of the confrontational nature of the American abortion controversy is the way that the American law on abortion was created.[6] In other countries abortion law was formed by a variety of political and legislative compromises. In the United States, however, the law was imposed not after political struggle and accommodation but by the sole fiat of the Supreme Court. Under the Constitution, the Court has the power to rule that laws that have been adopted by Congress or by any of the states are unconstitutional, that is, are invalid because they are inconsistent with constraints the Constitution imposes on the government. Once the Supreme Court has spoken, no other branch of government can contravene its decision, no matter how great a majority of the people oppose it. True, the people *can* reverse a Supreme Court decision by amending the Constitution explicitly to give legislators the power the Supreme Court said that they lack. But it is extremely difficult to do this, and, in practice, politicians and people who hate a Supreme Court decision can only hope that new justices will be appointed who agree with them, and that one day a revamped Supreme Court will overrule its own past decision, which it has the power to do.

In 1973, in the famous case of *Roe* v. *Wade*, the Court declared (by a vote of seven to two) that the abortion law of Texas, which made abortion a crime except when performed to save a mother's life, was unconstitutional.[7] It went further: it said, in effect, that *any* state law that forbade abortion in order to protect a fetus within the first two trimesters of pregnancy—before the seventh month—was unconstitutional.[8] It said that states can prohibit abortion in order to protect a fetus's life only in the third trimester (when only .01 percent of abortions, most of them necessary for medical reasons, are performed anyway). At a stroke, a court of nine judges in Washington, D.C., who were appointed rather than elected to their offices, and who were not even unanimous in their decision, had radically changed the laws of almost every one of the fifty American states. Many people, particularly women, were delighted. Others, particularly members of various religious groups, felt they had been kicked in the stomach: a distant court had told them they had to condone what their instincts and religions told them was the wholesale murder of innocent unborn children. The war over abortion began and has not flagged since. "Pro-life" groups, some of them organized and orchestrated by the Catholic church, turned to politics. They tried to persuade Congress to begin the process of amending the Constitution explicitly to declare that fetuses were to be treated as persons under that document, that their lives were to be protected as fully as any other person's life.

That campaign failed. But "pro-life" groups battled on many other fronts as well. They waged a public-relations war, distributing films and ultrasonic photographs of advanced fetuses that already looked like babies and that, when prodded, moved in ways that suggested pain. They staged sit-ins and rallies and demonstrations, like the violent and frightening riots in Wichita, Kansas, in 1991, aimed at stopping patients from entering abortion clinics. And they urged their members to vote only for politicians dedicated to changing the law so that abortion would be illegal once again.

Republican presidential platforms called for a constitutional amendment forbidding abortion, and also called for "appointment of judges who respect traditional family values and the sanctity of innocent human life," by which they meant judges who would vote to overrule *Roe* v. *Wade* and return control over abortion to the legislators of each state.[9] Presidents Reagan and Bush, elected under that promise, imposed the most stringent ideological tests for judicial appointments ever seen in America, not only for appointments to the Supreme Court but to all the subordinate federal courts as well. Until June 1992, most experts anticipated that at least four of the five justices those two presidents had appointed to the Supreme Court would vote to overrule *Roe* v. *Wade* as soon as an appropriate opportunity arose, joining the two original dissenting justices, William Rehnquist (by 1992 the Chief Justice) and Byron White, to provide more than enough votes for overruling.

But in that month, the Supreme Court handed down its decision in *Planned Parenthood of Southeastern Pennsylvania* v. *Casey*, upholding certain restrictions that Pennsylvania had placed on abortion. Much to almost everyone's surprise, in the course of that decision three of the Reagan-Bush appointees—Justices O'Connor, Kennedy, and Souter—announced that they *supported Roe* v. *Wade*, or at least what they called its "central holding."[10] Since two of the other justices then on the Court—Justice Blackmun, who had written the Court's opinion in *Roe*, and Justice John Paul Stevens—also declared their continuing firm support for *Roe*, five out of nine members of the Court endorsed a constitutional right to abortion. Later in 1992, this time by a six-three vote, the Court refused to review a lower-court decision striking down Guam's new anti-abortion statute.[11]

Roe is still under threat, however. In *Casey*, the four remaining justices—Rehnquist and White and the two other Reagan-Bush appointees, Antonin Scalia and Clarence Thomas—made it plain that they would vote to reverse *Roe* as soon as another occasion presented itself. In his separate opinion, Justice Blackmun reminded the nation that he was eighty-three, and could not serve on the Court "forever." President Clinton indicated, during the 1992 presidential campaign, that he would not appoint anyone to the Supreme Court who would vote to overturn *Roe,* and if Blackmun or any other justice retires during the Clinton presidency, the decision will presumably still be safe. But so long as the abortion issue remains as divisive in America as it has been, fate and a different president may one day supply the fifth vote that would make the famous decision only history.

A CRUCIAL DISTINCTION

Some commentators believe that if *Roe* were one day overruled, the American people would then reflect and bargain together, state by state, in the normal political way, to produce compromises everyone could live with. But there is little evidence so far that this is what would happen. During the period in which it was widely expected that *Roe* would soon be reversed, some American jurisdictions, including not only Guam but Louisiana and Utah, passed new, very strong anti-abortion statutes that showed no sign of compromise or accommodation—Guam's permitted no exceptions for rape or incest, for example.

Several books have recently been published urging that common ground be found between the two sides, or, if that is impossible, that Americans learn to live together disagreeing about abortion as they disagree about other matters.[12] But the authors who urge compromise urge it, understandably, on terms that protect what they themselves believe to be fundamental principles of justice. Those who believe that women have a fundamental right to make their own decisions about abortion, for example, insist that any acceptable solution must respect that principle. But no proposal that does respect it could possibly be accepted by people who believe that abortion is murder, that it violates the most fundamental rights and interests of unborn children.

That is why reasonable-sounding proposals that the abortion issue should somehow be resolved by compromise seem unrealistic. For these proposals do not challenge the standard view of the *character* of the abortion argument—the standard view of what the argument is *about*—according to which the issue turns on what answer one gives to a polarizing question. Is a fetus a helpless unborn child with rights and interests of its own from the moment of conception? If so, then permitting abortion is permitting murder, and having an abortion is worse than abandoning an inconvenient infant to die. If not, then people who claim to be "pro-life" are either acting in deep error or are sadistic, puritanical bigots, eager not to save lives but to punish women for what they regard as sexual sin.

Self-respecting people who give opposite answers to the question of whether a fetus is a person can no more compromise, or agree to live together allowing others to make their own decisions, than people can compromise about slavery or apartheid or rape. For someone who believes that abortion violates a person's most basic interests and most precious rights, a call for tolerance or compromise is like a call for people to make up their own minds about rape, or like a plea for second-class citizenship, rather than either full slavery or full equality, as a fair compromise of the racial issue.

So long as the argument is put in those polarized terms, the two sides cannot reason together, because they have nothing to reason, or to be reasonable, about. One side thinks that a human fetus is already a moral subject, an unborn child, from the moment of conception. The other thinks that a just-conceived fetus is merely a collection of cells under the command not of a brain but of only a genetic code, no more a child, yet, than a just-fertilized egg is a chicken. Neither side can offer any argument that the other must accept—there is no biological fact waiting to be discovered or crushing moral analogy waiting to be invented that can dispose of the matter. It is a question of primitive conviction, and the most we can ask, of each side, is not understanding of the other, or even respect, but just a pale civility, the kind of civility one might show an incomprehensible but dangerous Martian. If the disagreement really is that stark, there can be no principled compromise but at best only a sullen and fragile standoff, defined by brute political power. If *Roe* v. *Wade* were to be overruled, then America would soon be divided like an irregular checkerboard between states in which anti-abortion forces were powerful, and abortion largely prohibited, and those in which these forces were weak and abortion more freely available.

It is a major theme of this book, however, that this conventional, pessimistic understanding of the character of the abortion argument is wrong, that it is based on a widespread intellectual confusion we can identify and dispel. Once the confusion has been identified, we will see that a responsible legal settlement of the controversy, one that will not insult or demean any group, one that everyone can accept with full self-respect, is indeed available.

I can describe this intellectual confusion at once in very general terms. The public argument over abortion has failed to recognize an absolutely crucial distinction. One side insists that human life begins at conception, that a fetus is a person from that moment, that abortion is murder or homicide or an assault on the sanctity of human life. But each of these phrases can be used to describe two very different ideas.

First, they can be used to make the claim that fetuses are creatures with interests of their own right from the start, including, preeminently, an interest in remaining alive, and that therefore they have the rights that all human beings have to protect these basic interests, including a right not to be killed. Abortion is wrong in principle, according to this claim, because abortion violates someone's right not to be killed, just as killing an adult is normally wrong because it violates the adult's right not to be killed. I shall call this the *derivative* objection to abortion because it presupposes and is derived from rights and interests that it assumes all human beings, including fetuses, have. Someone who accepts this objection, and who believes that government should prohibit or regulate abortion for this reason, believes that government has a derivative responsibility to protect a fetus.

The second claim that the familiar rhetoric can be used to make is very different: that human life has an intrinsic, innate value; that human life is sacred just in itself; and that the sacred nature of a human life begins when its biological life begins, even before the creature whose life it is has movement or sensation or interests or rights of its own. According to this second claim, abortion is wrong in principle because it disregards and insults the intrinsic value, the sacred character, of any stage or form of human life. I shall call this the *detached* objection to abortion, because it does not depend on or presuppose any particular rights or interests. Someone who accepts *this* objection, and argues that abortion should be prohibited or regulated by law for *this* reason, believes that government has a detached responsibility for protecting the intrinsic value of life.

This distinction between derivative and detached grounds for protecting human life is even easier to understand in the context of euthanasia. In 1989, the Supreme Court of Missouri decided that the parents of Nancy Cruzan—a young woman who had been injured in a car crash that had left her in what doctors call a persistent vegetative state—had no right to order a hospital to withdraw the feeding tubes that were keeping their daughter alive. The court said that Missouri was entitled to keep Nancy Cruzan alive out of respect for the sanctity of life. The United States Supreme Court later upheld this decision.[13] Chief Justice Rehnquist, in a complex opinion I shall discuss in chapter 7, amplified the Missouri court's claim about the sanctity of life: he said that Missouri, as a community, had legitimate reasons for keeping Nancy Cruzan alive, even on the assumption that remaining alive was against her own interests, because the state was entitled to say that it is *intrinsically* a bad thing when anyone dies deliberately and prematurely. Justice Scalia, concurring, was even more explicit in stating that the intrinsic value of human life does not depend on any assumption about a patient's rights or interests; states have the power, he said, to prevent the suicide of competent people who rightly think they would be better off dead, a power that plainly is not derived from any concern about their rights and interests. If such people's taking their own lives is wrong, this is in spite of, not because of, their rights. It is because their lives have intrinsic value—are sacred—even if it is not in their *own* interests to continue living.

Similarly, the idea that abortion is sinful or wicked because human life is sacred is very different from the claim that it is sinful or wicked because a fetus has a right to live. The former offers an argument against abortion that does not in any way presume that a fetus is a person with rights or interests of its own. For just as someone can think it wrong to remove life support from a permanently vegetative patient or to assist a dying cancer patient to kill himself, whether or not death is in the patient's interests, so one can think it wrong to destroy a fetus whether or not a fetus has any interests to protect. The belief that human life in any form has intrinsic, sacred value can therefore provide a reason for people to object violently to abortion, to regard it as wicked in all circumstances, without in any way believing that a tiny collection of cells just implanted in the womb, with as yet no organs or brain or nervous system, is already something with interests and rights. Someone who does not regard a fetus as a person with rights and interests may thus object to abortion just as strenuously as someone who insists it is. But he will object for a different reason and, as I shall try to show, with very different implications for the political question of whether and when the state ought to prohibit or permit abortion.

The confusion that I believe has poisoned the public controversy about abortion, and made it more confrontational and less open to argument and accommodation than it should be, is the confusion between these two kinds of reasons for believing that abortion is often, perhaps always, morally wrong. The scalding rhetoric of the "pro-life" movement seems to presuppose the derivative claim that a fetus is from the moment of its conception a full moral person with rights and interests equal in importance to those of any other member of the moral community. But very few people—even those who belong to the most vehemently anti-abortion groups—actually believe that, whatever they say. The disagreement that actually divides people is a markedly less polar disagreement about how best to respect a fundamental idea we almost all share in some form: that individual human life is sacred. Almost everyone who opposes abortion really objects to it, as they might realize after reflection, on the detached rather than the derivative ground. They believe that a fetus is a living, growing human creature and that it is intrinsically a bad thing, a kind of cosmic shame, when human life at any stage is deliberately extinguished. Much of this book is an extended argument for this unorthodox view of the abortion controversy, and about the legal and political consequences of seeing the controversy in that light.

Commentators are often struck by what they take to be signal inconsistencies in Americans' opinions about abortion as revealed in polls. Though poll results differ considerably, many of them report a continuing widespread moral condemnation of abortion. A Gallup poll taken in 1991, for example, on behalf of an organization called Americans United for Life, asked those it polled to choose from a list the statement that best represented their views. Of those who responded, 36.8 percent chose "Abortion is just as bad as killing a person who has already been born, it is murder"; 11.5 percent chose "Abortion is murder, but it is not as bad as killing someone who has already been born"; and 28.3 percent chose "Abortion is not murder, but it does involve the taking of human life." A 1990 Wirthlin poll commissioned by the United States Catholic Conference asked people to assess the statement "All human life, including that of the unborn, should be protected." Thirty-one percent of respondents found that statement extremely convincing, 29 percent found it very convincing, 22 percent found it not very convincing, and 11 percent found it not convincing at all. Those polled were divided, in approximately the same way, about the statement "Every unborn child has a basic right to life."[14]

But polls also show that a great and growing number of Americans believe that abortion should not be prohibited by law. A *Time*/CNN poll conducted in August 1992 reported that 49 percent of those interviewed agreed that "a woman should be able to get an abortion if she decides she wants one no matter what the reason," and a further 38 percent agreed that abortion should be legal in certain circumstances. Only 10 percent said that abortion should be illegal in all circumstances.[15] An NBC News/*Wall Street Journal* poll conducted in July 1992 reported that only 26 percent of those responding thought that abortion should be illegal, while 67 percent did not.[16] The same Wirthlin/Catholic Conference poll that reported 60 percent of respondents as finding it either extremely or very convincing that the life of the unborn should be protected, and that unborn children have a right to life, also reported that only 7 percent said that abortion should be illegal in all circumstances, and only 14 percent said that it should be legal only when necessary to save the life of the mother.[17] Even allowing for mistakes, for variations among the groups sampled in different polls, and for the inevitable distorting effect of different ways of framing the same questions, these results may seem baffling.

They are baffling, however, only if we interpret people's statements that abortion is murder, or as bad or nearly as bad as murder, or that unborn life must be protected, or that unborn children have a "right" to live, as expressing what I called the derivative view that a fetus has rights and interests of its own. No one can consistently hold that a fetus has a right not to be killed and at the same time hold it wrong for the government to protect that right by the criminal law. The most basic responsibility of government, after all, is to protect the interests of everyone in the community, particularly the interests of those who cannot protect themselves.

But there is no inconsistency whatsoever if we suppose that people who condemn abortion as morally wrong are actually relying on what I called the detached explanation of why it is wrong—if we suppose, that is, that they share a profound conviction that it is intrinsically wrong deliberately to end a human life. It is perfectly consistent to hold that view, even in an extreme form, and yet believe that a decision whether to end human life in early pregnancy must nevertheless be left to the pregnant woman, the person whose conscience is most directly connected to the choice and who has the greatest stake in it.

That combination of views is not only consistent but is in keeping with a great tradition of freedom of conscience in modern pluralistic democracies. It is a very popular view that government has no business dictating what its citizens should think about ethical and spiritual values, especially religious ones. Many people consider the religious practices (or nonpractices) of others to be deeply contemptuous of cosmic truths of the greatest possible importance. They believe, for example, that atheists grossly misunderstand the source and character of the objective value of human life. A few centuries ago, people killed one another because they thought that some forms of heresy or disbelief were too wicked, too insulting to the fundamental basis of the moral order, to be tolerated. But now most Americans and most people in other Western democracies take the opposite view. We think that it is a terrible form of tyranny, destructive of moral responsibility, for the community to impose tenets of spiritual faith or conviction on individuals. If the great battles over abortion and euthanasia are really about the intrinsic, cosmic value of a human life, as I claim they are, then those battles have at least a quasi-religious nature, and it is hardly surprising that many people believe both that abortion and euthanasia are profoundly wrong and that it is no part of the proper business of government to try to stamp them out with the jackboots of the criminal law.[18]

So the polls suggest one reason for rejecting the conventional explanation that the abortion debate is about whether a fetus has rights and interests, and for replacing it with the explanation I have proposed. We also have another, rather different, reason for the same choice: that it is very hard to make any sense of the idea that an early fetus has interests of its own, in particular an interest in not being destroyed, from the moment of its conception.

Not everything that can be destroyed has an interest in not being destroyed, of course. A beautiful sculpture can be smashed, and that would be a terrible insult to the intrinsic value that great works of art embody and also very much against the interests of people who take pleasure in seeing or studying them. But a sculpture has no interests of its own; a savage act of vandalism is not unfair to *it*. Nor is it enough, for something to have interests, that it be alive and in the process of developing into something more mature—it is not against the interests of a baby carrot that it be picked early and brought to the table as a delicacy—nor even that it be something that will naturally develop into something different or more marvelous: a butterfly is much more beautiful than a caterpillar, but it is not better for the *caterpillar* to become one. Nor is it enough, for something to have interests, that it might, if treated in the right way, grow or develop into a human being. Imagine that (as some scientists apparently think conceivable) doctors were able to produce a child from an unfertilized ovum, by parthenogenesis.[19] Menstruation would still not be against an ovum's interests; a woman who used contraception would not be violating some creature's fundamental right every month.

Nor is it even enough, for something to have interests, that it be actually en route to becoming a full human being. Imagine that, just as Dr. Frankenstein reached for the lever that would bring life to the assemblage of body parts on his laboratory table, someone appalled at the experiment smashed the apparatus. That act, whatever we think of it, would not have been harmful or unfair to the assemblage, or against its interests. It might be objected that a newly conceived fetus, unlike an unfertilized ovum or a collection of spare body parts, is growing into a full human being on its own, with no outside help needed. But that isn't true—external help, either from a pregnant woman or from scientific ingenuity, is essential. In any case, the difference is irrelevant to the present question; the collection of body parts wouldn't have interests— stopping the experiment before it came to life wouldn't be harmful to it—even if Dr. Frankenstein had designed the procedure to work automatically unless interrupted, and that automatic procedure had already begun. It makes no sense to suppose that something has interests of *its own*—as distinct from its being important what happens to it—unless it has, or has had, some form of consciousness: some mental as well as physical life.[20]

Creatures that can feel pain have an interest in avoiding it, of course. It is very much against the interests of animals to subject them to pain, in trapping them or experimenting on them, for example. It is also very much against the interests of a fetus with a nervous system sufficiently

developed to feel pain to inflict pain on it. But a fetus cannot be aware
of pain until late in its mother's pregnancy, because its brain is not
sufficiently developed before then. True, electrical brain activity arises
in a fetus's brain stem, and it is capable of reflex movement, by approximately the seventh week after conception.[21] But there is no ground for
supposing that pain is possible before a connection is made between the
fetus's thalamus, into which peripheral nerve receptors flow, and its
developing neocortex; and though the timing of that connection is still
uncertain, it almost certainly takes place after mid-gestation. (One recent study concluded that "thalamic fibers pass into the human neocortex at about 22–23 weeks' gestation."[22]) These thalamic fibers do not
begin to form synapses with cortical neurons until some later time,
moreover, which has been estimated to be at about twenty-five weeks.
According to a leading embryologist, "This process of vastly enhanced
connectivity among cortical neurons presages a change in the electrical
patterns observed in the brain via electroencephalograms. The patterns
tend to become more regular and to show resemblance to adult patterns
associated with sleeping and waking states. Such criteria lead some
investigators to suggest that an adequate neural substrate for experi-
enced pain does not exist until about the seventh month of pregnancy
(thirty weeks), well into the period when prematurely born fetuses are
viable with intensive life support. . . . To provide a safe margin against
intrusion into possible primitive sentience," that expert continued, "the
cortical maturation beginning at about thirty weeks is a reasonable
landmark until more precise information becomes available. Therefore,
since we should use extreme caution in respecting and protecting possible sentience, a provisional boundary at about twenty-six weeks should
provide safety against reasonable concerns. This time is coincident with
the present definition of viability."[23]

Of course, many acts that cause people no physical pain are against
their interests. Someone acts against my interests when he chooses
someone else for a job I want, or sues me, or smashes into my car, or
writes a bad review of my book, or brings out a better mousetrap and
prices it lower than mine, even when these actions cause me no physical
pain and, indeed, even when I am unaware that they have happened. My
interests are in play in these circumstances not because of my capacity
to feel pain but because of a different and more complex set of capacities:
to enjoy or fail to enjoy, to form affections and emotions, to hope and

expect, to suffer disappointment and frustration. Since a creature can be killed painlessly, even after it has the capacity to feel pain, it is these more complex capacities, not the capacity to feel pain, that ground a creature's interests in continuing to live. It is not known when these more complex capacities begin to develop, in primitive or trace or shadowy form, in human beings. But it seems very unlikely that they develop in a human fetus before the point of cortical maturation, at around thirty weeks of gestational age, at which cortical electrical activity becomes more complex and periods of wakefulness can be distinguished by electroencephalogram from periods of sleep.[24] "Electrical activity of the brain begins to show intermittent patterns resembling some of those seen in normal adults" only at that point.[25]

Embryology has much more to discover about the development of the fetal nervous system, of course. As the expert I just quoted remarked, "The designation of twenty-six weeks as a safe barrier against the invasion of sentience . . . almost certainly will change as more sophisticated and penetrating information accumulates on the time of advent of sentience. That time is far more likely to be later than twenty-six weeks than earlier."[26] But it seems beyond challenge that a fetus does not have the neural substrate necessary for interests of any kind until some point relatively late in its gestation.

This important point—that an immature fetus cannot have interests and therefore cannot have an interest in surviving—is often overlooked because people are mistakenly drawn to an argument to the contrary something like this: It is very much in my interests that I am alive now and was not killed at any moment in the past. So when I was a just-conceived fetus, it must have been in my interests not to be aborted. Therefore any fetus has interests from the moment of its conception, and abortion is against those interests. This argument is fallacious, but we will have to take care to see why.

Once creatures with interests exist, then it makes sense to say, in retrospect, that certain events would have been against those interests if they had happened in the past. But it doesn't follow that if these events had happened they would have been against anyone's interests when they did. It is in the interests of every human being now alive, we might assume, that the earth did not explode in a collision with a gigantic meteor millions of years ago. But it does not follow that it would have been against any human being's interests if the earth had exploded then, because there would then never have been any human beings against whose interests that *could* have been. It is in my interests that my father didn't go on a long business trip the day before I was conceived. But it would not have been against anyone's interests, in that way, if he had done so because, once again, there would never have been anyone whose interests it could have harmed.

Of course, when a fetus is aborted, there is a creature for whom someone might think this bad; there is at least a candidate for that role. But the fetus's existence before it is aborted makes no difference to the logical point. If Frankenstein's monster were actually brought to life, and felt and acted like a real person, then it would have interests like any other such person, and it would plainly have been against those interests, in retrospect, if Frankenstein's apparatus had been smashed before the monster was created. But it doesn't follow that the collection of body parts on the laboratory table had interests before the switch was thrown, even though those body parts did exist, as just body parts, at that time. Whether abortion is against the interests of a fetus must depend on whether the fetus itself has interests at the time the abortion is performed, not whether interests will develop if no abortion takes place.

That distinction may help explain what some observers have found puzzling. Many people who believe that abortion is morally permissible nevertheless think it wrong for a pregnant woman to smoke or otherwise behave in ways injurious to the child she intends to bear. Critics find that contradictory; they say that because killing something is worse than injuring it, it cannot be wrong to smoke and yet not wrong to abort. The mistake in this criticism is just the mistake we have been analyzing. If a woman smokes during her pregnancy, a human being may later exist whose interests will have been seriously damaged by her behavior; but if she aborts, no one will exist whose interests her behavior will have damaged. This does not mean, of course, that there is nothing wrong with abortion, nor even that abortion is not morally worse than risking the health of a child who will be born. But it does mean that if early abortion is wrong, it is not for this reason; it is not because abortion is against the interests of the fetus whose life it terminates.

So my suggestion that most people who oppose abortion do so on the "detached" grounds I described has important advantages. It makes that opposition more self-consistent than the "derivative" interpretation can, and ties it to an important tradition of religious toleration with substantial roots in all genuine modern democracies. It avoids attributing to people the scarcely comprehensible idea that an organism that has never had a mental life can still have interests. But you may nevertheless find my suggestion arrogant, because it seems to claim to understand people's views about abortion better than they do themselves. After all, many people do say, and many of them carry banners declaring, that abortion is murder and that unborn people have a right to live. These phrases do seem to claim that fetuses have interests and rights.

But we must be careful to distinguish the public rhetoric in which people frame their opinions from the opinions themselves, which can sometimes be recovered only by a more careful examination than polls and demonstrations provide. Most people do not have grand theories about the metaphysical premises of their opinions about abortion, and very few have reflected about, or perhaps even noticed, the distinction I made between derivative and detached grounds for opposing abortion. Many people who are asked to state their views in a general and abstract way find it natural to use the strident and heated rhetoric that leaders of various interest groups have made prominent, whether or not it fits their actual instincts and convictions. They may act very differently from what their rhetoric suggests when making actual decisions in concrete circumstances involving their own family or friends or themselves. In the 1992 presidential campaign, for example, both President Bush and Vice President Quayle, who have each expressed "pro-life" views in the strongest orthodox terms, said they would support their own daughter or granddaughter who decided on abortion.[27] They would hardly do that if they really thought that abortion meant the murder of their grandchildren or great-grandchildren. A 1980 *New York Times*/CBS News poll illustrates the uncertain match between rhetoric and actual beliefs, and the independent emotive power of rhetoric. Only 29 percent of those polled agreed with the statement that there should be a constitutional amendment prohibiting abortion, but 50 percent of the same group, answering a later, differently phrased version of the same question, said that they favored a constitutional amendment protecting the life of an unborn child.[28]

People who use the heated public rhetoric of "murder" and "homicide" to express their opposition to abortion might nevertheless, on reflection, agree that they hold the detached rather than the derivative view. They declare that abortion is murder, or just as bad as murder, and they insist that human life begins at conception, or that a fetus is a person from the beginning, not because they think a fetus has rights and interests but just to emphasize the depth of their feeling that abortion is wrong because it is the deliberate destruction of the life of a human organism. We shall see, in chapter 2, that "murder" and "homicide" are words that have been used, historically, in that way. Some people also express views about euthanasia using similar terms: it seems natural for them to say, for example, that allowing Nancy Cruzan to die was a form of murder. But they mean that her life, even in that horribly reduced state, was still a human life; they do not necessarily mean that allowing her to die was against her interests. They might even agree that, on the contrary, it was in her interests to die.

My claim is not, then, that people do not know what they think, but rather that we cannot discover what they think simply by fixing on the high rhetoric of the public debate. We must be careful not to be misled by emotionally charged descriptions about human life and persons and murder that reveal strong emotions but are not a clear guide to the beliefs that people are emotional about. We must be especially careful about the highly ambiguous claims that human life begins at conception and that a fetus is a person from that moment. When someone makes one or the other of these claims, we cannot tell whether he means to make the derivative claim—that a fetus already has interests and rights of its own from the instant of conception, and that abortion is wrong for that reason—or the detached claim—that from the moment of conception a fetus embodies a form of human life which is sacred, a claim that does not imply that a fetus has interests of its own.

The familiar questions about when life begins and whether a fetus is a person are not simply but multiply ambiguous, and because these questions have become such familiar parts of the abortion debate, it is important that we understand the multiple ambiguities. Consider the question of whether human life begins at conception. Scientists disagree about exactly when the biological life of any animal begins, but it seems undeniable that a human embryo is an identifiable living organism at least by the time it is implanted in a womb, which is approximately fourteen days after its conception. It is also undeniable that the cells that compose an implanted embryo already contain biological codes that will govern its later physical development. When an opponent of abortion insists that a fetus is a human being, he may mean only to report these undeniable biological facts.[29]

But it does not follow from those facts that a fetus also has rights or interests of the kind that government might have a derivative responsibility to protect. That is plainly a further question, and it is in large part a moral rather than a biological one. Nor does it follow that a fetus already embodies an intrinsic value that government might claim a detached responsibility to guard. That is also a different question, and also a moral rather than a biological one. The question of whether a fetus is a human being, either at conception or at some later point in pregnancy, is simply too ambiguous to be useful. The crucial questions are the two moral ones I have just described, and we should consider these directly and unambiguously. When does a human creature acquire interests and rights? When does the life of a human creature begin to embody intrinsic value, and with what consequences? We do not have to decide whether a fetus is a full human being at conception, or at what point it becomes one, or whether that process is gradual or abrupt, in order to answer those crucial questions.

Is a fetus a person? That is an even more treacherous question, because the term "person" has a great many uses and senses that can easily be confused. Suppose it is discovered that pigs are much more intelligent and emotionally complex than zoologists now think they are, and someone then asks whether a pig should therefore be considered a person. We might treat that as a philosophical question, asking us to refine our conception of what a person really is to see whether pigs, on the basis of our new information, qualify for that title. Or we might treat the question as a practical one, asking whether we should now treat pigs as we treat creatures we regard as people, acknowledging that pigs have a right to life so that it is wrong to kill them for food and a right not to be enslaved so that it is wrong to imprison them in pens. Of course, we might think that the two questions are connected: that if pigs are persons in the philosophical sense, they should be treated as other persons are, and that if they are not, they should not. But that does not necessarily follow, in either direction. We might believe philosophically that pigs are persons but that human beings have no reason to treat them as we treat one another; or, on the contrary, we might decide that pigs are not persons according to our best understanding of that complex concept but that nevertheless their capacities entitle them to the treatment persons give one another.

Once again it would be wise, therefore, to set aside the question of whether a fetus is a person, not because that question is unanswerable or metaphysical, as many judges and commentators have declared, but because it is too ambiguous to be helpful. Once again, we must ask, instead, the key moral questions I distinguished. Does a fetus have interests that should be protected by rights, including a right to life? Should we treat the life of a fetus as sacred, whether a fetus has interests or not? Once again, we do not need to decide whether a fetus is a person in order to answer these questions, and these are the questions that count.

Nevertheless, I shall have to use the word "person" in some of the arguments and discussions of this book, for two reasons. First, as we shall see, the Fourteenth Amendment to the United States Constitution uses the term "person" in a crucial context: it declares that all persons must be treated as equals. The question is therefore inescapable whether a fetus is a person for the purposes of that clause—whether a fetus is a *constitutional* person. Second, the word "person" has figured explicitly in some of the arguments of other people that I shall have to consider, including the argument some philosophers have made that even if a fetus is a person, abortion should nevertheless be permitted in certain circumstances.

But when I discuss these issues I shall be using the word "person" only in what I called the practical sense. In that sense, the claim that a fetus is a person means only that it has a right to be treated *as* a person, that is, in the way we believe creatures that are undeniably persons, like you and me, should be treated.[30] I therefore take the legal question— whether a fetus is a constitutional person—to be the question of whether the Constitution requires states to treat a fetus as having the same rights as children and adults; and the moral question—whether a fetus is a moral person—to be the question of whether a fetus should be given the same moral rights as children and adults undeniably have. (In this practical sense, we might argue, for example, that newborn infants are constitutional persons without deciding whether or not they satisfy whatever standards of consciousness we might think necessary for personhood in the philosophical sense.[31])

We must therefore distinguish two possible controversies about abortion. The first is an argument about whether a fetus has two morally relevant properties: interests, including an interest in continuing to live, and rights that protect those interests. If the answer to this first question is yes, then there is a derivative objection to abortion, and a derivative justification for laws prohibiting or regulating it. If the answer is no, then there is no such objection or justification. The second is a different question: about whether abortion is sometimes morally wrong not because it is unfair or unjust to anyone but because it denies and offends the sanctity or inviolability of human life. If the answer to that second question is yes, then there is a detached objection to abortion, and perhaps a detached justification for outlawing or regulating it, even though there is no derivative objection or justification.

We can distinguish two controversies about euthanasia in the same way. Is it in the best interests of a patient who has fallen into a permanent coma to be kept alive? If so, then doctors have a derivative reason not to withdraw life-support systems from such patients. If not, they have no such reason. Is it wrong to allow such a patient to die, even if dying is in his own best interests, because respect for the sanctity of human life requires that every effort be made to prolong life? If so, then doctors have a detached moral reason for not withdrawing life support.

THE ARGUMENT TO COME

Combatants and commentators alike talk as if the abortion controversy were of the first, inevitably confrontational, kind, as if it centered on the rights and interests of a fetus. That is how politics have shaped the argument. But this is a serious mistake. In chapter 2, I shall claim that if we look more closely, we shall find that for almost everyone—liberals and conservatives, groups as well as individuals, Catholics as well as feminists—the abortion argument is rather of the second kind. It is an argument about how and why human life has intrinsic value, and what that implies for personal and political decisions about abortion. This realization is of great importance, not only because it clarifies the debate but because it contradicts the pessimistic conclusion that argument is irrelevant and accommodation impossible.

Many readers may initially find the idea that human life has intrinsic value to be vague and mysterious. In chapter 3, I shall try to convince such skeptics that they must nevertheless confront that idea and try to understand it, because many of their most profound convictions presuppose it. I shall have to explore, moreover, the equally familiar but widely misunderstood idea of the *sacred,* because the important idea we share is that human life has not just intrinsic but sacred value. Some readers, I know, will take particular exception to the term "sacred" because it will suggest to them that the conviction I have in mind is necessarily a theistic one. I shall try to explain why it is not, and how it may be, and commonly is, interpreted in a secular as well as in a conventionally religious way. But "sacred" does have ineliminable religious connotations for many people, and so I will sometimes use "inviolable" instead to mean the same thing, in order to emphasize the availability of that secular interpretation.

I shall also aim to show that the idea of the sacred, so far from being alien or mysterious, is familiar, almost commonplace—many people's opinions about art or nature implicitly assume that these phenomena, too, have a kind of sacred value. I shall rely on these common opinions about art and nature to explain what the claim that human life is sacred really means and why it has a secular as well as a religious basis. I shall also try to show something even more important: how the assumption that most people accept the sanctity of human life but disagree in complex ways about its implications for abortion explains the great controversy in a more illuminating and optimistic way than the orthodox account can.

Chapters 4 through 6 consider the constitutional and political implications of my recommendations. In those chapters I hope to show that we cannot make sense of the constitutional controversy in the United States—the great legal and political argument about *Roe* v. *Wade*—if we construe that controversy as being centrally about the rights and interests of a fetus. It is widely assumed that the critical question in *Roe* v. *Wade* is the question of whether states have the constitutional power to treat a fetus as a person; but if that were true, then *Roe* would be obviously, almost uncontroversially, correct, and the great opposition to it, among not only anti-abortion activists but some renowned constitutional scholars as well, would be wholly inexplicable. What was really at stake in that important case was whether state legislatures have the constitutional power to decide which intrinsic values all citizens must respect, and how, and whether legislatures may prohibit abortion on that ground. That is a much more difficult and complex issue, and it is hardly surprising that constitutional scholars disagree about it.

This more difficult issue requires us to decide the broader question of whether the Constitution should be understood as a limited list of the particular individual rights that statesmen now dead thought important, or as a commitment to abstract ideals of political morality that each generation of citizens, lawyers, and judges must together explore and reinterpret. I shall argue that the first answer is indefensible, in spite of its apparent popularity among conservative members of the present Supreme Court. I shall reappraise *Roe* v. *Wade* in the light of my several conclusions, and I shall revise and defend an argument many lawyers have found intuitively appealing but legally unsound—that freedom of choice about abortion is a necessary implication of the religious freedom guaranteed by the First Amendment, and that women therefore have a right to that freedom for that reason, though for others as well. The discussion of these chapters focuses on the United States Constitution, but the underlying question is a more universal issue of political morality. Should *any* political community make intrinsic values a matter of collective decision rather than individual choice?

Chapters 7 and 8 turn to tragedy at the other edge of life in earnest— to euthanasia. The idea that human life is sacred or inviolable is as central to discussions of that topic as it is to discussions about abortion, and the argument of those chapters will therefore draw on the analytical base of earlier ones. Should the law allow doctors to kill terminally ill patients who are in great pain and who plead to die? Should it allow relatives of patients who are unconscious "vegetables" to decide that life-support machines, which can keep people alive in that condition for many years, should be shut off? Should it allow doctors or relatives not to treat people in the advanced stages of Alzheimer's disease, or other irreversible forms of dementia, who develop pneumonia or cancer? These questions, once taboo, are now more openly discussed not only among doctors but in politics as well. But the discussion suffers from a failure to notice how far these questions about death require us also to think about life.

Three distinct issues come together in decisions about euthanasia. We must be concerned how best to respect the patient's autonomy, his best interests, and the intrinsic value or sanctity of his life. We can properly understand none of these issues, however, or whether they argue for or against euthanasia in a given circumstance, until we better understand why some people want to remain biologically alive so long as they can, even in appalling circumstances, and why others in such straits want to die as soon as possible. Both these ambitions will seem unintelligible if we try to understand them as reflecting people's opinions about the relative badness of future experiences, for it makes no sense to ask whether it feels worse to be permanently unconscious or wholly demented or dead. We must ask, instead, about the *retrospective* meaning of death or the diminution of life, about how the last stage of a life affects its overall character. We understand how one life can be more pleasant or enjoyable or full of achievement than another. But the suggestion that a period of unconsciousness or dementia before death might make that life worse as a whole than if death had come sooner introduces a very different kind of standard for judging lives; it judges lives not just by reckoning overall sums of pleasure or enjoyment or achievement, but more structurally, as we judge a literary work, for example, whose bad ending mars what went before.

Once again, the idea that lives can be judged in that structural way will strike some readers as mysterious. But I shall try to show that many of our deepest convictions about how to live and when to die are inexplicable without it. I shall also try to show how judging life in that way presupposes an even more basic premise: that we are ethically responsible for making something worthwhile of our lives, and that this responsibility stems from the same, even more fundamental idea that I argued is at the root of the abortion controversy as well, the idea that each separate human life has an intrinsic, inviolable value.

Revising our view about the central issue in the abortion debate allows us to make this important connection between abortion and euthanasia—between mortal questions at the two edges of normal life. If people's instincts and opinions about abortion all turned on whether they thought that a fetus had interests and rights, as the conventional view of the abortion debate insists, these instincts and opinions would be logically disconnected from their other convictions and from the rest of their lives. They would have no necessary connection with any of their opinions about euthanasia, or capital punishment, or war, or the importance of social welfare programs, or anything else of great importance. But if the controversy about abortion has the shape I claim—if it is a controversy about whether human life itself is sacred, and why, and about which acts show respect and which disrespect for human life—then someone's opinions about abortion will inevitably reflect his more basic instincts and attitudes and ideas, instincts that inevitably color his reactions to all the other great moral and political issues. If someone believes that no circumstance or interest can possibly justify deliberately killing a fetus, even though a fetus has no interests of its own, then he is very likely also to believe that nothing can justify allowing a terminally ill patient to die, even though the patient may have no interests to protect, either. On the other hand, if someone thinks that it is morally permissible to terminate a pregnancy when the fetus is seriously abnormal—when the baby would be born with Tay-Sachs disease or without a brain, for example—then he is also likely to think that it is preferable to end the life of a desperately suffering patient who wants to die or a patient who is in a persistent vegetative state. The idea that I said binds us all together, that our lives have intrinsic, inviolable value, also deeply and consistently divides us, because each person's own conception of what that idea *means* radiates throughout his entire life.

PHILOSOPHY FROM THE INSIDE OUT

This book offers an argument, a case for certain specific conclusions, rather than a history or a survey or a review. I shall discuss a variety of issues in constitutional law, moral philosophy, theology, and social and political thought; I shall discuss these only because—and only to the extent that—my overall argument intersects them. I am not apologizing for this selectivity, or for constructing the book as an extended argument rather than as a more discursive study. On the contrary, I hope that the book may serve as an example of a now neglected genre: an argumentative essay that engages theoretical issues but begins with, and remains disciplined by, a moral subject of practical political importance.

Political philosophers, philosophers of law, social theorists, linguists, structuralists, pragmatists, and deconstructionists have in recent years produced innovative and sometimes compelling theories, which other people have tried to apply to social and political issues. But these theories have not yet improved the quality of public political argument as much as they might have, and that is partly because though the theories plainly do have implications for particular contemporary political controversies, they were not constructed for or in response to them.

Theory can connect with practice in two different ways or directions. It can connect from the outside in: we can construct general theories of justice or personal ethics or constitutional interpretation from general assumptions about human nature or the structure of language or thought, or from first principles of some other character, and then try to apply those general theories to concrete problems. Or we can proceed in the opposite direction, from the inside out, which is what I aim to do. We can begin with practical problems, like the question of whether the law should ever permit abortion or euthanasia, and if so in which circumstances, and then ask which general philosophical or theoretical issues we must confront in order to resolve those practical problems.

The difference is not in the level of abstraction or theoretical depth one finally reaches. Some of the discussions of this book, for example, are evidently philosophical and abstract, and the questions they try to answer are as deep as anyone might wish. The difference is in how the abstract issues are chosen, combined, and formulated. When we reason from the outside in, a practical issue must shop from among ready-made theories on the racks to see which theory asks and tries to answer questions that best fit its own dimensions. When we reason from the inside out, theories are bespoke, made for the occasion, Savile Row not Seventh Avenue. Theories homemade in that way, rather than wholesaled or imported, may be more likely to succeed in the political forum. They may be better suited to the academy, too, but that is another story.

2

THE
MORALITY OF
ABORTION

Sometimes people who disagree passionately with one another have no clear grasp of what they are disagreeing about, even when the dispute is violent and profound. Most people assume that the great, divisive abortion argument is at bottom an argument about a moral and metaphysical issue: whether even a just-fertilized embryo is already a human creature with rights and interests of its own, a person in the sense I defined in chapter 1, an unborn child, helpless against the abortionist's slaughtering knife. The political rhetoric is explicit that this is the issue in controversy. The "human life" amendment that anti-abortion groups have tried to make part of the United States Constitution declares, "The paramount right to life is vested in each human being from the moment of fertilization without regard to age, health, or conditions of dependency." The "pro-choice" world defends abortion by claiming that an embryo is no more a child than an acorn is an oak. Theological, moral, philosophical, and even sociological discussions of abortion almost all presume that people disagree about abortion because they disagree about whether a fetus is a person with a right to life from the moment of its conception, or becomes a person at some point in pregnancy, or does not become one until birth. And about whether, if a fetus is a person, its right to life must yield in the face of some stronger right held by pregnant women.

I have suggested some preliminary reasons for thinking that this account of the abortion debate, in spite of its great popularity, is fatally misleading. We cannot understand most people's actual moral and political convictions about when abortion is permissible, and what government should do about abortion, in this way. The detailed structure of most conservative opinion about abortion is actually inconsistent with the assumption that a fetus has rights from the moment of conception, and the detailed structure of most liberal opinion cannot be explained only on the supposition that it does not.

Of course, people's opinions about abortion do not come in only two varieties, conservative and liberal. There are degrees of opinion, ranging from extreme to moderate, on both sides, and there are also differences of opinion that cannot be located on a conservative-liberal spectrum at all—neither view about whether a later abortion is worse than an earlier one seems distinctly more liberal or more conservative, for example. Nevertheless, in this part of my argument, I shall suppose that people are spread along a conservative-liberal spectrum because this will make it easier to describe my main points.

We have seen that a great many people who are morally very conservative about abortion—who believe that it is never, or almost never, morally permissible, and who would be appalled if any relative or close friend chose to have one—nevertheless think that the law should leave women free to make decisions about abortion for themselves, that it is wrong for the majority or for the government to impose its view upon them. Even many Catholics take that view: Governor Mario Cuomo of New York among them, as he made explicit in a well-known 1984 speech at Notre Dame University in Indiana.[1]

Some conservatives who take that position base it, as Cuomo did, on the principle that church and state should be separate: they believe that freedom of decision about abortion is part of the freedom people have to make their own religious decisions. Others base their tolerance on a more general notion of privacy and freedom: they believe that the government should not dictate to individuals on any matter of personal morality. But people who really consider a fetus a person with a right to live could not maintain either version. Protecting people from murderous assault—particularly people too weak to protect themselves—is one of government's most central and inescapable duties.

Of course, a great many people who are very conservative about abortion do not take this tolerant view: they believe that governments should ban abortion, and some of them have devoted their lives to achieving that end. But even those conservatives who believe that the law should prohibit abortion recognize some exceptions. It is a very common view, for example, that abortion should be permitted when necessary to save the mother's life.[2] Yet this exception is also inconsistent with any belief that a fetus is a person with a right to live. Some people say that in this case a mother is justified in aborting a fetus as a matter of self-defense; but any safe abortion is carried out by someone else—a doctor—and very few people believe that it is morally justifiable for a third party, even a doctor, to kill one innocent person to save another.

Abortion conservatives often allow further exceptions. Some of them believe that abortion is morally permissible not only to save the mother's life but also when pregnancy is the result of rape or incest.[3] The more such exceptions are allowed, the clearer it becomes that conservative opposition to abortion does not presume that a fetus is a person with a right to live. It would be contradictory to insist that a fetus has a right to live that is strong enough to justify prohibiting abortion even when childbirth would ruin a mother's or a family's life but that ceases to exist when the pregnancy is the result of a sexual crime of which the fetus is, of course, wholly innocent.

On the other side, a parallel story emerges. Liberal views about abortion do not follow simply from denying that a fetus is a person with a right to live; they presuppose some other important value at stake. I exempt here the views of people who think that abortion is never even morally problematic—Peggy Noonan, a White House speech writer in Ronald Reagan's administration, said that when she was in college she "viewed abortion as no more than a surgical procedure"[4]—and that women who have scruples about abortion, or regret or remorse, are silly. Most people who regard themselves as liberal about abortion hold a more moderate, more complex view. I will construct an example of such a view, though I do not mean to suggest that all moderate liberals accept all parts of it.

A paradigm liberal position on abortion has four parts. First, it rejects the extreme opinion that abortion is morally unproblematic, and insists, on the contrary, that abortion is always a grave moral decision, at least from the moment at which the genetic individuality of the fetus is fixed and it has successfully implanted in the womb, normally after about fourteen days. From that point on, abortion means the extinction of a human life that has already begun, and for that reason alone involves a serious moral cost. Abortion is never permissible for a trivial or frivolous reason; it is never justifiable except to prevent serious damage of some kind. It would be wrong for a woman to abort her pregnancy because she would otherwise have to forfeit a long-awaited European trip, or because she would find it more comfortable to be pregnant at a different time of year, or because she has discovered that her child would be a girl and she wanted a boy.

Second, abortion is nevertheless morally justified for a variety of serious reasons. It is justified not only to save the life of the mother and in cases of rape or incest but also in cases in which a severe fetal abnormality has been diagnosed—the abnormalities of thalidomide babies, for example, or of Tay-Sachs disease—that makes it likely that the child, if carried to full term, will have only a brief, painful, and frustrating life.[5] Indeed, in some cases, when the abnormality is very severe and the potential life inevitably a cruelly crippled and short one, the paradigm liberal view holds that abortion is not only morally permitted but may be morally required, that it would be wrong knowingly to bring such a child into the world.

Third, a woman's concern for her own interests is considered an adequate justification for abortion if the consequences of childbirth would be permanent and grave for her or her family's life. Depending on the circumstances, it may be permissible for her to abort her pregnancy if she would otherwise have to leave school or give up a chance for a career or a satisfying and independent life. For many women, these are the most difficult cases, and people who take the paradigm liberal view would assume that the expectant mother would suffer some regret if she decided to abort. But they would not condemn the decision as selfish; on the contrary, they might well suppose that the contrary decision would be a serious moral mistake.

The fourth component in the liberal view is the political opinion that I said moral conservatives about abortion sometimes share: that at least until late in pregnancy, when a fetus is sufficiently developed to have interests of its own, the state has no business intervening even to prevent morally impermissible abortions, because the question of whether an abortion is justifiable is, ultimately, for the woman who carries the fetus to decide. Others—mate, family, friends, the public—may disapprove, and they might be right, morally, to do so. The law might, in some circumstances, oblige her to discuss her decision with others. But the state in the end must let her decide for herself; it must not impose other people's moral convictions upon her.

I believe that these four components in the paradigm liberal view represent the moral convictions of many people—at least a very substantial minority in the United States and other Western countries. The liberal view they compose is obviously inconsistent with any assumption that an early-stage fetus is a person with rights and interests of its own. That assumption would, of course, justify the view that abortion is always morally problematic, but it would plainly be incompatible with the fourth component of the package, that the state has no right to protect a fetus's interests through the criminal law, and even more plainly with the third component: if a fetus does have a right to live, a mother's interests in having a fulfilling life could hardly be thought more important than that right. Even the second component, which insists that abortion may be morally permissible when a fetus is seriously deformed, is hard to justify if one assumes that a fetus has a right to remain alive. In cases when a child's physical deformities are so painful or otherwise crippling that we believe it would be in the best interests of the child to die, we might say that abortion, too, would have been in the child's best interests. But that is not so in every case in which the paradigm liberal view allows abortion; even children with quite terrible deformities may form attachments, give and receive love, struggle, and to some degree conquer their handicaps. If their lives are worth a great deal, then, how could it have been better for *them* to have been killed in the womb?

But though the presumption that a fetus has no rights or interests of its own is *necessary* to explain the paradigm liberal view, it is not sufficient because it cannot, alone, explain why abortion is ever morally wrong. Why should abortion raise any moral issue at all if there is no one whom it harms? Why is abortion then *not* like a tonsillectomy? Why should a woman feel any regret after an abortion? Why should she feel more regret than she does after sex with contraception? The truth is that liberal opinion, like the conservative view, presupposes that human life itself has intrinsic moral significance, so that it is in principle wrong to terminate a life even when no one's interests are at stake. Once we see this clearly, then we can explain why liberal and conservative opinions differ in the ways they do.

My discussion so far has emphasized individual moral opinion. But people do not respond to great moral or legal issues only as individuals; on the contrary, many people insist that their views on such important issues reflect and flow from larger, more general commitments or loyalties or associations. They have views, they think, not just as individuals, but as Catholics or Baptists or Jews or protectors of family values or feminists or atheists or socialists or social critics or anarchists or subscribers to some other orthodox or radical view about justice or society. We must consider how far the hypothesis I am now defending—that the abortion debate is about intrinsic value, not about a fetus's rights or interests—helps us better to understand the claims, insights, doctrines, and arguments of these large institutions or movements. I shall raise that question with reference to two of the most prominent groups in the controversy: traditional religions and the women's movement.

RELIGION

Throughout the Western world, even where church and state are normally separated, the battle over abortion has often had the character of a conflict between religious sects. In the United States, opinions about abortion correlate dramatically with religious belief. According to the 1984 American National Election Study, 22 percent of Baptists and fundamentalists, 16 percent of Southern Baptists, and 15 percent of Catholics then believed that abortion should never be permitted. The same survey showed that Lutherans (9 percent of whom would permit no abortions) and Methodists (8 percent) were more liberal denominations, Episcopalians (5 percent) and Jews (4 percent) even more so. Regular churchgoers of all faiths in America are much more likely to hold conservative views about abortion than nonchurchgoers or people who attend church only sporadically. Since religion tends to correlate, at least roughly, with other social divisions in America—with economic class, for example—these divisions may express other influences. But the controversy over abortion in the United States does seem to have a strong religious dimension.[6]

The anti-abortion movement is led by religious groups, uses religious language, invokes God constantly, and often calls for prayer. It embraces members of many religions, as the statistics I just described suggest, including not only fundamentalists but Orthodox Jews, Mormons, and Black Muslims. But Catholics have provided the organizational leadership. In 1980, John Dooling, a federal court judge in New York, declared that the Hyde amendment—which Congress had adopted in 1976 and which prohibited the use of federal medicaid funds to finance abortions—was unconstitutional because it denied people's right to free exercise of religion.[7] In the course of an extraordinarily thorough opinion, Dooling, himself a devout Catholic, said, "Roman Catholic clergy and laity are not alone in the pro-life movement, but the evidence requires the conclusion that it is they who have vitalized the movement, given it organization and direction, and used ecclesiastical channels of communication in its support."[8]

But it is important to note that leaders of many other religious faiths have also spoken out on the subject, including many who hold liberal rather than conservative views, and Dooling cited testimony from a number of them. Many of these statements, both those condemning abortion and those approving it in certain carefully limited circumstances, do not rely on the presumption that a fetus is a person. They all assert the different idea underlying most people's views about abortion: that any instance of human life has an intrinsic, sacred value that one must strive not to sacrifice. Not surprisingly, they all declare or suggest a particular source of that intrinsic, sacred value; they regard human life as the most exalted creation of God.

Dooling quoted, for example, the testimony of Dr. James E. Wood, Jr., executive director of the Baptist Joint Committee on Public Affairs, who reported that Baptists were divided about abortion and that there was no official Baptist position. But Dr. Wood also said that in 1973 the joint committee, reacting to the decision of Catholic bishops to work for a constitutional amendment reversing *Roe* v. *Wade*, objected to a campaign that "would coerce all citizens to accept a moral judgment affirmed by one member of the Body of Christ." Similarly, the 1976 Southern Baptist Convention rejected any "indiscriminate attitude toward abortion, as contrary to the biblical view" but refused to adopt a submitted resolution that declared, "Every decision for an abortion, for whatever reason, must necessarily involve the decision to terminate the life of an innocent human being." Dr. Wood said that in his own opinion, sound Baptist faith condemned abortion for frivolous reasons but recognized it as permissible when pregnancy was involuntary (including pregnancies of very young girls not of an age to consent and of women whose contraceptive devices had failed), cases of fetal deformity, and cases where significant family reasons argued against a pregnancy.[9]

The Reverend John Philip Wagoman, a Methodist minister who in 1980 was dean of the Wesley Theological Seminary in Washington, D.C., and had been president of the American Society of Christian Ethics, testified, in Judge Dooling's words, that "it was a common view among Protestant Christian theologians, and to some extent among other religious bodies, that human personhood—in the sense in which the person receives its maximum value in relation to the Christian faith—does not exist in the earlier stages of pregnancy . . . there is not a fully human person until that stage in development where someone has begun to have experience of reality." But, said Dooling, Dean Wagoman nevertheless insisted that "nearly no aspect of life is more sacred, closer to being human in relation to God, than bringing new life into the world to share in the gift of God's grace. . . . In bringing new life into the world human beings must be sure that the conditions into which the new life is being born will sustain that life in accordance with God's intention for the life to be fulfilled. . . . It matters whether a new life . . . might threaten to undermine the theologically understood fulfillment of already existing human beings." A pregnant woman "responding out of faith and love of God to the love which God has provided to human beings" might decide to have an abortion when the new life would be unlikely to receive the nurture necessary for human fulfillment, either because she is herself only a teenager, for example, or because she is close to menopause or because the existence of a new child would make life much harder for the existing family.[10]

According to the testimony of Rabbi David Feldman, "in Jewish law a fetus is not a person, and no person is in existence until the infant emerges from the womb into the world," so in Jewish law abortion is not murder. (If it were, Rabbi Feldman pointed out, it would not be permissible for a doctor to perform an abortion even to save the mother's life, because that would mean killing one innocent person to save another.)

But Judaism nevertheless holds that abortion is in principle wrong. In the stricter Jewish tradition, Rabbi Feldman said, abortion is objectionable for any reason except to protect the mother's life or sanity or personal well-being; a more liberal tradition, he said, allows more exceptions: protecting a woman from "mental anguish," for example. In both traditions, however, abortion is not merely permissible but mandatory in some cases. In those cases, abortion is required by a woman's sound sense of religious duty, because it is a choice, sanctioned by the Jewish faith, for life in this world as against life in any other. In 1975, the Biennial Convention of the United Synagogues of America declared that abortions, "though serious even in the early stages of pregnancy, are not to be equated with murder, hardly more than is the decision not to become pregnant." It added, "abortions involve very serious psychological, religious, and moral problems, but the welfare of the mother must always be our primary concern." [11]

Each of these declarations insists that any decision about abortion requires reflection about an important value: the intrinsic value of human life. Each interprets that value as resting on God's creative power and love, but each insists that a proper religious attitude must recognize and balance a different sort of threat to the sanctity of life: the threat to a woman's health and well-being that an unwanted pregnancy may pose. To show a proper respect for God's creation, in such cases, requires judgment and balance, not asserting the automatic priority of the biological life of a fetus over the developed life of its mother.

Some conservative theologians and religious leaders have also explicitly said that the crucial question about abortion is not whether a fetus is a person but how best to respect the intrinsic value of human life. The late Professor Paul Ramsey of Princeton, an influential Protestant theologian, was a fierce opponent of abortion. Writing before *Roe* v. *Wade* was decided, he insisted that even the use of intrauterine contraceptive devices, which prevent the implantation of a fertilized egg, was sinful, and he suggested that all young girls be given German measles deliberately to immunize them from that disease so that it would not be necessary to abort any fetuses damaged because a woman contracted the disease in pregnancy. But Ramsey made plain that his strong opinions were based not on the assumption of fetal personhood or rights but on respect for the divine dignity that is "alien" to man but "surrounds" him.

"From this point of view," he said, "it is *relatively* unimportant to say exactly when among the products of human generation we are dealing with an organism that is human and when we are dealing with organic life that is not human. . . . A man's dignity is an overflow from God's dealings with him, and not primarily an anticipation of anything he will ever be by himself alone. . . . The Lord did not set his love upon you, nor choose you because you were already intrinsically more than a blob of tissue in the uterus."[12] Ramsey argued that it is respect for God's creative choice and love of mankind, not any rights of a "blob of tissue in the uterus," that makes abortion sinful.

The Roman Catholic church's condemnation of abortion does seem an important counterexample, however, to my claim that for most people the abortion controversy is not about whether a fetus is a person with a right to live but about the sanctity of life understood in a more impersonal way. The church's present official position about fetal life is set out in its *Instruction on Respect for Human Life in Its Origin and on the Dignity of Procreation*, published in 1987 by the Vatican's Congregation for the Doctrine of the Faith with the consent of the pope. The *Instruction* declares that "every human being" has a "right to life and physical integrity from the moment of conception until death. . . ."[13] But most American Catholics do not seem to accept that view, and it has been the clear official view of the church itself for little more than a century, a fraction of Catholicism's long history. For substantial periods, if there was any reigning opinion within the church hierarchy it was to the contrary: that a fetus becomes a person not at conception but only at a later stage of pregnancy, later than the stage at which almost all abortions now take place. I do not mean that the church ever sanctioned early abortions. Quite the opposite: from its earliest beginnings, the church's condemnation of early as well as late abortion was clear and imperative; it was, as a prominent Catholic layman has put it, a nearly absolute value in the church's history.[14] But it relied not on the derivative claim that a fetus is a person with a right not to be killed, but on the different, detached view that abortion is wrong because it insults God's creative gift of life.

The detached reason for condemning abortion is historically firmer than the view set out in the Vatican's 1987 *Instruction* and also, according to many Catholic philosophers, better grounded in traditional Catholic theology. It also unites the church's opposition to abortion with its other

historical concerns about sexuality, including its opposition to contraception. For many centuries, Catholic theologians stressed these connections, but the claim that a fetus is a person from the moment of
conception dissipates them. The church's official view that abortion is
sinful in nearly all circumstances would not change dramatically if it
were now to abandon the new fetus-is-a-person justification and return
to the older one. That step would have the important advantage, as we
shall see, of changing the nature of the confrontation between the
church and its members in the United States and other countries who
hold strikingly more liberal views about abortion.

Abortion was common in the Greco-Roman world; but early Chris-
tianity condemned it. In the fifth century, St. Augustine called even
married women "in the fashion of harlots" who in order to avoid the
consequences of sex "procure poisons of sterility, and if these do not
work, they extinguish and destroy the fetus in some way in the womb,
preferring that their offspring die before it lives, or if it was already alive
in the womb, to kill it before it was born."[15] None of the early denuncia-
tions of abortion presupposed that a fetus has been ensouled—granted
a soul by God—at the moment of conception. Augustine declared
himself uncertain on that point, and so allowed that in early abortion an
"offspring" may die "before it lives." St. Jerome said that "seeds are
gradually formed in the uterus, and it is not reputed homicide until the
scattered elements received their appearance and members."[16] Catholicism's great thirteenth-century philosopher-saint, Thomas Aquinas,
held firmly that a fetus does not have an intellectual or rational soul at
conception but acquires one only at some later time—forty days in the
case of a male fetus, according to traditional Catholic doctrine, and later
in the case of a female.

Aquinas and almost all later Catholic theologians rejected Plato's
view that a human soul can exist in a wholly independent and disem-
bodied way or can be combined with any sort of substance. Under the
Platonic view, God might combine a human soul with a rock or a tree.
Aquinas accepted instead the Aristotelian doctrine of hylomorphism,
which holds that the human soul is not some independent free-floating
substance that can be combined with anything, but is logically related
to the human body in the same way as the shape or form of any object
is logically related to the raw material out of which it is made. No statue
can have a given form unless it—the whole stone, or wood, or wax, or

plaster—has that form. Even God could not bring it about that a huge unformed block of stone actually had the shape of Michelangelo's David. By the same token, nothing can embody a human soul, on this view, unless it already is a human body, which meant, for Aquinas and later Catholic doctrine, a body with the shape and organs of a human being. Aquinas therefore denied that a human soul is already instinct in the embryo that a woman and a man together create through sex. That initial embryo, he thought, is only the raw material of a human being, whose growth is directed by a series of souls, each appropriate to the stage it has reached, and each corrupted and replaced by the next, until it has finally achieved the necessary development for a distinctly human soul.

Aquinas's views about fetal development, which he took from Aristotle, were remarkably prescient in some respects. He understood that an embryo is not an extremely tiny but fully formed child who simply grows larger until birth, as some later scientists with primitive microscopes decided, but an organism that develops through an essentially vegetative stage, then a stage at which sensation begins, and, finally, a stage of intellect and reason. But he was wrong about the biology of reproduction in two important respects. He believed that the active power that causes a new human being to grow is what he called the "generative" soul of the father, acting at a distance through "froth" in the semen, and that the mother contributes only nourishment sustaining that growth. Of course, we now know that both parents contribute chromosomes to the embryo, which has a genetic structure different from that of either of them. Aquinas also apparently thought that the fetal brain and other organs necessary to provide the bodily form required for a sentient or intellectual soul are in place by the time of fetal "quickening" or movement. Modern embryologists believe that the neural substrate necessary to make any sentience possible has not formed until much later.[17]

Catholic philosophers are currently engaged in a strenuous debate about whether Aquinas would have modified his view about when a fetus is ensouled if he had been aware of what biological science has now discovered. One group argues that he would then have maintained that a fetus has a soul from conception: they say that because he believed that the organic development of a fetus must be directed by a soul, and because science has shown that this cannot be the soul of the father acting alone in the way Aquinas supposed, he would have decided that embryological development is directed by the fetus's own soul, which must therefore be present from the start.[18] But this argument seems doubtful. Aquinas thought that the father's soul controlled fetal development at a distance, through some frothy power in the semen. If he had formed his view in the light of modern embryology, he might well have said that the generative souls of both parents direct fetal development together, acting at a distance through the chromosomes each contributes, an opinion that seems much closer to the spirit of his original view than the more radical claim of immediate ensoulment.

The rival group of Catholic philosophers, who argue that Aquinas would not have changed his view, say that his most fundamental reason for denying immediate ensoulment was his hylomorphism—his conviction that a full human soul, which is essentially intellectual, cannot be the form of a creature that has never had the material shape necessary for even the most rudimentary stage of thought or sentience. Joseph Donceel, S.J., puts the point this way: "If form and matter are strictly complementary, as hylomorphism holds, there can be an actual human soul only in a body endowed with the organs required for the spiritual activities of man. We know that the brain, and especially the cortex, are the main organs of those highest sense activities without which no spiritual activity is possible."[19] Donceel and others seem to me right in taking that position (which is the Aristotelian version of the view I defended that a fetus cannot have interests of its own before it has a mental life) to be fundamental to Aquinas's views about ensoulment. But this implies not simply that Aquinas would have continued to deny immediate ensoulment, even if he had had the benefit of modern discoveries, but that he might well have thought that a fetus is ensouled later than he said it was—perhaps not until twenty-six weeks, which is, according to the expert opinion I cited, a cautious choice for a point in fetal development before which sentience is not possible. The combination of traditional Thomist metaphysics and contemporary science might therefore produce a spiritual version of the main distinction drawn in *Roe* v. *Wade:* a fetus has no human soul, and abortion cannot be considered murder, until approximately the end of the second trimester of pregnancy. In any case, however, it is at least problematic whether the now official Catholic view, that a fetus has a full human soul at conception, is consistent with the Thomist tradition.

Nor was that view thought necessary, in the past, to justify the strongest condemnation of even very early abortion. For many centuries, Catholic doctrine, following Aquinas, held that abortion in the early weeks of pregnancy, before the fetus is "formed," is not murder because the soul is not yet present. An instruction manual described as the most influential book of seminary instruction in the nineteenth century still declared, "The fetus, although not ensouled, is directed to the forming of a man; therefore its ejection is anticipated homicide." But though early abortion was not considered murder during this long period, it was certainly considered a grave sin, as the expression "anticipated homicide" insists. Though Jerome did not think an early fetus had a soul, and Augustine was uncertain on the matter, neither of them distinguished between the sinfulness of early and later abortion. Augustine condemned contraception, early abortion—before the fetus "lives"—and later abortion in the same terms. In the Middle Ages, the term "homicide" was sometimes used to name any offense, including contraception, against the natural order of procreation and thus against the sanctity of life conceived as God's divine gift. Decrees of Pope Gregory IX provided that anyone who treated a man or woman "so that he cannot generate, or she conceive, or offspring be born, let it be held as homicide."[20] This expanded conception of homicide, to include not just the killing of an actual human being but any interference with God's creative force, united the church's various concerns with procreation. Masturbation, contraception, and abortion were together seen as offenses against the dignity and sanctity of human life itself. That idea was restated in 1968, in Pope Paul VI's influential encyclical letter about contraception, *Humanae Vitae*.

> Just as man does not have unlimited dominion over his body in general, so also, and with more particular reason, he has no such dominion over his specifically sexual facilities, for these are concerned by their very nature with the generation of life, of which God is the source. For Human life is sacred—all men must recognize that fact, Our Predecessor, Pope John XXIII, recalled, "since from its first beginnings it calls for the creative action of God." Therefore . . . the direct interruption of the generative processes already begun, and, above all, direct abortion, even for therapeutic reasons, are to be absolutely excluded as lawful means of control-

ling the birth of children. Equally to be condemned . . . is direct
sterilization, whether of the man or of the woman, whether permanent or temporary. Similarly excluded is an action, which either
before, at the moment of, or after sexual intercourse, is specifically
intended to prevent procreation—whether as an end or as a
means.[21]

For many centuries, this traditional church view—that abortion is
wicked because it insults the sanctity of human life even when the fetus
killed has not yet been ensouled—was believed capable of sustaining a
firm and unwavering moral opposition to early abortion. Even in 1974,
when the doctrine that a fetus has a right to life from conception had
become fixed in official Catholic doctrine, a declaration by the Sacred
Congregation for the Doctrine of the Faith declared that its opposition
to abortion did not depend on "questions of the moment when the
spiritual soul is infused"—on which, it said, authors are still in disagreement—because even if ensoulment is delayed there is nevertheless a
human life preparing for a soul, which is enough to ground a "moral
affirmation" that abortion is sinful. The declaration noted that the
church's opposition to abortion was just as strong in the long period
when this doctrine was denied.[22] Canon and secular law waxed and
waned in severity about abortion, but even the severest condemnation
of early abortion was thought consistent with denying immediate ensoulment: for a brief period in the sixteenth century, for example, even
excommunication was thought a permissible punishment, as it is now,
for an early abortion. It is true that the church's present position about
abortion is particularly severe by historical standards, not just in the
punishment it provides for early abortions but, even more significantly,
in the exceptions it refuses to recognize for late ones. In 1930, for
example, a papal encyclical made the church's refusal to permit a late-
stage abortion to save the life of a mother more rigid; that change had
nothing to do with any shift in theological doctrine about ensoulment
or the status of an unformed fetus.

It is widely thought that a papal decree in 1869, in which Pius IX
declared that even an early abortion is punishable by excommunication,
marked the first official rejection of the traditional view that a fetus is
ensouled sometime after conception and official adoption of the contem-

porary immediate-ensoulment view. There is considerable debate among religious historians and philosophers about what prompted the change. Some Catholic philosophers suggest that modern biological discoveries were responsible, but as we saw, these discoveries were at least as likely to lead church leaders to believe that ensoulment takes place not earlier but later than Aquinas thought. Some historians suggest a theological rather than philosophical inspiration for the change in doctrine. In 1854, Pius IX pronounced the dogma of Immaculate Conception, that "the Virgin Mary was, in the first instant of her conception, preserved untouched by any taint of original sin," which seems to presuppose that the Virgin had a soul from that moment. But, as Michael Coughlan has argued, alternate constructions of the dogma are available that suppose that God made an exception in this case, for which there are ample historical precedents.[23]

Though it remains controversial whether any philosophical or doctrinal thesis adequately explains the church's official change of view, there is no doubt that the change gave it a considerable political advantage in its campaign against abortion. Since the eighteenth century, Western democracies had begun to resist explicitly theological arguments in politics. In the United States, the First Amendment to the Constitution provides that Congress has no power to establish any particular religion or to legislate in service of any religion's dogma or metaphysics. By the late nineteenth century, the idea that church and state should be separate was becoming orthodox wisdom in many nations of Europe as well. In a political culture that insists on secular justifications for its criminal law, the detached argument that early abortion is sin because any abortion insults and frustrates God's creative power cannot count as a reason for making abortion a crime. It is revealing that though anti-abortion statutes were enacted throughout the United States in the mid-nineteenth century, religious groups and arguments played almost no part in the campaign, which was conducted largely by doctors newly organized into professional associations. (Some of the campaigning doctors opposed abortion on moral grounds; others wanted to stop competition from nondoctors who performed abortion.)

The Roman Catholic church's change to the doctrine of immediate ensoulment greatly strengthened its political position. People who believe, for whatever reason, that a fetus is a person from the instant of its conception are free to argue that even early abortion is the murder of an unborn child, an argument they cannot make if they believe a fetus acquires a soul or becomes a person only later. In other words, Catholic doctrine now allowed a derivative secular as well as a detached religious argument. Just as any religious body can properly argue, even in a pluralist community that separates church from state, that the rights of children or minorities or the poor should not be neglected, so it can argue that the rights of unborn children must not be sacrificed either. God need not be mentioned in the argument. The declaration by the Sacred Congregation I mentioned, published the year after *Roe* v. *Wade*, emphasized this point. "It is true that it is not the task of the law to choose between points of view or to impose one rather than another. But the life of the child takes precedence over all opinions. One cannot invoke freedom of thought to destroy this life. . . . It is at all times the task of the State to preserve each person's rights and to protect the weakest."[24]

The immediate-ensoulment doctrine had another practical political advantage. The older, traditional doctrine—that early abortion is a sin because it insults the inherent value of God's gift of life—was part of a larger general view of sexuality and creation that condemned abortion, masturbation, and contraception as different manifestations of the sin of disrespect of God and life, all aspects of "homicide" in the broadest sense. The church continues to condemn contraception in the strongest terms; in *Humanae Vitae,* Pope Paul VI denounced as "intrinsically deliberate contraception wrong."[25] But contraception is so firmly a fact of life in many Western countries and has seemed so desirable a part of the attempts made to curb population growth and improve economic life in the nations of the Third World that the church needs a sharp and effective way to distinguish abortion from contraception; in the United States, this became particularly important after the Supreme Court's 1965 decision in *Griswold* v. *Connecticut,* which, together with other decisions in its wake, altogether prohibited states to outlaw contraception. Of course, even according to the traditional view, abortion can be distinguished as much the graver insult to God's creative power, and many deeply religious people plausibly believe that contraception, which frustrates no investment in an actual human life, is no insult at all. But the doctrine of immediate ensoulment makes a more dramatic distinction, because it claims that a conceptus has a divine soul, though a sperm or an ovum does not.

The doctrine has had the conspicuous disadvantage, however, of making official Catholic dogma much more remote from the opinions and practices of most Catholics. In 1992, a Gallup poll reported that 52 percent of American Catholics thought that abortion should be legal in "many or all" circumstances, a further 33 percent in "rare" circumstances, and only 13 percent under no circumstances. It also reported that 15 percent of Catholics believe that abortion is morally acceptable in all circumstances, a further 26 percent in many circumstances, 41 percent in rare circumstances, and only 13 percent in none.[26] As I said, in America, Catholic women are actually no less likely to have an abortion than women generally.

Practicing Catholics could not accept the exceptions that most of them do if they really believed that a fetus is a person with a right to life from the moment of conception. Even in Ireland, a country long dominated by conservative Catholicism, where abortion is constitutionally forbidden, most Catholics apparently reject that view. As I mentioned earlier, when an Irish court forbade a fourteen-year-old rape victim to have an abortion in Britain, the order produced a furor. On appeal, the Irish Supreme Court held that the constitutional ban exempted abortions necessary to save a mother's life, and that because the young woman had threatened to kill herself if forced to bear the child, the exception applied in this case. As Catholic critics pointed out, that opinion would seem to permit abortion not just abroad but in Ireland as well on any occasion on which a pregnant woman threatened to kill herself if abortion was refused and a doctor believed her. But the Irish Supreme Court nevertheless felt compelled by public opinion to find some way of permitting the abortion. The series of events provoked the November 1992 referendum I mentioned, in which a majority refused a constitutional amendment declaring that abortion might be lawful when necessary to save the mother's life, but nevertheless approved constitutional changes allowing Irishwomen to have abortions abroad and information about foreign abortion services to be distributed within Ireland. Though the first of these votes was widely understood as a refusal to liberalize abortion, the law that resulted from the referendum plainly presupposes that a fetus is not a person from conception; if it were, a state would certainly be justified in ordering its citizens not to kill a fetus in a foreign country—indeed, it would be morally obliged to do so. (What if some impoverished country decided to permit infanticide in order to encourage tourism? It would certainly be proper for other countries to forbid their citizens to take unwanted young children there.)

So the Irish people's latest vote is further confirmation that even people who believe, on religious grounds, that the state should prohibit almost all abortions do not actually think that a fetus is a person from the moment of conception. They believe something different but more firmly grounded in Catholic tradition: that abortion is a fierce and rarely justified waste of the divine gift of human life. People who oppose abortion for that reason might well find it acceptable that citizens be permitted to have an abortion abroad. Almost no one is such a moral relativist as to believe that infanticide is morally proper if done where the laws permit it, but many people do think that each nation should be permitted to decide for itself what may be done on its soil, out of respect for fundamental intrinsic values, when no one's rights are violated.

These statistics and events tend to support Gary Wills's strong claim that "most Catholics have concluded that their clerical leaders are unhinged on the subject of sex."[27] If the church were to return to its traditional view about the moral status of a fetus, early and late, it would no longer find itself in such sharp doctrinal confrontation with its own members. According to its present view, Catholics who accept the permissibility of abortion in cases of rape or serious fetal deformity are condoning the murder of innocent persons; official doctrine permits no other description. But in the more traditional view, the differences between hierarchy and laity could be regarded as differences in interpretation of a shared and fundamental commitment—to human life as the gift of God—that all Catholics share. For, of course, Catholics who reject the doctrine of immediate ensoulment and deny that an early abortion is murder may nevertheless agree that early abortion is a very grave act, sinful except in the most pressing circumstances. Joseph Donceel, S.J., does not believe that an early fetus is a person, but he nevertheless insists, "Although a prehuman embryo cannot demand from us the absolute respect which we owe to the human person, it deserves a very great consideration, because it is a living being, endowed with a human finality, on its way to hominization. Therefore it seems to me that only very serious reasons should allow us to terminate its existence."[28] Donceel might well recognize exceptions that more conservative Catholics would not, but the ground of judgment he proposes—whether an exception is permitted by the best understanding of the respect owed to any example of developing human life—encourages conservative and liberal alike to understand their differences as less important than their shared respect for human life as intrinsically and overwhelmingly valuable.

Perhaps Catholic doctrine is already moving in this direction, if not explicitly or self-consciously. One of the most interesting religious developments today is the emergence, among Catholics and Protestants who are firmly opposed to any abortion, of the doctrine some of them call the Consistent Ethic of Life. This doctrine insists that people who oppose abortion must show a consistent respect for human life in their views about other social issues. Joseph Cardinal Bernardin, the archbishop of Chicago, has been a pioneer in developing and defending that thesis. In a series of important essays and speeches, he argues that Catholics who oppose abortion out of respect for human life must, if they are consistent, also oppose the death penalty (at least when its deterrent value is in doubt), work toward a fairer health-care policy for the poor, promote welfare policies that will improve the quality and length of human life, and oppose the legalization of active euthanasia even for terminally ill patients.[29]

Cardinal Bernardin has not, so far as I know, cast any explicit doubt on the official contemporary Catholic view that a fetus is a person from conception. In a recent speech, he urged his listeners to help "save the lives of millions of our unborn sisters and brothers."[30] But his argument—that it is *inconsistent* to support capital punishment or euthanasia while condemning abortion—presupposes that principled opposition to abortion is based on respect for the intrinsic value of life, rather than on any assumption that a fetus is a person with a right to life. For someone who based his condemnation of abortion on the latter ground—that a fetus does have such a right—would *not* be inconsistent in endorsing capital punishment if he also thought (as Bernardin does) that a murderer has forfeited his right to live.[31] Nor would he be inconsistent in supporting euthanasia if he agreed with Bernardin's view about why euthanasia is wrong.

Bernardin explicitly bases his own opposition to euthanasia on a detached, not a derivative, argument. "The grounding principle . . . is found in the Judeo-Christian heritage which has played such an influential role in the formation of our national ethos. In this religious tradition, the meaning of human life is grounded in the fact that it is sacred because God is its origin and its destiny." That principle explains, he says, why it is wrong to judge euthanasia by looking only to the question whether it benefits or injures the patient as an individual, rather than to the deeper question of whether it harms a "social good" which can be in "tension" with "personal rights." It would be inconsistent to oppose abortion and support euthanasia only if opposition to abortion necessarily embraced a parallel detached view: that abortion, too, is wrong not just because a fetus has a right to live, if it does, but because abortion insults the "social good" of respect for life, which it would do even if a fetus had no such right. Of course, I do not mean that Cardinal Bernardin or others drawn to his views cannot also insist that a fetus is indeed a person with rights and interests. But their attractive call for consistency assumes that the case against abortion in no way depends on that view.

FEMINISM

I have been arguing that doctrinal religious opinion about abortion can be better understood as based on the detached assumption that human life has intrinsic value rather than on the derivative idea that a fetus is a person with its own interests and rights. I should like to make an opposite but parallel claim about a large and diverse movement rallying its forces mainly on the "pro-choice" side: I suggest that feminist arguments and studies are grounded not just in denying that a fetus is a person or claiming that abortion is permissible even if it is, but also in positive concerns that recognize the intrinsic value of human life.

Of course, it is a crude mistake to treat all women who regard themselves as feminists, or as part of the women's movement in the general sense, as parties to the same set of convictions. There are serious divisions of opinion within feminism about the best strategies for improving the political, economic, and social position of women—for example, about the ethics and wisdom of censoring literature some feminists find demeaning to women. Feminists also disagree about deeper questions: about the character and roots of sexual and gender discrimination, about whether women are genetically different from men in moral sensibility or perception, and about whether the goal of feminism should be simply to erase formal and informal discrimination or to aim instead at a thoroughly genderless world in which roughly as many fathers are in primary charge of children as mothers and roughly as many women hold top military positions as men. Feminists even disagree about whether abortion should be permitted: there *are* "pro-life" feminists.[32] The feminist views I shall discuss are those that are central to this book, those that are concerned with the special connection between a pregnant woman and the fetus she carries.

In the United States, during the decades before *Roe* v. *Wade*, feminists were leaders in the campaigns to repeal anti-abortion laws in various states: they argued, with an urgency and power unmatched by any other group, for the rights that *Roe* finally recognized. They have since expressed deep disgust with Supreme Court decisions that have allowed states to restrict those rights in various ways,[33] and they have demonstrated in support of their position, risking, in some cases, violent injury at the hands of anti-abortion protesters. Nevertheless, some feminists are among the most savage critics of the arguments Justice Blackmun used in his opinion justifying the *Roe* decision; they insist that the Court reached the right result but for very much the wrong reason. Some of them suggest that the decision may in the end have worked to the detriment rather than the benefit of women.

Blackmun's opinion argued that women have a general constitutional right to privacy and that it follows from that general right that they have the right to an abortion before the end of the second trimester of their pregnancy. Some feminists object that the so-called right to privacy is a dangerous illusion and that a woman's freedom of choice about abortion in contemporary societies, dominated by men, should be defended not by an appeal to privacy but instead as an essential aspect of any genuine attempt to improve sexual equality. It is not surprising that feminists should want to defend abortion rights in as many ways as possible, and certainly not surprising that some should call attention to sexual inequality as part of the reason why women need such rights. But why should they be eager not only to claim an additional argument from equality but actually to reject the right-to-privacy argument on which the Court had relied? Why shouldn't they urge both arguments, and as many others as seem pertinent?

Many of the reasons feminist writers offer to explain their rejection of the right to privacy are indeed unconvincing, but it is important to see *why* in order to identify the illuminating and revealing reasons they also offer. Professor Catharine MacKinnon of the Michigan law school, for example, a prominent feminist lawyer, argues that the right-to-privacy argument presupposes what she regards as a fallacious distinction between matters that are in principle private, like the sexual acts and decisions of couples, which government should not attempt to regulate or supervise, and those that are in principle public, like foreign economic policy, about which government must of course legislate.[34] That distinction, she believes, is mistaken and dangerous for women in several ways. It supposes that women really are free to make decisions for themselves within the private space they occupy, though in fact, she insists, women are often very unfree in the so-called private realm; men often force sexual compliance upon them in private, and this private sexual domination both reflects and helps sustain the political and economic subordination of women in the public community.

Appealing to a right to privacy is dangerous, MacKinnon suggests, in two ways. First, insisting that sex is a private matter implies that the government has no legitimate concern with what happens to women behind the bedroom door, where they may be raped or mauled. Second, the claim that abortion is a private matter seems to imply that government has no responsibility to help finance abortion for poor pregnant women as it helps finance childbirth for them. (Other feminists expand on this point: basing the right to an abortion on a right to privacy seems to suggest, they say, that government does all it needs to do for sexual equality by allowing women this free choice, and ignores the larger truth that any substantial advance toward equality will require considerable public expenditure on welfare and other programs directed to women.) MacKinnon argues that the Supreme Court's 1980 decision in *Harris* v. *McRae,* which reversed Judge John Dooling's decision that the Hyde amendment prohibiting the use of federal funds to finance abortion was unconstitutional, was a direct result of the Court's rhetoric about privacy in *Roe* v. *Wade.*

Is this persuasive? It is certainly true that many women are sexually intimidated and that a presumption of much criminal and civil law—that women who have sexual intercourse have either been raped or have freely and willingly consented—is much too crude, and the American law of sexual harassment has begun slowly to change (in part thanks to MacKinnon's work) to reflect that realization. But there is no evident connection between these facts and MacKinnon's claims about the rhetoric of privacy. The right to privacy that the Court recognized in *Roe v. Wade* in no way assumes that all or even some women are genuinely free agents in sexual decisions. On the contrary, that women are often dominated by men makes it more rather than less important to insist that women should have a constitutionally protected right to control the use of their own bodies. MacKinnon, it is true, disparages the motives of men who favor women's right to abortion. Liberal abortion rules, she says, allow men to use women sexually with no fear of any consequences of paternity; allow them, she says, quoting a feminist colleague, to fill women up, vacuum them out, and fill them up again. But her suspicion of men who are her allies, even if it were well founded, would offer no ground for being more critical of the right-to-privacy argument than of any other argument for liberal abortion rules that men might support.

Nor is the second reason she gives against the right-to-privacy argument—that recognizing privacy in sex means that the law will not protect women from marital rape or help to finance abortions—any more persuasive, for she conflates different senses of "privacy." Sometimes privacy is territorial: people have a right to privacy in the territorial sense when they are entitled to do as they wish in a certain specified space—inside their own home, for example. Sometimes privacy is a matter of confidentiality: we say that people may keep their political convictions private, meaning that they need not disclose how they have voted. Sometimes, however, privacy means something different from either of these senses: it means sovereignty over personal decisions. The Supreme Court has cited, for example, as precedents for the right to privacy in contraception and abortion decisions, its earlier rulings that the Constitution protects the right of parents to send their children to a private school or a school in which a foreign language is taught.[35] That is a matter of sovereignty over a particular parental decision that the Court believed should be protected; it is not a matter of either territorial privacy or secrecy. (It is true that in *Griswold* v. *Connecticut*, the contraception case I described earlier, one justice said that the law must not forbid contraceptives because if it did, policemen would have to search bedrooms. But he alone urged that rationale, and the Court explicitly rejected it in a decision soon after when it held that the right to privacy meant that teen-agers were free to buy contraceptives in drugstores.[36])

The right to privacy that the Court endorsed in *Roe* v. *Wade* is plainly privacy in the sense of sovereignty over particular, specified decisions, and it does not follow, from the government's protecting a woman's sovereignty over the use of her own body for procreation, that it is indifferent to how her partner treats her—or how she treats him—inside her home. On the contrary: a right not to be raped or sexually violated is another example of a right to control how one's body is used. Nor does it follow that the government has no responsibility to assure the economic conditions that make the exercise of the right possible and its possession valuable. On the contrary: recognizing that women have a constitutional right to determine how their own bodies are to be used is a prerequisite, not a barrier, to the further claim that the government must ensure that this right is not illusory.[37]

These explanations that MacKinnon and some other feminists give for their opposition to the language of privacy do not go to the heart of the matter. But other passages in their work suggest a far more compelling explanation: claiming that a right to *privacy* protects a woman's decision whether to abort assimilates pregnancy to other situations that are very unlike it; the effect of that assimilation is to obscure the special meaning of pregnancy for women and to denigrate, by overlooking, its unique character. The claim of privacy, according to these feminists, treats pregnancy as if a woman and her fetus were morally and genetically separate entities. It treats pregnancy, MacKinnon says, as if it were just another case in which two separate entities have either deliberately or accidentally become connected in some way and one party plainly has a "sovereign right" to sever the connection if it wishes. She offers these examples of other such cases: the relationship between an employee and her employer, or between a tenant on short lease and his landlord, or (in a reference to a well-known article about abortion by the philosopher Judith Jarvis Thomson that many feminists dislike) between a sick violinist and a woman who wakes to find that the violinist has been connected by tubes to her body, an attachment that must be maintained for nine months if the violinist is to remain alive. MacKinnon insists that pregnancy is not like those relationships; in a striking passage, she describes what pregnancy is like from the perspective of a woman.

In my opinion and in the experience of many pregnant women, the fetus is a human form of life. It is alive. . . . More than a body part but less than a person, where it is, is largely what it is. From the standpoint of the pregnant woman, it is both me and not me. It "is" the pregnant woman in the sense that it is in her and of her and is hers more than anyone's. It "is not" her in the sense that she is not all that is there.[38]

MacKinnon also cites the poet Adrienne Rich's comment, "The child that I carry for nine months can be defined *neither* as me nor as not-me."[39]

By ignoring the unique character of the relationship between pregnant woman and fetus, by neglecting the mother's perspective and assimilating her situation to that of a landlord or a woman strapped to a violinist, the privacy claim obscures, in particular, the special *creative* role of a woman in pregnancy. Her fetus is not merely "in her" as an inanimate object might be, or something alive but alien that has been transplanted into her body. It is "of her and is hers more than anyone's" because it is, more than anyone else's, her creation and her responsibility; it is alive because *she* has made it come alive. She already has an intense physical and emotional investment in it unlike that which any other person, even its father, has; because of these physical and emotional connections it is as wrong to say that the fetus is separate from her as to say that it is not. All these aspects of a pregnant woman's experience—everything special, complex, ironic, and tragic about pregnancy and abortion—is neglected in the liberal explanation that women have a right to abortion because they are entitled to sovereignty over personal decisions, an explanation that would apply with equal force to a woman's right to choose her own clothing.

The most characteristic and fundamental feminist claim is that women's sexual subordination must be made a central feature of the abortion debate. MacKinnon put the point in a particularly striking way: if women were truly equal with men, she said, then the political status of a fetus would be different from what it is now. That seems paradoxical: how can the inequality of women, however unjustified, doom fetuses—half of whom are female—to a lower status, and a lesser right to live, than they would otherwise have? But this objection to MacKinnon's suggestion, like so much else in the public and philosophical debate about abortion, presupposes that the pivotal issue is whether a fetus is a person with interests and rights of its own. The objection would be sound if that were the central issue—if the debate were about a fetus's status in *that* sense. But MacKinnon's point becomes not only sensible but powerful if we take her to be discussing a fetus's status in the detached sense I have distinguished. Then the crucial question is whether and when abortion is an unjustifiable waste of something of intrinsic importance, and MacKinnon's point is the arresting one that the intrinsic importance of a new human life may well depend on the meaning and freedom of the act that created it.

If women were free and equal to men in their sexual relationships, feminists say—if they had a more genuinely equal role in forming the moral, cultural, and economic environment in which children are conceived and raised—then the status of a fetus would be different because it would be more genuinely and unambiguously the woman's own intended and wanted creation rather than something imposed upon her. Abortion would then more plainly be, as of course many women now think it is, a kind of self-destruction, a woman destroying something into which she had mixed herself. Women cannot take that view of abortion now, some feminists argue, because too much sexual intercourse is rape to a degree, and pregnancy is too often the result not of creative achievement but of uncreative subordination, and because the costs of pregnancy and child-rearing are so unfairly distributed, falling so heavily and disproportionately on them.

This argument, at least put in the way I have put it here, may be overstated. It takes no notice of the creative function of the father, for example, and though it shows what is objectionable in relying wholly on the concept of privacy to defend a woman's right to an abortion, it does not prove that the Supreme Court was misguided in relying on that concept in deciding the constitutional issue in *Roe* v. *Wade*. After all, appealing to privacy does not deny the ways in which pregnancy is a unique relationship or the ambivalent and complex character of many pregnant women's attitudes toward the embryos they carry. In fact, the best argument for applying the constitutional right of privacy to abortion, as we shall see in chapter 6, emphasizes the special psychic as well as physical costs of unwanted pregnancies. I do not believe, finally, that even a great and general improvement in gender equality in the United States would either undercut the argument that women have a constitutional right to abortion or obviate the need for such a right.

In spite of these important reservations, the feminist argument has added a very important dimension to the abortion debate. It is true that many women's attitudes toward abortion are affected by a contradictory sense of both identification with and oppression by their pregnancies, and that the sexual, economic, and social subordination of women contributes to that undermining sense of oppression. In a better society, which supported child rearing as enthusiastically as it discourages abortion, the status of a fetus probably would change, because women's sense of pregnancy and motherhood as creative would be more genuine and less compromised, and the inherent value of their own lives less threatened. The feminist arguments reveal another way, then, in which our understanding is cramped and our experience distorted by the one-dimensional idea that the abortion controversy turns only on whether a fetus is a person from the moment of conception. Feminists do not hold that a fetus is a person with moral rights of its own, but they do insist that it is a creature of moral consequence. They emphasize not the woman's right suggested by the rhetoric of privacy, but a woman's responsibility to make a complex decision she is best placed to make.

That is explicitly the message of another prominent feminist lawyer, Professor Robin West, who argues that if the Supreme Court one day overrules *Roe* v. *Wade,* and the battle over abortion shifts from courtrooms to legislatures, women will not succeed in defending abortion rights if they emphasize their right to privacy, which suggests selfish, willful decisions taken behind a veil of immunity from public censure. Instead, she says, women should emphasize responsibility, and she offers what she calls a responsibility-based argument to supplement the right-based claims of *Roe.*

> Women need the freedom to make reproductive decisions not merely to vindicate a right to be left alone, but often to strengthen their ties to others: to plan responsibly and have a family for which they can provide, to pursue professional or work commitments made to the outside world, or to continue supporting their families or communities. At other times the decision to abort is necessitated, not by a murderous urge to end life, but by the harsh reality of a financially irresponsible partner, a society indifferent to the care of children, and a workplace incapable of accommodating or supporting the needs of working parents. . . . Whatever the reason, the

decision to abort is almost invariably made within a web of inter-
locking, competing, and often irreconcilable responsibilities and
commitments.[40]

West is obviously assuming that the audience to which this argument
is addressed has firmly rejected the view that a fetus is a person. If her
claims were interpreted as proposing that a woman may murder another
person in order to "strengthen her ties to others," or because her husband
is financially irresponsible, or because society does not mandate mater-
nity leave, these claims would be politically suicidal for the feminist
cause. West assumes what I have been arguing throughout this chapter:
that most people recognize, even when their rhetoric does not, that the
real argument against abortion is that it is irresponsible to waste human
life without a justification of appropriate importance.

West and other feminists often refer to the research of the sociologist
Professor Carol Gilligan of Harvard University. In a much-cited study,
Gilligan argued that, at least in American society, women characteristically think about moral issues in ways different from men.[41] Women
who are faced with difficult moral decisions, she said, pay less attention
to abstract moral principles than men do, but feel a greater responsibility
to care for and nurture others, and to prevent hurt or pain. She relied
on, among other research studies, interviews with twenty-nine women
contemplating abortion who had been referred to her research program
by counseling services. These women were not typical of all women
considering abortion; although twenty-one of them did have abortions
following the discussions (of the others, four had their babies, two
miscarried, and two could not be reached to learn of their decision), they
were all at least willing to discuss their decisions with a stranger and to
delay their abortions to do so.

One feature of the responses is particularly striking. Though many of
the twenty-nine women in the study were in considerable doubt about
what was the right decision to make, and agonized over it, none of them,
apparently, traced that doubt to any uncertainty or perplexity over the
question of whether a fetus is a person with a right to live. At least
one—a twenty-nine-year-old Catholic nurse—said she believed in the
principle that a fetus is a person and that abortion is murder, but it is
doubtful that she really did believe that, as she also said that she had
come to think that abortion might sometimes be justified because it fell

into "a 'gray' area," just as she now thought, on the basis of her nursing experience, that euthanasia might sometimes be justified in spite of her church's teaching to the contrary. In any case, even she worried, like the others, not about the metaphysical status of the fetus but about a conflict of responsibilities she believed she owed to family, to others, and to herself.

The women in the study did not see this conflict as one between simple self-interest and their responsibilities to others but rather as a conflict between genuine responsibilities on both sides, of having to decide—as a twenty-five-year-old who had already had one abortion put it—how to act in a "decent, human kind of way, one that leaves maybe a slightly shaken but not totally destroyed person." Some of them said that the selfish choice would be to have their babies. One nineteen-year-old felt that "it is a choice of hurting myself [by an abortion] or hurting other people around me. What is more important?" Or, as a seventeen-year-old put it, "What I want to do is to have the baby, but what I feel I should do, which is what I need to do, is have an abortion right now, because sometimes what you want isn't right." When she wanted the child, she said, she wasn't thinking of the responsibilities that go with it, and that was selfish.

All of Gilligan's subjects talked and wondered about responsibility. They sometimes talked of responsibility to the child, but they meant the future hypothetical child, not the existing embryo—they meant that it would be wrong to have a child one could not care for properly. They also worried about other people who would be affected by their decision. One, in her late twenties, said that a right decision depends on awareness of "what it will do to your relationship with the father or how it will affect him emotionally." They talked of responsibility to themselves, but they had in mind not their pleasure, or doing what they wanted now, but their responsibilities to make something of their own lives. One adolescent said, "Abortion, if you do it for the right reasons, is helping you to start over and do different things." A musician in her late twenties said that her choice for abortion was selfish because it was for her "survival," but she meant surviving in her work, which, she said, was "where I derive the meaning of what I am."

Gilligan says, in summary, "Here the conventional feminine voice emerges with great clarity, defining the self and proclaiming its worth on the basis of the ability to care for and protect others." But her subjects

talked of another, more abstract, kind of responsibility as well: responsibility to what they called "the world." One said, "I don't need to pay off
my imaginary debts to the world through this child, and I don't think
that it is right to bring a child into the world and use it for that purpose."
Another said that it would be selfish for her to decide to have an abortion
because it denied "the survival of the child, another human being," but
she did not mean that abortion was murder or that it violated any fetal
rights. She put it in very different, more impersonal and abstract terms:
"Once a certain life has begun it shouldn't be stopped artificially."

This is a brief but carefully accurate statement of what, beneath all
the screaming rhetoric about rights and murder, most people think is the
real moral defect in abortion. Abortion wastes the intrinsic value—the
sanctity, the inviolability—of a human life and is therefore a grave
moral wrong unless the intrinsic value of other human lives would be
wasted in a decision *against* abortion. Each of Gilligan's subjects was
exploring and reacting to that terrible conflict. Each was trying, above
all, to take the measure of her responsibility for the intrinsic value of her
own life, to locate the awful decision she had to make in that context, to
see the decisions about whether to cut off a new life as part of a larger
challenge to show respect for all life by living well and responsibly
herself. Deciding about abortion is not a unique problem, disconnected
from all other decisions, but rather a dramatic and intensely lit example
of choices people must make throughout their lives, all of which express
convictions about the value of life and the meaning of death.

OTHER NATIONS

In democracies, people's convictions about the nature of the abortion
controversy are often reflected not just in their own opinions as individuals and in the positions of groups to which they belong but also
in the details of the legal restrictions on abortion that their governments
enact. In the United States, since 1973, such legislation has been restricted
by the Supreme Court's *Roe* v. *Wade* decision. But there has been a good
deal of legislation about abortion in Europe in recent decades, and like
the Irish referendum I described it supports the view that most people's
concerns about abortion are based on detached rather than derivative
reasons.

Professor Mary Ann Glendon of the Harvard Law School wrote an influential book, published in 1987, comparing the American laws of abortion and divorce with those of other Western countries. She argued that the abortion law imposed by *Roe* v. *Wade* is very much out of step with the law of many Western European countries. Some of those nations permit early abortions subject to either few or no practical constraints. But they also, in different ways, recognize and seek to protect the intrinsic value of human life in any form, which Glendon said *Roe* v. *Wade* does not because it unduly emphasizes individual rights and individual liberty, and encourages "autonomy, separation, and isolation in the war of all against all" in contrast with European emphasis on "social solidarity."⁴² She suggested that the Supreme Court should revise its holdings so as to permit American states each to reach its own resolution of the abortion dilemma, forbidding only laws that, in the words of an Italian decision she quoted, place "a total and absolute priority" on survival of the fetus. She hoped that a spirit of reasonable compromise would then produce, state by state, compromises along the lines of the European laws she discussed.

I disagree with much of Glendon's analysis. I believe the contrast she draws between "individual rights" and "social solidarity," though now very popular among conservative critics of the liberal tradition, is both simplistic and dangerous. The United States' historical commitment to individual human rights has not proved isolating or Hobbesian, as she and other critics have suggested, nor has it undermined a national sense of community. On the contrary. The United States is a nation of continental size, covering many very different and very large regions, and it is pluralist in almost every possible aspect: racial, ethnic, and cultural. In such a nation, individual rights, to the extent they are recognized and actually enforced, offer the only possibility of genuine community in which all individuals participate as equals. The United States can be a *national* community, moreover, only if the most fundamental rights are national, too, only if the most important principles of freedom recognized in some parts of the country are honored in all others as well. It is true that many of the claims that different groups in America now make about what they are entitled to have by right are inflated and sometimes preposterous. But the possibility of abuse no more refutes the need for genuine individual rights than fascism or communism, each of which has claimed authority in the name of "social solidarity," refutes Glendon's appeals for a greater sense of common goal and purpose.

The European nations that Glendon said have chosen solidarity over rights are increasingly recognizing the poverty and danger of that contrast, moreover. The most distinctive contemporary movement within Western European law is not any communitarian striving to place the virtues of "other important values" above the "values of tolerance," as she recommends.[43] Europe remembers only too well the results of that ordering in its recent past, and is horrified at its return in some parts of Eastern Europe now. No, the most important legal trend is toward constitutionally embedded individual rights adjudicated and enforced by courts—not just national courts, but also the international courts in Luxembourg and Strasbourg, which strive to unite Europe as a community of principle as well as commerce.[44]

Europe is different from America in many ways that make Glendon's hopes that American states will one day follow the European pattern of compromise about abortion seem unrealistic. The United States is much less homogeneous, racially and culturally, than France, Britain, Germany, Spain, Italy, or other European nations, and in some regions of the country, politics are more dominated by religious attitudes and groups than the national politics of many of those countries are.[45] In that respect, parts of America are more like Ireland than they are like Britain, France, Germany, or Italy. As I said, several American states and the territory of Guam, each hoping to persuade the Supreme Court to overrule *Roe* v. *Wade*, recently adopted very stern anti-abortion statutes—Gaum's did not allow exceptions even for rape—and several other states would be likely to produce such laws if that decision is ever overruled. Nor does it seem likely that either the national Congress or many state legislatures will soon provide the welfare and other support for poor young mothers that is an important part of the European dedication to human life.

Nevertheless, in spite of these important reservations about Glendon's overall argument, I find her comparisons of American law with that of other countries extremely informative and revealing. They confirm, internationally, the hypothesis I have been defending: that the argument over abortion is not well understood as an argument about whether a fetus is a person, but must be reconstructed as an argument of a very different character.

One European country—Ireland, as we have seen—has very strict anti-abortion laws. Five others—Albania, Northern Ireland, Portugal,

Spain, and Switzerland—nominally restrict abortion, even in early pregnancy, to circumstances in which the mother's general health is threatened and, in Spain and Portugal, to cases of rape, incest, or fetal deformity. The remaining Western European countries, including Belgium, Britain, France, Italy, Germany, and the Scandinavian countries, have laws that either explicitly or in practice allow abortion almost on demand in the first stages of pregnancy—during the first three months in most, though until 1991 up to twenty-eight weeks in Britain, which is *beyond* the point at which *Roe* allows American states to prohibit it. Glendon believes that these restrictions do not significantly reduce the level of abortion. The Netherlands, which has one of the most liberal abortion laws, also has one of the lowest rates of abortion, lower than nearly all countries with stricter laws.[46] But, she argues, the European laws nevertheless contrast with *Roe* because whatever their practical effect on the incidence of abortion, they affirm the central communal value of human life and educate people to respect that value.

Glendon points to the French law, which permits abortion in the first ten weeks only if the pregnant woman is "in distress." The law allows a woman to decide herself whether or not she is in distress, and does not require a medical certificate or any other party's approval, though it does require her to accept "counseling." The government pays at least 70 percent of the cost of the abortion, moreover—all of it if the grounds are wholly medical. The practical effect of the French law may therefore be almost the same as if it had explicitly allowed abortion on demand for ten weeks. Any moral condemnation of abortion implicit in the language of the law seems undercut by the nation's willingness to help pay the costs. But Glendon insists on a different point: the language of the law, by requiring that women declare themselves in "distress," instructs that abortion for whimsical reasons or only for convenience is morally wrong.

Professor Laurence Tribe of the Harvard Law School has said that the "French solution, within an Anglo-American legal system . . . seems to teach mostly hypocrisy."[47] The French law would indeed be duplicitous if the French legislature had claimed, as justification for it, that a fetus is a person with a right to live. It would be hypocritical to declare that a woman is free to take the life of another person if she thinks she is "in distress," and even worse to show no collective interest in the good faith or plausibility of her decision. But the statute is not duplicitous but, rather, finely judged if it aims at a detached rather than a derivative goal: that people recognize the moral gravity of a decision about abortion and take personal moral responsibility for it. It lays down an official standard that a woman is expected to interpret and define for herself as an exercise of personal responsibility, and it provides for an occasion of counseling at which the moral gravity of the act can be explored without usurping her own right and duty to make the moral decision for herself.

Glendon rightly calls attention to an important decision of the Federal Republic of Germany's Constitutional Court. In 1974, the West German parliament adopted a liberal abortion statute providing that abortion was permissible for any reason until the twelfth week of pregnancy but illegal after that time except for serious reasons: fetal deformity or a threat to the health of the mother. In 1975, in a complicated and very controversial opinion, the Constitutional Court held that law unconstitutional on the ground that it did not sufficiently value human life.

The court relied, among other provisions, on Article 2(2) of the 1949 West German Basic Law, which declares, "Everyone shall have the right to life and to inviolability of his person." This suggests a derivative ground for the court's decision; it suggests that the court may have believed that even an early fetus has a right to life as powerful as the right of any other person. But the argument the court offered, and the decision it actually reached, are inconsistent with that proposition. The decision can only be understood as resting on the different, detached, ground that any German law of abortion must be drafted so as to acknowledge the intrinsic importance of human life.[48] For the court did not declare that any statute that permitted abortion except, perhaps, to save a mother's life, would be unconstitutional, as it should logically have done if it really meant to declare that every fetus has a guaranteed right to life. Instead, it held that the 1974 statute was invalid because it formally required no reason at all for abortion during the first twelve weeks, and so evidenced no sign of the moral gravity of deliberately ending a human life. The court held that the statute's complete disregard for what, at least after fourteen days of gestation, was plainly a form of human life was inconsistent with the meaning of the 1949 Basic Law, which rests, as the court put it, on "an affirmation of the fundamental value of human life," an affirmation intended wholly to repudiate the utter contempt the Nazis had shown for that value.

The court made plain that it was not ruling out abortions, even on grounds that any conservative would reject as improper. It invited the parliament to adopt a new statute allowing abortion but showing more respect for the intrinsic value of life than the 1974 statute had. By way of illustration, and to ensure that abortion was available for good cause in the interval before a new law was completed, the court drafted and imposed its own "transitional" abortion scheme, which made plain, again, that it did not really affirm a fetal right to life. The transitional rules provided, for example, that abortion was permissible not only in cases of rape, or fetal deformity, or when the mother's health was threatened, but also "in order to avert the danger of a grave emergency" of some other kind to the pregnant woman.

Glendon suggests that the practical differences between these transitional rules the court itself drafted and the law that it had declared unconstitutional were speculative. The real difference, she says, is in the social meaning of the court's declaration that, in principle, abortion is not a matter for whim or caprice but is an issue of moral gravity. In 1976, the West German parliament enacted a new statute whose practical difference from the overruled 1974 law, in terms of what each law in practice prohibits, is even more marginal. The 1976 law provided that abortion is permissible within twelve weeks if continued pregnancy would place a woman in a situation of serious hardship, and up to the twenty-second week if fetal deformity would make it unreasonable to require a woman to continue the pregnancy. It also provided, like the French law, for mandatory counseling before even an early abortion, and for a three-week waiting period between counseling and abortion. As I noted in chapter 1, the unified German parliament adopted a new, even more liberal law in 1992, and the Constitutional Court was expected to rule on the constitutionality of that new law early in 1993.

In 1985, the Spanish Constitutional Court, obviously influenced by the German decision of 1975, considered the constitutionality of new Spanish laws that had repealed old and very strict constraints on abortion and introduced new rules allowing abortion in cases of rape, fetal deformity, and threat to the mother's physical or mental health. The court made the distinction I have been pressing, between the derivative claim that a fetus has rights as a "person" and the detached idea that human life has an intrinsic value that must be recognized and endorsed collectively. It denied that a fetus is a person for purposes of the Spanish constitution, or has the rights of a person, but it said that the Spanish constitution does endorse human life as a value that the nation's laws must respect.[49] By a close vote, it held the new abortion law unconstitutional but neverthe-less set out guidelines for amendment it said would make the law constitutional: that a doctor must certify any claimed threat to the mother's physical and mental health, and that abortion facilities must be licensed.[50] The Spanish parliament accepted these guidelines and amended the law accordingly. The changes did not, as a practical mat-ter, substantially strengthen restrictions on abortion, but they did signal the collective concern for the gravity of abortion that a majority of the Constitutional Court thought essential.

In 1992, the European Court of Human Rights made an important decision that also presupposed that a fetus is not a person with rights or interests of its own, and that laws prohibiting or regulating abortion can be justified only on the different ground that abortion is thought to jeopardize the inherent value of human life.[51] Before the 1992 referen-dum, Irish law forbade any organization to supply to a pregnant woman within Ireland the name, address, or telephone number of an abortion clinic in Great Britain, and an Irish court had issued a permanent injunction against two abortion-counseling services that did provide that information. The judge had considered the argument that an in-junction would violate a pregnant woman's constitutional right to infor-mation, but he had declared that "I am satisfied that no right could constitutionally arise to obtain information the purpose of which was to defeat the constitutional right of the unborn child." The counseling services appealed to the European Court, arguing that the injunction violated the European Convention of Human Rights, to which Ireland is a party. That court did not decide whether the convention guarantees a right to abortion, because it did not need to. But the court did decide that the ban on information violated Article 10 of the Convention, which protects freedom of speech and information. Among other arguments, it said that since information about abortion clinics is available from other sources in Ireland—for example, from British telephone books there—the ban on organizations supplying that information to pregnant women who request it would not prevent enough abortions to justify the con-straint on freedom of information. It used, in other words, a test of "proportionality" between the degree to which the ban on information would aid Ireland's policy of protecting fetal life and the degree to which it would harm freedom of speech; it held that the gain to the policy was not significant enough to justify the cost to freedom. But that proportionality test would be bizarre if, as the Irish government argued, a fetus is a person with a right to life: if it is, then a government would be entitled to try to prevent the murder of even one additional fetus, and a ban on direct information about foreign abortion clinics would be appropriate even if most pregnant women had other ways of obtaining that information. The Irish law has now been changed, but the European Court's decision remains important because its proportionality test presupposes that the point of laws banning abortion is not to prevent murder but to protect a public sense of the inherent value of life. It is proper to argue that minor or very marginal gains in achieving *that* goal would not justify substantial abridgments of other rights, including the rights protected by the Convention's Article 10.

THE NEXT STEP

Though this chapter has covered much ground, it has been dedicated mainly to a single claim: that we cannot understand the moral argument now raging around the world—between individuals, within and between religious groups, as conducted by feminist groups, or in the politics of several nations—if we see it as centered on the issue of whether a fetus is a person. Almost everyone shares, explicitly or intuitively, the idea that human life has objective, intrinsic value that is quite independent of its personal value for anyone, and disagreement about the right interpretation of that shared idea is the actual nerve of the great debate about abortion. For that reason, the debate is even more important to most people than an argument about whether a fetus is a person would be, for it goes deeper—into different conceptions of the value and point of human life and of the meaning and character of human death.

I have tried to show the inadequacy of the conventional explanation. But so far I have said little to make the concept of intrinsic value, or of sanctity or inviolability, more precise or to answer the objection that these ideas are too mysterious to figure in a genuine explanation of anything. Nor have I yet explained, except in the most tentative way, how we can make sense of the abortion debate in light of these ideas. These are crucial challenges, and we must confront them at once.

3

WHAT IS

SACRED?

Scientists sometimes cannot explain their observations about the known universe except by assuming the existence of something not yet discovered—another planet or star or force. So they assume that something else does exist, and they look for it. Astronomers discovered the planet Neptune, for example, only after they realized that the movements of the planet Uranus could be explained only by the gravitational force of another celestial body, yet unknown, orbiting the sun still farther out.

I have been arguing that most of us—liberals as well as conservatives—cannot explain our convictions in the way that many politicians, self-appointed spokesmen, moralists, and philosophers think we can. They say that the different opinions we have about when and why abortion is morally wrong, and about how the law should regulate abortion, all follow from some foundational conviction each of us has about whether a fetus is a person with rights or interests of its own, and, if so, how far these trump the rights and interests of a pregnant woman. But when we look closely at the kinds of convictions most people have, we find that we cannot explain these simply by discovering people's views about whether a human fetus is a person. Our convictions reflect another idea we also hold, whose gravitational force better explains the shape of our beliefs and our disagreements.

I have already said what that different idea is. We believe that it is

68

intrinsically regrettable when human life, once begun, ends prematurely. We believe, in other words, that a premature death is bad in itself, even when it is not bad for any particular person. Many people believe this about suicide and euthanasia—that a terrible thing has happened when someone takes his own life or when his doctor kills him at his own request even when death may be in that person's own best interests. We believe the same about abortion: that it is sometimes wrong not because it violates a fetus's rights or harms its interests, but in spite of a fetus's having no rights or interests to violate. The great majority of people who have strong views about abortion—liberal as well as conservative—believe, at least intuitively, that the life of a human organism has intrinsic value in any form it takes, even in the extremely undeveloped form of a very early, just-implanted embryo. I say "at least intuitively" because many people have not related their views about abortion or euthanasia to the idea that human life has intrinsic value. For them, that idea is the undiscovered planet that explains otherwise inexplicable convictions.

The idea of life's intrinsic value may seem mysterious, and I must try to make it seem less so. I shall have to overcome, first, an objection that philosophers have raised, which denies the very possibility that *anything* has intrinsic value. David Hume and many other philosophers insisted that objects or events can be valuable only when and because they serve someone's or something's interests. On this view, nothing is valuable unless someone wants it or unless it helps someone to get what he does want. How can it be important that a life continue unless that life is important for or to someone? How can a life's continuing be, as I am suggesting, simply important in and of itself?

That may seem a powerful objection. But much of our life is based on the idea that objects or events can be valuable in themselves. It is true that in ordinary, day-to-day life people do spend most of their time trying to get or make things they value because they or someone else enjoys or needs them. They try to make money and buy clothes or food or medicine for that reason. But the idea that some events or objects are valuable in and of themselves—that we honor them not because they serve our desires or interests but for their own sakes—is also a familiar part of our experience. Much of what we think about knowledge, experience, art, and nature, for example, presupposes that in different ways these are valuable in themselves and not just for their utility or for the pleasure or satisfaction they bring us. The idea of intrinsic value is commonplace, and it has a central place in our shared scheme of values and opinions.

It is not enough, however, simply to say that the idea of intrinsic value is familiar. For we are concerned with a special application of that idea—the claim that human life even in its most undeveloped form has intrinsic value—and that application raises unique puzzles. Why does it not follow, for example, that there should be as much human life as possible? Most of us certainly do not believe that. On the contrary, it would be better, at least in many parts of the world, if there were less human life rather than more. Then how can it be intrinsically important that human life, once begun, continue? Those are important questions, and in answering them we will discover a crucial distinction between two categories of intrinsically valuable things: those that are *incrementally* valuable—the more of them we have the better—and those that are not but are valuable in a very different way. I shall call the latter *sacred* or *inviolable* values.

There is another, quite independent puzzle. I claim not only that most of us believe that human life has intrinsic value, but also that this explains why we disagree so profoundly about abortion. How can that be? How can a shared assumption explain the terrible divisions about abortion that are tearing us apart? The answer, I believe, is that we interpret the idea that human life is intrinsically valuable in different ways, and that the different impulses and convictions expressed in these competing interpretations are very powerful and passionate.

It is obvious enough that the abstract idea of life's intrinsic value is open to different interpretations. Suppose we accept this abstract idea, and also accept that in at least some circumstances a deliberate abortion would show a wrongful contempt for the intrinsic value of life. Which circumstances are these? The list of questions we must pose in deciding this is very long. Is an abortion at a late stage of pregnancy a worse insult to the intrinsic value of life than one at an early stage? If so, why? What standard of measurement or comparison do and should we use in making that kind of judgment?

What else, besides abortion, fails to show the required respect for human life? Does a doctor show respect for life when he allows a mother to die in order to save a fetus? Which decision that a doctor might make in such circumstances would show more and which less respect for the intrinsic value of human life? Why? Suppose a pregnancy is the result of rape: which decision then shows greater respect for the intrinsic value of human life—a decision for or against abortion? Suppose a fetus is horribly deformed: does it show respect or contempt for life to allow it to be born? What standard of measuring respect or contempt for human life should we use in making these judgments?

Different people with sharply different convictions about a range of religious and philosophical matters answer these various questions differently, and the different answers they give in fact match the main divisions of opinion about abortion. If we can understand the abortion controversy as related to other differences of religious and philosophical opinion in that way, then we shall understand much better how and why we disagree. We shall also be in a better position to emphasize how we agree, to see how our divisions, deep and painful though they are, are nevertheless rooted in a fundamental unity of humane conviction. What we share is more fundamental than our quarrels over its best interpretation.

THE IDEA OF THE SACRED

What does it mean to say that human life is intrinsically important? Something is *instrumentally* important if its value depends on its usefulness, its capacity to help people get something else they want. Money and medicine, for example, are only instrumentally valuable: no one thinks that money has value beyond its power to purchase things that people want or need, or that medicine has value beyond its ability to cure. Something is *subjectively* valuable only to people who happen to desire it. Scotch whiskey, watching football games, and lying in the sun are valuable only for people, like me, who happen to enjoy them. I do not think that others who detest them are making any kind of a mistake or failing to show proper respect for what is truly valuable. They just happen not to like or want what I do.

Something is intrinsically valuable, on the contrary, if its value is *independent* of what people happen to enjoy or want or need or what is good for them. Most of us treat at least some objects or events as intrinsically valuable in that way: we think we should admire and protect them because they are important in themselves, and not just if or because we or others want or enjoy them. Many people think that great paintings, for example, are intrinsically valuable. They are valuable, and must be respected and protected, because of their inherent quality as art, and not because people happen to enjoy looking at them or find instruction or some pleasurable aesthetic experience standing before them. We say that we want to look at one of Rembrandt's self-portraits because it is wonderful, not that it is wonderful because we want to look at it. The thought of its being destroyed horrifies us— seems to us a terrible desecration—but this is not just because or even if that would cheat us of experiences we desire to have. We are horrified even if we have only a very small chance of ever seeing the painting anyway—perhaps it is privately owned and never shown to the public, or in a museum far away—and even if there are plenty of excellent reproductions available.[1]

We treat not just particular paintings or other works of art that way, but, more generally, human cultures. We think it a shame when any distinctive form of human culture, especially a complex and interesting one, dies or languishes. Once again, this cannot be fully explained merely in terms of the contribution that cultural variety makes to the excitement of our lives. We create museums to protect and sustain interest in some form of primitive art, for example, not just because or if we think its objects splendid or beautiful, but because we think it a terrible waste if any artistic form that human beings have developed should perish as if it had never existed. We take much the same attitude toward parts of popular or industrial culture: we are troubled by the disappearance of traditional crafts, for example, not just if we need what it produced—perhaps we do not—but because it seems a great waste that an entire form of craft imagination should disappear.

Is human life subjectively or instrumentally or intrinsically valuable? Most of us think it is all three. We treat the value of someone's life as instrumental when we measure it in terms of how much his being alive serves the interests of others: of how much what he produces makes other people's lives better, for example. When we say that Mozart's or Pasteur's life had great value because the music and medicine they created served the interests of others, we are treating their lives as instrumentally valuable. We treat a person's life as subjectively valuable when we measure its value to him, that is, in terms of how much *he* wants to be alive or how much being alive is good for him. So if we say that life has lost its value to someone who is miserable or in great pain, we are treating that life in a subjective way.

Let us call the subjective value a life has for the person whose life it is its *personal* value. It is personal value we have in mind when we say that normally a person's life is the most important thing he or she has. It is personal value that a government aims to protect, as fundamentally important, when it recognizes and enforces people's right to life. So it is understandable that the debate about abortion should include the question of whether a fetus has rights and interests of its own. If it does, then it has a personal interest in continuing to live, an interest that should be protected by recognizing and enforcing a right to life. I have argued that an early fetus has no interests and rights, and that almost no one thinks it does; if personal value were the only pertinent kind of value at stake in abortion, then abortion would be morally unproblematic.

If we think, however, that the life of any human organism, including a fetus, has intrinsic value whether or not it also has instrumental or personal value—if we treat any form of human life as something we should respect and honor and protect as marvelous in itself—then abortion remains morally problematical. If it is a horrible desecration to destroy a painting, for example, even though a painting is not a person, why should it not be a much greater desecration to destroy something whose intrinsic value may be vastly greater?

We must notice a further and crucial distinction: between what we value incrementally—what we want more of, no matter how much we already have—and what we value only once it already exists. Some things are not only intrinsically but incrementally valuable. We tend to treat knowledge that way, for example. Our culture wants to know about archaeology and cosmology and galaxies many millions of light-years away—even though little of that knowledge is likely to be of any practical benefit—and we want to know as much of all that as we can.[2] But we do not value human life that way. Instead, we treat human life as sacred or inviolable. (As I said in chapter 1, I use those terms—and also the terms "sanctity" and "inviolability"—interchangeably.) The hallmark of the sacred as distinct from the incrementally valuable is that the sacred is intrinsically valuable because—and therefore only once—

it exists. It is inviolable because of what it represents or embodies. It is not important that there be more people. But once a human life has begun, it is very important that it flourish and not be wasted.

Is that a peculiar distinction? No: we make the same distinction about other objects or events that we think are intrinsically valuable. We treat much of the art we value as sacredly rather than incrementally valuable. We attach great value to works of art once they exist, even though we care less about whether more of them are produced. Of course we may believe that the continued production of *great* art is tremendously important—that the more truly wonderful objects a culture produces the better—and we believe the same about great lives: even those who are most in favor of controlling population growth would not want fewer Leonardo da Vincis or Martin Luther Kings. But even if we do not regret that there are not more works by a given painter, or more examples of a particular artistic genre, we insist on respecting the examples we do in fact have. I do not myself wish that there were more paintings by Tintoretto than there are. But I would nevertheless be appalled by the deliberate destruction of even one of those he did paint.

Something is sacred or inviolable when its deliberate destruction would dishonor what ought to be honored. What makes something sacred in that way? We can distinguish between two processes through which something becomes sacred for a given culture or person. The first is by association or designation. In ancient Egypt, for example, certain animals were held sacred to certain gods; because cats were associated with a certain goddess, and for no other reason, it was sacrilegious to injure them. In many cultures, people take that attitude toward national symbols, including flags. Many Americans consider the flag sacred because of its conventional association with the life of the nation; the respect they believe they owe their country is transferred to the flag. Of course, the flag's value to them is not subjective or instrumental. Nor is the flag incrementally valuable; even the most flag-reverent patriot does not believe that there must be as many flags as possible. He values the flag as sacred rather than incrementally valuable, and its sacred character is a matter of association.

The second way something may become sacred is through its history, how it came to be. In the case of art, for example, inviolability is not associational but genetic: it is not what a painting symbolizes or is associated with but how it came to be that makes it valuable. We protect even a painting we do not much like, just as we try to preserve cultures we do not especially admire, because they embody processes of human creation we consider important and admirable.

We take a parallel attitude, we must now notice, toward aspects of the natural world: in our culture, we tend to treat distinct animal species (though not individual animals) as sacred. We think it very important, and worth considerable economic expense, to protect endangered species from destruction at human hands or by a human enterprise—a market in rhinoceros tusks, valued for their supposed aphrodisiac power; dams that threaten the only habitat of a certain species of fish; or timbering practices that will destroy the last horned owls. We are upset—it would be terrible if the rhinoceros ceased to exist—and we are indignant: surely it is wrong to allow such a catastrophe just so that human beings can make more money or increase their power.

Why are individual species so valuable that it would be dreadful if some useful enterprise destroyed one or a few of the many thousands of species in the world? Someone might say: we protect endangered species because we want the pleasure of continuing to see animals of each species, or because we want the useful information we might gain by studying them, or because it is more interesting for us that there be more rather than fewer species. But none of these arguments rings true. Many—perhaps most—of the people who consider endangered species important are very unlikely ever to encounter any of the animals they want to protect. I doubt that many who have labored to protect the horned owl have any plans to visit the habitat of those birds or to look them up in zoos, nor do I think they believe that in keeping horned owls alive we will learn enough useful information to justify the expense. These people struggle to protect the species simply because they think it would be a shame if human acts and decisions caused it to disappear.

So this is another important example of something many of us take to be of intrinsic rather than instrumental value. It is also an example of sacred rather than incremental value: few people believe the world would be worse if there had always been fewer species of birds, and few would think it important to engineer new bird species if that were possible. What we believe important is not that there be any particular number of species but that a species that now exists not be extinguished by us. We consider it a kind of cosmic shame when a species that nature has developed ceases, through human actions, to exist.

I put the point that way—about not destroying what nature has created—to emphasize the similarity I claim between our reverence for art and our concern for the survival of species. Both art and species are examples of things inviolable to us not by association but in virtue of their history, of how they came to exist. We see the evolutionary process through which species were developed as itself contributing, in some way, to the shame of what we do when we cause their extinction now. Indeed, people who are concerned to protect threatened species often stress the connection between art and nature themselves by describing the evolution of species as a process of creation.

For most Americans, and for many people in other countries, the evolutionary process is quite literally creative, for they believe that God is the author of nature. On that assumption, causing a species to disappear, wholly to be lost, is destroying a creative design of the most exalted artist of all. But even people who do not take that view, but who instead accept the Darwinian thesis that the evolution of species is a matter of accidental mutation rather than divine design, nevertheless often use artistic metaphors of creation. They describe discrete animal species as not just accidents but as achievements of adaptation, as something that nature has not just produced but wrought. The literature of conservation is studded with such personifications of nature as creative artist. They are part of the fertile ground of ideas and associations in which the roots of conservationist concern are buried. Indeed, so thoroughly have the metaphors of artistic and cultural creation come to dominate pleas for the preservation of species that the analogy is now used in reverse. An anthropologist recently pleaded that we should treat the threatened death of a primitive language with as much concern and sympathy as we show snail darters and horned owls and other near-extinct species of animal life.[3]

Our concern for the preservation of animal species reaches its most dramatic and intense form, of course, in the case of one particular species: our own. It is an inarticulate, unchallenged, almost unnoticed, but nevertheless absolute premise of our political and economic planning that the human race must survive and prosper. This unspoken assumption unites the two different examples of sanctity we have so far identified. Our special concern for art and culture reflects the respect in which we hold artistic creation, and our special concern for the survival of animal species reflects a parallel respect for what nature, understood either as divine or as secular, has produced. These twin bases of the sacred come together in the case of the survival of our own species, because we treat it as crucially important that we survive not only biologically but culturally, that our species not only lives but thrives. That is the premise of a good part of our concern about conservation and about the survival and health of cultural and artistic traditions. We are concerned not only about ourselves and others now alive, but about untold generations of people in centuries to come.

We cannot explain our concern about future humanity, of course, as concern for the rights and interests of particular people. Suppose that through great stupidity we were to unleash radioactivity whose consequence was that human beings were extinct by the twenty-second century. It is absurd to argue that we would then have done terrible injury or injustice to people who would otherwise have lived, unless we think that in some very crowded mystical space people are waiting to be conceived and born. We sometimes talk that way, and may even fall into ways of thinking that would make sense only if there were such mystical worlds of possible people with a right to exist. But in fact our worries about humanity in centuries to come make sense only if we suppose that it is intrinsically important that the human race continue even though it is not important to the interests of particular people.

We also consider it important that people live well, and we therefore think we have a responsibility not only not to destroy the possibility of future generations but also to leave them a fair share of natural and cultural resources. That is the presupposition of what philosophers call the problem of justice between generations: the idea that each generation of people must in fairness leave the world fit for habitation not only by their children and grandchildren, whom they already know and love, but for generations of descendants whose identity is in no way yet fixed, at least in ways we can understand, but depends on what we must consider billions of independent accidents of genetic coupling. Philosophers speak of this as a matter of justice, and so do politicians and columnists: they argue, for example, that the huge national debt that the government has allowed the United States to develop in recent decades is unfair to generations yet unborn. But that way of putting it is misleading, because our concern for the future is not concern for the rights or interests of specific people. The decisions we now make about conservation and the economy will affect, in ways we cannot understand, let alone anticipate, not only what resources our descendants will have but which people they will be. It hardly makes sense to say that we owe it to some particular individual not selfishly to squander the earth's resources if that individual will exist only if we do squander them. Or, for that matter, only if we don't. Our concern for future generations is not a matter of justice at all but of our instinctive sense that human flourishing as well as human survival is of sacred importance.

Through this canvass of things, events, and processes that many people take to be inviolable, I have tried to show how general the idea of the sacred really is, and therefore to forestall the objection that the principle that I believe is at the root of most people's convictions about abortion— the principle that human life, even the life of a very early embryo, is inviolable—is bizarre or odd. But the examples have the further value of suggesting that at least in many of the most familiar cases, the nerve of the sacred lies in the value we attach to a process or enterprise or project rather than to its results considered independently from how they were produced. We are horrified at the idea of the deliberate destruction of a work of art not just because we lose the art but because destroying it seems to demean a creative process we consider very important. Similarly, we honor and protect cultures, which are also, more abstractly, forms of art, because they are communal products of the kinds of enterprise we treat as important. Our attitudes toward individual works of art and discrete cultures, then, display a deep respect for the enterprises that give rise to them; we respect these enterprises independently of their particular results.

Our concern for the preservation of animal species is also based on respect for the way they came into being rather than for the animals considered independently of that history. The natural processes of evolution and development themselves have a normative significance for us, and this is not because the species they generated—the rhinoceros or the horned owl, for example—are superior on some independent test of animal worth to others that might have evolved if they had not, but because we consider it wrong, a desecration of the inviolable, that a species that evolution did produce should perish through our acts. Geneticists have created plants that we find instrumentally valuable: they produce food and may save lives. But we do not think that these artificially produced species are intrinsically valuable in the way that naturally produced species are.

For many people, as I said, the respect we owe nature is respect for God conceived as the divine creator. We respect all God's creatures, on this view, not one by one, not each robin or horse or horned owl or snail darter, but as imaginative designs produced by God's inspired genius, to be honored as such, as God commanded Noah to honor his designs by keeping species, not individual animals, alive in the ark. Some conservationists who do not think of themselves as religious may nevertheless hold a powerful, intuitive conviction that nature is *itself* alive, a mysterious, inexorable force unifying all life in Life itself. Walt Whitman was the poet of that conviction—in *Leaves of Grass* and *Song of Myself* he celebrated the "procreant urge of the world"[4]—and another poet, David Plante, speaks of an elemental "pulse in the mud" as the mysterious source of all life. People with either of these views—the conventionally religious one or some version of the idea that nature itself is purposive—believe that destroying a species is wrong because it wastes an important and creative achievement of God or the procreant world. They mean that we should regret the loss of a species just as—though to a much greater degree than—we would regret the foundering of some project on which we or others had long labored. We regret the waste of a creative investment not just for what we do not have, but because of the special badness of great effort frustrated.

But many people who wish to protect endangered animal species or other important or beautiful natural products do not believe in a creative God or in a mysterious intelligence guiding nature. For them, the analogy between nature and art is only an analogy: they speak of nature as creative only as a metaphorical way of reporting their primitive but strong conviction that nature and art are both processes whose products are, in principle, inviolable. They believe that it is a shame for human beings to destroy what was created over aeons of natural selective evolution, not because some divine or cosmic artist created it but just because, in some primal way, it *is* a shame, an intrinsically bad thing to do. When they say that the extinction of a species is a waste of nature's investment, they mean not that nature is a conscious investor but that even unconscious natural processes of creation should be treated as investments worthy of respect.[5] Perhaps future generations will mock the idea as ridiculously sentimental. But it is nevertheless very wide-spread now, and there is nothing irrational or disreputable about it. It is no more sentimental to treat what nature has created as an investment we should not waste than it is to take the same view of an ancient work of art, whose unknown author perished many centuries ago, or of some ancient language or craft created by people who never thought they were investing in anything.

I must emphasize, finally, two further features of our convictions about the sacred and inviolable. First, for most of us, there are degrees of the sacred just as there are degrees of the wonderful. It would be sacrilegious for someone to destroy a work by a minor Renaissance artist but not as bad as destroying a Bellini. It is regrettable when a distinctive and beautiful species of exotic bird is destroyed, but it would be even worse if we stamped out the Siberian tiger. And though we would no doubt regret the entire extinction of pit vipers or sharks, our regret might be mixed; we might think it not as bad when a species is destroyed that is dangerous to us. Second, our convictions about inviolability are selective. We do not treat everything that human beings create as sacred. We treat art as inviolable, but not wealth or automobiles or commercial advertising, even though people also create these. We do not treat everything produced by a long natural process—coal or petroleum deposits, for example—as inviolable either, and many of us have no compunction about cutting down trees to clear space for a house or slaughtering complex mammals like cows for food. And we consider only some species of animals as sacred: few people care when even a benign species of insect comes to an end, and even for those who believe that viruses are animals, the eradication of the AIDS virus would be an occasion for celebration untinged by even a trace of regret.

So in different ways we are selective about which products of which kinds of creative or natural processes we treat as inviolable. As we would expect, our selections are shaped by and reflect our needs and, in a reciprocal way, shape and are shaped by other opinions we have. We honor human artistic effort, for example, because it can produce marvel-ous things, like great paintings of beauty and insight and wonder, and then, because we honor that form of human creative enterprise, we respect everything it produces, including paintings we do not find mar-velous. We honor nature because it has produced striking geological formations and majestic plants and living creatures we find extraordinary, including us, and we protect examples of that production—mountains or rivers or forests or animals—in a special and more intense way because they are natural. The reciprocity between our admiration for processes and our admiration for product is complex, and its result, for most people, is not a single overarching principle from which all their convictions about the inviolable flow, but a complex network of feelings and intuitions.

It is not my present purpose to recommend or defend any of these widespread convictions about art and nature, in either their religious or secular form. Perhaps they are all, as some skeptics insist, inconsistent superstitions. I want only to call attention to their complexity and characteristic structure, because I hope to show that most people's convictions about abortion and euthanasia can be understood as resting on very similar, though in some important ways different, beliefs about how and why *individual* human life, in any form, is also inviolable.

THE SANCTITY OF EACH HUMAN LIFE

An obscure nineteenth-century Austrian philosopher, Joseph Popper-Lynkeus, said that the death of any human being, except of a murderer or a suicide, was "a far more important happening than any political or religious or national occurrence, or the sum total of the scientific and artistic and technological advances made throughout the ages by all the peoples of the world."[6] He added that anyone tempted to regard this extraordinary claim as an exaggeration should "imagine the individual concerned to be himself or his best beloved." His addition confuses the intrinsic value of human life with what I called its personal value. My life may be personally more important to me than anything else, but it does not follow that it is intrinsically more important, and once that distinction is made, it is ludicrous to suppose that even a premature and tragic death, let alone a natural death after a long life, is intrinsically a worse event than the destruction of all human art and knowledge would be. But Popper-Lynkeus's claim does capture, in hyperbolic form, a conviction that must now be our main concern: that in some circumstances the deliberate ending of a single human life is intrinsically bad—objectively a shame—in the same way as the destruction of great art or the loss of important knowledge would be.

We are now in a better position to appreciate that conviction. I said that we treat the preservation and prosperity of our own species as of capital importance because we believe that we are the highest achievements of God's creation, if we are conventionally religious, or of evolution, if we are not, and also because we know that all knowledge and art and culture would disappear if humanity did. That combination of nature and art—two traditions of the sacred—supports the further and more dramatic claim that each individual human life, on its own, is also inviolable, because each individual life, on its own, can be understood as the product of both creative traditions. The first of these traditions—the idea that nature is creative—has had a prominent role as a basis for that claim. The dominant Western religious traditions insist that God made humankind "in His own image," that each individual human being is a representation and not merely a product of a divine creator, and people who accept that article of faith will understandably think that each human being, not just the species as a whole, is a creative masterpiece. A secular form of the same idea, which assigns the masterpiece to nature rather than God, is also a staple of our culture—the image of a human being as the highest product of natural creation is one of Shakespeare's most powerful, for example. "What a piece of work is a man!" says Hamlet, and James Tyrrel, who arranges the murder of the princes in the Tower for Richard III, quotes a killer as being appalled at realizing that he has "smothered the most replenished sweet work of Nature that from the prime creation e'er she framed." In these and other ways, the idea that human beings are special among natural creations is offered to explain why it is horrible that even a single human individual life should be extinguished.

The role of the other tradition of the sacred in supporting the sanctity of life is less evident but equally crucial: each developed human being is the product not just of natural creation, but also of the kind of deliberative human creative force that we honor in honoring art. A mature woman, for example, is in her personality, training, capacity, interests, ambitions, and emotions, something like a work of art because in those respects she is the product of human creative intelligence, partly that of her parents and other people, partly that of her culture, and also, through the choices she has made, her *own* creation. The Greeks used two words for life that bring out the distinction: *zoe*, by which they meant physical or biological life, and *bios*, by which they meant a life as *lived*, as made up of the actions, decisions, motives, and events that compose what we now call a biography.[7]

The idea that each individual human life is inviolable is therefore rooted, like our concern for the survival of our species as a whole, in two combined and intersecting bases of the sacred: natural *and* human creation. Any human creature, including the most immature embryo, is a triumph of divine or evolutionary creation, which produces a complex, reasoning being from, as it were, nothing, and also of what we often call the "miracle" of human reproduction, which makes each new human being both different from and yet a continuation of the human beings who created it. Levin—Tolstoy's fictional self-projection in *Anna Karenina*—is struck by wonder, in spite of himself, at the birth of his son:

> Meanwhile, at the foot of the bed, in Lizaveta Petrovna's skillful hands flickered the life of a human being, like the small uncertain flame of a night-light—a human being who had not existed a moment ago but who, with the same rights and importance to itself as the rest of humanity, would live and create others in its own image. . . . Whence, wherefore had it come, and who was it? He could not understand at all, nor accustom himself to the idea. It seemed to him too much, a superabundance, to which he was unable to get used for a long time.[8]

The natural miracle that so moved Levin begins much earlier than birth: it begins in the genetic identity of an embryo. The second form of sacred creation, the human as distinct from the natural investment, is also immediate when pregnancy is planned, because a deliberate decision of parents to have and bear a child is of course a creative one. Any surviving child is shaped in character and capacity by the decisions of parents and by the cultural background of community. As that child matures, in all but pathological cases, his own creative choices progressively determine his thoughts, personality, ambitions, emotions, connections, and achievements. He creates his life just as much as an artist creates a painting or a poem. I am not suggesting, as some nineteenth-century Romantic writers did, that a human life is literally a work of art. That is a dangerous idea, because it suggests that we should value a person in the same way that we value a painting or a poem, valuing him for beauty or style or originality rather than personal or moral or intellectual qualities. But we can—and do—treat leading a life as itself a kind of creative activity, which we have at least as much reason to honor as artistic creation.

The life of a single human organism commands respect and protection, then, no matter in what form or shape, because of the complex creative investment it represents and because of our wonder at the divine or evolutionary processes that produce new lives from old ones, at the processes of nation and community and language through which a human being will come to absorb and continue hundreds of generations of cultures and forms of life and value, and, finally, when mental life has begun and flourishes, at the process of internal personal creation and judgment by which a person will make and remake himself, a mysterious, inescapable process in which we each participate, and which is therefore the most powerful and inevitable source of empathy and communion we have with every other creature who faces the same frightening challenge. The horror we feel in the willful destruction of a human life reflects our shared inarticulate sense of the intrinsic importance of each of these dimensions of investment.

THE METRIC OF DISRESPECT

I must now try to show how this understanding of the sacredness of human life allows us better to explain the two opposing attitudes toward abortion than does the traditional account, which supposes that these attitudes are based on different views about whether and when a fetus is a person with a right to life. I shall assume that conservatives and liberals all accept that in principle human life is inviolable in the sense I have defined, that any abortion involves a waste of human life and is therefore, in itself, a bad thing to happen, a shame. And I shall try to show how that assumption explains why the two sides both agree and disagree in the ways that they do.

I begin with their agreement. Conservatives and liberals both suppose, as I said, that though abortion is always morally problematic and often morally wrong, it is worse on some occasions than on others. They suppose, in other words, that there are degrees of badness in the waste of human life. What measure are they assuming in those judgments? Let us put that question in a more general form. We all assume that some cases of premature death are greater tragedies than others, not only when we are puzzling about abortion, but in the context of many other events as well. Most of us would think it worse when a young woman dies in a plane crash than when an elderly man does, for example, or a boy than a middle-aged man. What measure of tragedy are we assuming when we think this? What measure should we assume?

This is not the question moral philosophers and medical ethicists often write about—the question of what *rights* different sorts of people have to live, or of how relatively wicked it is to deny them lifesaving resources or to kill them. We might believe that it is worse—that there has been a greater waste of life—when a young person dies than when an old one does, or when an emotionally healthy person dies than a suicidal one, or when a man with young children dies than a bachelor, without suggesting that it would be any less wicked to kill an old than a young person, or a depressive than a happy one, or a bachelor than a father. Nor even—though this is obviously a different and harder question—that it would be any fairer to deny an old man scarce lifesaving resources, like kidney machines, when there is not enough for everyone who needs them, or to deny those resources to depressives and bachelors so that they could be used for spirited fathers of six.

These judgments about murder and fairness belong to the system of rights and interests, the system of ideas I said could not explain our most common convictions about abortion. Most people think (and our laws certainly insist) that people have an equal right to life, and that the murder of a depressive handicapped octogenarian misanthrope is as heinous, and must be punished as seriously, as the murder of anyone younger or healthier or more valuable to others. Any other view would strike us as monstrous. It is more complicated, as I just conceded, how these differences between people should affect the distribution of scarce medical resources. Doctors in most countries assume that such resources should be devoted to younger rather than older people, and for many doctors, quality of life and value to others come into the equation as well. But even these questions of fairness are different from the question of the intrinsic goodness or badness of events that we are considering. We might insist, for example, that the interests of a seriously depressed and gravely handicapped person should be respected just as much as those of an emotionally healthy person in allocating scarce medical resources, and yet think (as some people might, though many do not) that it is a greater tragedy when the latter dies young than the former. I am now asking, then, not about justice or rights or fairness, but about tragedy and the waste of life. How should we measure and compare the waste of life, and therefore the insult to the sanctity of life, on different occasions?

We should consider, first, a simple and perhaps natural answer to that question. Life is wasted, on this simple view, when life is lost, so that the question of how much has been wasted by a premature death is answered by estimating how long the life cut short would probably otherwise have lasted. This simple answer seems to fit many of our intuitive convictions. It seems to explain the opinion I just mentioned, for example: that the death of a young woman in an airplane crash is worse than the death of an old man would be. The young woman would probably otherwise have had many more years left to live.

The simple answer is incomplete, because we can measure life—and therefore loss of life—in different ways. Should we take into account only the duration of life lost with no regard to its quality? Or should we take quality into account as well? Should we say that the loss of the young woman who died in the crash would be greater if she had been looking forward to a life full of promise and pleasure than if she was physically or psychologically handicapped in some permanent and grave way? Should we also take into account the loss her death would cause to the lives of others? Is the death of a parent of young children, or of a brilliant employer of large numbers of people, or of a musical genius, a worse waste of life than the death at the same age of someone whose life was equally satisfying to himself but less valuable to others?

We should not puzzle over these alternatives, however, because this simple answer, which measures waste of life only in terms of life lost, is unacceptable whether we define that loss only as duration of life or include quality of life or benefit to others. It is unacceptable, in any of these forms, for two compelling reasons.

First, though the simple answer seems to fit some of our convictions, it contradicts other important and deeply held ones. If the waste of life were to be measured only in chronological terms, for example, then an early-stage abortion would be a worse insult to the sanctity of life, a worse instance of life being wasted, than a late-stage abortion. But almost everyone holds the contrary assumption: that the later the abortion—the more like a child the aborted fetus has already become—the worse it is. We take a similar view about the death of young children. It is terrible when an infant dies but worse, most people think, when a three-year-old child dies and worse still when an adolescent does. Almost no one thinks that the tragedy of premature death decreases in a linear way as age increases. Most people's sense of that tragedy, if it were rendered as a graph relating the degree of tragedy to the age at which death occurs, would slope upward from birth to some point in late childhood or early adolescence, then follow a flat line until at least very early middle age, and then slope down again toward extreme old age. Richard's murder of the princes in the Tower could have no parallel, for horror, in any act of infanticide.

Nor does the simple interpretation of how death wastes life fit our feelings better in the more elaborate forms I mentioned. Our common view that it is worse when a late-stage fetus is aborted or miscarries than an early-stage one, and worse when a ten-year-old child dies than an infant, makes no assumptions about the quality of the lives lost or their value for others.

The simple view of wasted life fails for a second, equally important reason. It wholly fails to explain the important truth I have several times emphasized: that though we treat human life as sacred, we do not treat it as incrementally good; we do not believe abstractly that the more human lives that are lived the better. The simple claim that a premature death is tragic only because life is lost—only because some period of life that might have been lived by someone will not be—gives us no more reason to grieve over an abortion or any premature death than we have to grieve over contraception or any other form of birth control. In both cases, less human life is lived than might otherwise be.

The "simple loss" view we have been considering is inadequate because it focuses only on future possibilities, on what will or will not happen in the future. It ignores the crucial truth that waste of life is often greater and more tragic because of what has already happened in the past. The death of an adolescent girl is worse than the death of an infant girl because the adolescent's death frustrates the investments she and others have already made in her life—the ambitions and expectations she constructed, the plans and projects she made, the love and interest and emotional involvement she formed for and with others, and they for and with her.

I shall use "frustration" (though the word has other associations) to describe this more complex measure of the waste of life because I can think of no better word to suggest the combination of past and future considerations that figure in our assessment of a tragic death. Most of us hold to something like the following set of instinctive assumptions about death and tragedy. We believe, as I said, that a successful human life has a certain natural course. It starts in mere biological development—conception, fetal development, and infancy—but it then extends into childhood, adolescence, and adult life in ways that are determined not just by biological formation but by social and individual training and choice, and that culminate in satisfying relationships and achievements of different kinds. It ends, after a normal life span, in a natural death. It is a waste of the natural and human creative investments that make up the story of a normal life when this normal progression is frustrated by premature death or in other ways. But how bad this is—how great the frustration—depends on the stage of life in which it occurs, because the frustration is greater if it takes places after rather than before the person has made a significant personal investment in his own life, and less if it occurs after any investment has been substantially fulfilled, or as sub-stantially fulfilled as is anyway likely.

This more complex structure fits our convictions about tragedy better than the simple loss-of-life measure does. It explains why the death of an adolescent seems to us worse in most circumstances than the death of an infant. It also explains how we can consistently maintain that it is sometimes undesirable to create new human lives while still insisting that it is bad when any human life, once begun, ends prematurely. No frustration of life is involved when fewer rather than more human beings are born, because there is no creative investment in lives that never exist. But once a human life starts, a process has begun, and interrupting that process frustrates an adventure already under way.

So the idea that we deplore the frustration of life, not its mere absence, seems adequately to fit our general convictions about life, death, and tragedy. It also explains much of what we think about the particular tragedy of abortion. Both conservatives and liberals assume that in some circumstances abortion is more serious and more likely to be unjustifiable than in others. Notably, both agree that a late-term abortion is graver than an early-term one. We cannot explain this shared conviction simply on the ground that fetuses more closely resemble infants as pregnancy continues. People believe that abortion is not just emotionally more difficult but morally worse the later in pregnancy it occurs, and increasing resemblance alone has no moral significance. Nor can we explain the shared conviction by noticing that at some point in pregnancy a fetus becomes sentient. Most people think that abortion is morally worse early in the second trimester—well before sentience is possible—than early in the first one (several European nations, which permit abortion in the first but not the second trimester, have made that distinction part of their criminal law). And though that widely shared belief cannot be explained by the simple lost-life theory, the frustration thesis gives us a natural and compelling justification of it. Fetal development is a continuing creative process, a process that has barely begun at the instant of conception. Indeed, since genetic individuation is not yet complete at that point, we might say that the development of a unique human being has not started until approximately fourteen days later, at implantation. But after implantation, as fetal growth continues, the natural investment that would be wasted in an abortion grows steadily larger and more significant.

HUMAN AND DIVINE

So our sense that frustration rather than just loss compromises the inviolability of human life does seem helpful in explaining what unites most people about abortion. The more difficult question is whether it also helps in explaining what divides them. Let us begin our answer by posing another question. I just described a natural course of human life—beginning in conception, extending through birth and childhood, culminating in successful and engaged adulthood in which the natural biological investment and the personal human investment in that life are realized, and finally ending in natural death after a normal span of years. Life so understood can be frustrated in two main ways. It can be frustrated by premature death, which leaves any previous natural and personal investment unrealized. Or it can be frustrated by other forms of failure: by handicaps or poverty or misconceived projects or irredeemable mistakes or lack of training or even brute bad luck; any one of these may in different ways frustrate a person's opportunity to redeem his ambitions or otherwise to lead a full and flourishing life. Is premature death always, inevitably, a more serious frustration of life than any of these other forms of failure?

Decisions about abortion often raise this question. Suppose parents discover, early in the mother's pregnancy, that the fetus is genetically so deformed that the life it would lead after birth will inevitably be both short and sharply limited. They must decide whether it is a worse frustration of life if the gravely deformed fetus were to die at once— wasting the miracle of its creation and its development so far—or if it were to continue to grow in utero, to be born, and to live only a short and crippled life. We know that people divide about that question, and we now have a way to describe the division. On one view, immediate death of the fetus, even in a case like this one, is a more terrible frustration of the miracle of life than even a sharply diminished and brief infant life would be, for the latter would at least redeem some small part, however limited, of the natural investment. On the rival view, it would be a worse frustration of life to allow this fetal life to continue because that would add, to the sad waste of a deformed human's biological creation, the further, heartbreaking waste of personal emotional investments made in that life by others but principally by the child himself before his inevitable early death.

We should therefore consider this hypothesis: though almost everyone accepts the abstract principle that it is intrinsically bad when human life, once begun, is frustrated, people disagree about the best answer to the question of whether avoidable premature death is always or invariably the most serious possible frustration of life. Very conservative opinion, on this hypothesis, is grounded in the conviction that immediate death is inevitably a more serious frustration than any option that postpones death, even at the cost of greater frustration in other respects. Liberal opinion, on the same hypothesis, is grounded in the opposite conviction: that in some cases, at least, a choice for premature death minimizes the frustration of life and is therefore not a compromise of the principle that human life is sacred but, on the contrary, best respects that principle.

What reasons do people have for embracing one rather than the other of these positions? It seems plain that whatever they are, they are deep reasons, drawn consciously or unconsciously from a great network of other convictions about the point of life and the moral significance of death. If the hypothesis I just described holds—if conservatives and liberals disagree on whether premature death is always the worst frustration of life—then the disagreement must be in virtue of a more general contrast between religious and philosophical orientations.

So I offer another hypothesis. Almost everyone recognizes, as I have suggested, that a normal, successful human life is the product of two morally significant modes of creative investment in that life, the natural and the human. But people disagree about the relative importance of these modes, not just when abortion is in question but on many other mortal occasions as well. If you believe that the natural investment in a human life is transcendently important, that the gift of life itself is infinitely more significant than anything the person whose life it is may do for himself, important though that may be, you will also believe that a deliberate, premature death is the greatest frustration of life possible, no matter how limited or cramped or unsuccessful the continued life would be.[9] On the other hand, if you assign much greater relative importance to the human contribution to life's creative value, then you will consider the frustration of that contribution to be a more serious evil, and will accordingly see more point in deciding that life should end before further significant human investment is doomed to frustration.

We can best understand some of our serious disagreements about abortion, in other words, as reflecting deep differences about the relative moral importance of the natural and human contributions to the inviolability of individual human lives. In fact, we can make a bolder version of that claim: we can best understand the full range of opinion about abortion, from the most conservative to the most liberal, by ranking each opinion about the relative gravity of the two forms of frustration along a range extending from one extreme position to the other—from treating any frustration of the biological investment as worse than any possible frustration of human investment, through more moderate and complex balances, to the opinion that frustrating mere biological investment in human life barely matters and that frustrating a human investment is always worse.

If we look at the controversy this way, it is hardly surprising that many people who hold views on the natural or biological end of that spectrum are fundamentalist or Roman Catholic or strongly religious in some other orthodox religious faith—people who believe that God is the author of everything natural and that each human fetus is a distinct instance of his most sublime achievement. Our hypothesis explains how orthodox religion can play a crucial role in forming people's opinions about abortion even if they do not believe that a fetus is a person with its own right to life.

That is a significant point. It is widely thought that religious opposition to abortion is premised on the conviction that every human fetus is a person with rights and interests of its own. It is therefore important to see that religious opposition to abortion need not be based on that assumption. I said that many religious traditions, including Roman Catholicism for most of its history, based their opposition to abortion on the different assumption that human life has intrinsic value. The present hypothesis shows how that assumption can ground very fierce, even absolute, opposition to abortion. A strongly orthodox or fundamentalist person can insist that abortion is always morally wrong because the deliberate destruction of something created as sacred by God can never be redeemed by any human benefit.

This is not to suggest, however, that only conventionally religious people who believe in a creator God are conservatives about abortion. Many other people stand in awe of human reproduction as a natural miracle. Some of them, as I said, embrace the mysterious but apparently powerful idea that the natural order is in itself purposive and commands respect as sacred. Some prominent conservationists, for example, though hardly religious in the conventional sense, seem to be deeply religious in that one and may be drawn a considerable distance toward the conservative end of the spectrum of opinion I described. They may well think that any frustration of the natural investment in human life is so grave a matter that it is rarely if ever justified—that the pulse in the mud is more profound than any other source of life's value. They might therefore be just as firmly opposed to aborting a seriously deformed fetus as any religiously orthodox conservative would be.

Nor does it follow, on the other hand, that everyone who is religious in an orthodox way or everyone who reveres nature is therefore conservative about abortion. As we have seen, many such people, who agree that unnecessary death is a great evil, are also sensitive to and emphatic about the intrinsic badness of the waste of human investment in life. They believe that the frustration of that contribution—for example, in the birth of a grievously deformed fetus whose investment in its own life is doomed to be frustrated—may in some circumstances be the worse of two evils, and they believe that their religious conviction or reverence for nature is not only consistent with but actually requires that position. Some of them take the same view about what many believe to be an even more problematic case: they say that their religious convictions entail that a woman should choose abortion rather than bear a child when that would jeopardize her investment in her *own* life.

I described extreme positions at two ends of the spectrum: that only natural investment counts in deciding whether abortion wastes human life, and that only human investment counts. In fact, very few people take either of these extreme positions. For most people, the balance is more complex and involves compromise and accommodation rather than giving absolute priority to avoiding frustration of either the natural or the human investment. People's opinions become progressively less conservative and more liberal as the balance they strike gives more weight to the importance of not frustrating the human investment in life; more liberal views emphasize, in various degrees, that a human life is created not just by divine or natural forces but also, in a different but still central way, by personal choice, training, commitment, and decision. The shift in emphasis leads liberals to see the crucial creative investment in life, the investment that must not be frustrated if at all possible, as extending far beyond conception and biological growth and well into a human being's adult life. On that liberal opinion, as I have already suggested, it may be more frustrating of life's miracle when an adult's ambitions, talents, training, and expectations are wasted because of an unforeseen and unwanted pregnancy than when a fetus dies before any significant investment of that kind has been made.

That is an exceptionally abstract description of my understanding of the controversy between conservative and liberal opinion. But it will become less abstract, for I shall try to show how the familiar differences between conservative and liberal views on abortion can be explained by the hypothesis that conservatives and liberals rank the two forms of frustration differently. We must not exaggerate that difference, however. It is a difference in emphasis, though an important one. Most people who take what I call a liberal view of abortion do not deny that the conception of a human life and its steady fetal development toward recognizable human form are matters of great moral importance that count as creative investments. That is why they agree with conservatives that as this natural investment continues, and the fetus develops toward the shape and capacity of an infant, abortion, which wastes that investment, is progressively an event more to be avoided or regretted. Many people who hold conservative opinions about abortion, for their part, recognize the importance of personal creative contributions to a human life; they, too, recognize that a premature death is worse when it occurs not in early infancy but after distinctly human investments of ambition and expectation and love have been made. Conservatives and liberals disagree not because one side wholly rejects a value the other thinks cardinal, but because they take different—sometimes dramatically different—positions about the relative importance of these values, which both recognize as fundamental and profound.

CONSERVATIVE EXCEPTIONS: RECONSIDERING THE NATURAL

I am defending the view that the debate over abortion should be understood as essentially about the following philosophical issue: is the frustration of a biological life, which wastes human life, nevertheless sometimes justified in order to avoid frustrating a human contribution to that life or to other people's lives, which would be a different kind of waste? If so, when and why? People who are very conservative about abortion answer the first of these questions No.

There is an even more extreme position, which holds that abortion is never justified, even when necessary to save the life of the mother. Though that is the official view of the Catholic church and of some other religious groups, only a small minority even of devout Catholics accept it, and even Justice Rehnquist, who dissented in *Roe* v. *Wade,* said that he had little doubt that it would be unconstitutional for states to prohibit abortion when a mother's life was at stake. So I have defined "very conservative" opinion to permit abortion in this circumstance. This exceedingly popular exception would be unacceptable to all conservatives, as I have said, if they really thought that a fetus is a person with protected rights and interests. It is morally and legally impermissible for any third party, such as a doctor, to murder one innocent person even to save the life of another one. But the exception is easily explicable if we understand conservative opinion as based on a view of the sanctity of life that gives strict priority to the divine or natural investment in life.

If either the mother or the fetus must die, then the tragedy of avoidable death and the loss of nature's investment in life is inevitable. But a choice in favor of the mother may well seem justified to very conservative people on the ground that a choice against her would in addition frustrate the personal and social investments in her life; even they want only to minimize the overall frustration of human life, and that requires saving the mother's life in this terrible situation.

The important debate is therefore between people who believe that abortion is permissible *only* when it is necessary to save the mother's life and people who believe that abortion may be morally permissible in other circumstances as well. I shall consider the further exceptions the latter group of people claim, beginning with those that are accepted even by people who regard themselves as moderately conservative about abortion and continuing to those associated with a distinctly liberal position.

Moderate conservatives believe that abortion is morally permissible to end a pregnancy that began in rape. Governor Buddy Roemer of Louisiana, for example, who has declared himself in favor of a ban on abortion, nevertheless vetoed an anti-abortion statute in 1991 because it excepted rape victims only in a manner that he said "dishonors women . . . and unduly traumatizes victims of rape."[10] On the a-fetus-is-a-person view, an exception for rape is even harder to justify than an exception to protect the life of the mother. Why should a fetus be made to forfeit its right to live, and pay with its life, for the wrongdoing of someone else? But once again, the exception is much easier to understand when we shift from the claim of fetal personhood to a concern for protecting the divine or natural investment in human life. Very conservative people, who believe that the divine contribution to a human life is everything and the human contribution almost nothing beside it, believe that abortion is automatically and in every case the worst possible compromise of life's inviolability, and they do not recognize an exception for rape. But moderately conservative people, who believe that the natural contribution normally *outweighs* the human contribution, will find two features of rape that argue for an exception.

First, according to every prominent religion, rape is itself a brutal violation of God's law and will, and abortion may well seem less insulting to God's creative power when the life it ends itself began in such an insult. Though rape would not justify violating the rights of an innocent person, it could well diminish the horror conservatives feel at an abortion's deliberate frustration of God's investment in life. In his opinion in *McRae* v. *Califano*, the Hyde amendment case I described in chapter 2, Judge John Dooling summarized testimony by Rabbi David Feldman: "In the stricter Jewish view abortion is a very serious matter permitted only where there is a threat to life, or to sanity, or a grave threat to mental health and physical well-being. Abortion for rape victims would be allowed, using a field and seed analogy: involuntary implantation of the seed imposes no duty to nourish the alien seed."[11]

Second, rape is a terrible desecration of its victim's investment in her own life, and even those who count a human investment in life as less important than God's or nature's may nevertheless recoil from so violent a frustration of that human investment. Rape is sickeningly, comprehensively contemptuous because it reduces a woman to a physical convenience, a creature whose importance is exhausted by her genital use, someone whose love and sense of self—aspects of personality particularly at stake in sex—have no significance whatsoever except as vehicles for sadistic degradation.

Requiring a woman to bear a child conceived in such an assault is especially destructive to her self-realization because it frustrates her creative choice not only in sex but in reproduction as well. In the ideal case, reproduction is a joint decision rooted in love and in a desire to continue one's life mixed with the life of another person. In Catholic tradition, and in the imagination of many people who are not Catholics, it is itself an offense against the sanctity of life to make love without that desire: that is the basis of many people's moral opposition to contraception. But we can dispute that sex is valuable only for reproduction, or creative only in that way—as most people do—while yet believing that sex is maximally creative when reproduction is contemplated and desired, and that reproduction frustrates creative power when it is neither. Of course, people in love often conceive by accident, and people not in love sometimes conceive deliberately, perhaps out of a misguided hope of finding love through children. Rape is not just the absence of contemplation and desire, however. For the victim, rape is the direct opposite of these, and if a child is conceived, it will be not only without the victim's desire to reproduce but in circumstances made especially horrible because of that possibility.

Moderate conservatives therefore find it difficult to insist that abortion is impermissible in cases of rape. It is sometimes said that conservatives who allow the rape exception but not, for example, an exception for unmarried teenagers whose lives would be ruined by childbirth must be motivated by a desire to punish unmarried women who have sex voluntarily. Though some conservatives may indeed believe that pregnancy is a fit punishment for sexual immorality, our hypothesis shows why conservatives who make only the rape exception do not necessarily hold that appalling view. The grounds on which I said conservatives might make an exception for rape do not extend so forcefully to pregnancies that follow voluntary intercourse. Though many religious people do think that unmarried sex also violates God's will, few consider it as grave as rape, and the argument that an unwanted pregnancy grotesquely frustrates a woman's creative role in framing her own life is weaker when the pregnancy follows voluntary sex. Of course, the difference would not be pertinent at all, as I said, if a fetus were a person with rights and interests of its own, because that person would be completely innocent whatever the nature or level of its mother's guilt.

LIBERAL EXCEPTIONS: PROTECTING LIFE IN EARNEST

Other, more permissive exceptions to the principle that abortion is wrong are associated with a generally liberal attitude toward abortion, and we should therefore expect, on the basis of the hypothesis we are testing, that they will reflect a greater respect for the human contribution to life and a correspondingly diminished concern with the natural. But we must not forget that people's attitudes about abortion range over a gradually changing spectrum from one extreme to the other, and that any sharp distinction between conservative and liberal camps is just an expository convenience.

Liberals think that abortion is permissible when the birth of a fetus would have a very bad effect on the quality of lives. The exceptions liberals recognize on that ground fall into two main groups: those that seek to avoid frustration of the life of the child, and those that seek to prevent frustration of the life of the mother and other family members.

Liberals believe that abortion is justified when it seems inevitable that the fetus, if born, will have a seriously frustrated life. That kind of justification is strongest, according to most liberals, when the frustration is caused by a very grave physical deformity that would make any life deprived, painful, frustrating for both child and parent, and, in any case, short. But many liberals also believe that abortion is justified when the family circumstances are so economically barren, or otherwise so unpromising, that any new life would be seriously stunted for that reason. It is important to understand that these exceptions are not based, as they might seem to be, on concern for the rights or interests of the fetus. It is a mistake to suppose that an early fetus has interests of its own; it especially makes no sense to argue that it might have an interest in being aborted. Perhaps we could understand that latter argument to mean that if the fetus does develop into a child, that child would be better off dead. But many liberals find abortion justified even when this is not so. I do not mean to deny that sometimes people would be better off dead—when they are in great and terminal pain, for example, or because their lives are otherwise irremediably frustrated. (We shall be considering the problems posed in such cases later in this book.) But this is rarely true of children born into even very great poverty. Nor is it necessarily true even of children born with terrible, crippling handicaps who are doomed shortly to die; sometimes such children establish relationships and manage achievements that give content and meaning to their lives, and it becomes plain that it is in their interests, and in the interests of those who love and care for them, that they continue living as long as possible. The liberal judgment that abortion is justified when the prospects for life are especially bleak is based on a more impersonal judgment: that the child's existence would be intrinsically a bad thing, that it is regrettable that such a deprived and difficult life must be lived.

Sometimes this liberal judgment is wrongly taken to imply contempt for the lives of handicapped children or adults, or even as a suggestion, associated with loathsome Nazi eugenics, that society would be improved by the death of such people. That is a mistake twice over. First, as I insisted earlier in this chapter, the general question of the relative intrinsic tragedy of different events is very different from any question about the *rights* of people now living or about how they should be treated. The former is a question about the intrinsic goodness or evil of events, the latter about rights and fairness. Second, in any case, the liberal opinion about abortion of deformed fetuses in no way implies that it would be better if even grievously handicapped people were now to die. On the contrary, the very concern the liberal judgment embodies—respect for the human contribution to life and anxiety that it not be frustrated—normally sponsors exactly the opposite conclusion. The investment a seriously handicapped person makes in his own life, in his struggle to overcome his handicap as best he can, is intense, and the investment his family and others make is likely to be intense as well. The liberal position insists that these investments in life should be realized as fully as possible, for as long and as successfully as the handicapped person and his community together can manage; and liberals are even more likely than conservatives to support social legislation that promotes that end. One may think that in the worst of such cases it would have been better had the life in question never begun, that the investment we are so eager to redeem should never have been necessary. But that judgment does not detract from concern for handicapped people; on the contrary, it is rooted in the same fundamental respect for human investment in human life, the same horror at the investment being wasted.

The second distinctly liberal group of exceptions, which take into account the effects of pregnancy and childbirth on the lives of mothers and other family members, are even harder to justify on any presumption that includes the idea that a fetus is a person with rights and interests. But the popularity of these exceptions is immediately explicable once we recognize that they are based on respect for the intrinsic value of human life. Liberals are especially concerned about the waste of the human contribution to that value, and they believe that the waste of life, measured in frustration rather than mere loss, is very much greater when a teenage single mother's life is wrecked than when an early-stage fetus, in whose life human investment has thus far been negligible, ceases to live. That judgment does not, of course, depend on comparing the quality of the mother's life, if her fetus is aborted, with that of the child, had it been allowed to live. Recognizing the sanctity of life does not mean attempting to engineer fate so that the best possible lives are lived overall; it means, rather, not frustrating investments in life that have already been made. For that reason, liberal opinion cares more about the lives that people are now leading, lives in earnest, than about the possibility of other lives to come.

The prospects of a child and of its mother for a fulfilling life obviously each depend very much on the prospects of the other. A child whose birth frustrates the chances of its mother to redeem her own life or jeopardizes her ability to care for the rest of her family is likely, just for that reason, to have a more frustrating life itself. And though many people have become superb parents to disabled or disadvantaged children, and some extraordinary ones have found a special vocation in that responsibility, it will sometimes be a devastating blow to a parent's prospects to have a crippled child rather than a normal one, or a child whose bearing and care will seriously strain family resources.

This is only another instance of the difficulty any theoretical analysis of an intricate personal and social problem, like abortion, must face. Analysis can proceed only by abstraction, but abstraction, which ignores the complexity and interdependencies of real life, obscures much of the content on which each actual, concrete decision is made. So we have no formulas for actual decision but only, at best, a schema for understanding the arguments and decisions that we and other people make in real life. I have argued that we do badly, in understanding and evaluating these decisions and arguments, if we try to match them to procrustean assumptions about fetal personhood or rights. We do better to see them as reflecting more nuanced and individual judgments about how and why human life is sacred, and about which decision of life and death, in all the concrete circumstances, most respects what is really important about life.

There will be disagreement in these judgments, not only between large parties of opinion, like those I have been calling conservative and liberal, but within these parties as well. Indeed, very few people, even those who share the same religion and social and intellectual background, will agree in every case. Nor is it possible for anyone to compose a general theory of abortion, some careful weighing of different kinds or modes of life's frustration from which particular decisions could be generated to fit every concrete case. On the contrary, we discover what we think about these grave matters not in advance of having to decide on particular occasions, but in the course of and by making them.

Where do we stand? I began this book by suggesting that we must redesign our explanation of the great abortion controversy, our sense of what the argument is an argument about. I have now completed my proposal for that redesign. I said that our new explanation would have important implications for political morality and for constitutional law.

I said that it would allow us to see the legal argument about the role of the United States Constitution in a new light, and even cautiously to raise our hopes that Americans and people in other countries where liberty is prized might find a collective solution to the political controversy that all sides could accept with dignity. I shall try to redeem those high promises in the next three chapters. But I shall anticipate my most important conclusion. Seeing the abortion controversy in the fresh light I described will not, of course, end our disagreements about the morality of abortion, because these disagreements are deep and may be perpetual. But if that fresh light helps us to identify those disagreements as at bottom *spiritual,* that should help bring us together, because we have grown used to the idea, as I said, that real community is possible across deep religious divisions. We might hope for even more—not just for greater tolerance but for a more positive and healing realization: that what we share—our common commitment to the sanctity of life—is itself precious, a unifying ideal we can rescue from the decades of hate.

4

ABORTION
IN COURT:
PART I

*R*oe v. *Wade* is undoubtedly the best-known case the United States
Supreme Court has ever decided: it is better known among
Americans—and, indeed, throughout the world—than *Marbury*
v. *Madison,* the 1803 case in which the Court first decided it had the
power to declare acts of Congress unconstitutional, or *Dred Scott* v.
Sandford, the 1857 case in which the Court helped to precipitate the Civil
War by deciding that a slave was only a piece of property and had to
be returned to his "owner," or even *Brown* v. *Board of Education,* the 1954
case in which the Court declared racially segregated schools unconstitutional and helped begin the civil rights movement that has transformed
the country. *Roe* v. *Wade* is more famous than any of these, and it has
been savagely criticized for two decades.

Roe's bitterest critics say that the Court licensed murder. They say
that a fetus is a person from the moment of conception and that a fetus's
right to live is more important than any reason a woman might have for
killing it. A great many of the decision's most sophisticated critics take
a different view, however. They argue not that the Court's opinion on
these great philosophical issues was wrong but that it had no business
ruling on the matter at all, because the Constitution gives democrat-
ically elected state legislatures, not unelected judges, the power to
decide whether and when abortion will be legal. On this view, the
Supreme Court's holding in *Roe* v. *Wade* was not justified by any legal

argument, but was, in the pejorative sense of the term, a *political* decision the Court had no right to make.

That is the view of very right-wing lawyers like Robert Bork, who wrote, in a book about the Senate's rejection of his nomination to the Supreme Court, "Unfortunately, in the entire opinion there is not one line of explanation, not one sentence that qualifies as a legal argument. Nor has the Court in the sixteen years since ever provided the explanation lacking in 1973. It is unlikely that it ever will, because the right to abort, whatever one thinks of it, is not to be found in the Constitution."[1] Bork's opinion is also the view of many distinguished constitutional scholars, including several who are not known as conservatives and some who themselves believe that state legislatures should not make abortion a crime.

Though *Roe* v. *Wade* is famous, and furiously attacked and defended, few people understand the constitutional issues raised by the case. People know, of course, that the *Roe* decision held, roughly, that states may not prohibit abortion at all before the second trimester of pregnancy, and may not prohibit it before the third trimester except in those rare cases when it would jeopardize the *mother's* health. They also know that as a result of the decision, the anti-abortion laws of most states were held to be unconstitutional, and that a great many more abortions took place than would otherwise have occurred. But most of *Roe*'s critics and even most of its defenders are unaware of what arguments persuaded the majority of justices, in 1973, to rule as they did.

Laws that prohibit abortion or make it difficult or expensive to procure one deprive pregnant women of a freedom or opportunity that is crucial to many of them. A woman who is forced to bear a child she does not want because she cannot have an early and safe abortion is no longer in charge of her own body: the law has imposed a kind of slavery on her. That is, moreover, only the beginning. For many women, bearing unwanted children means the destruction of their own lives, because they are still children themselves, because they will no longer be able to work or study or live in ways important to them, or because they cannot support the children. (Of course, these different kinds of harm are multiplied and intensified if the pregnancy begins in rape or incest, or if the child is born with grave physical or mental handicaps.) Adoption, even when it is available, does not remove the injury, for many women would suffer great emotional pain for many years if they turned a child over to others to raise and love. (One of Carol Gilligan's subjects in the abortion study I described—a Catholic nurse—had already put one child up for adoption and could not face doing it again, even though the alternative was abortion. "Psychologically," she said, "there was no way that I could hack another adoption. It took me about four and a half years to get my head on straight. There was just no way I was going to go through it again.")

For many women, these are not simply undesirable but terrible injuries that flow from society's criminalization of abortion. They dread them and would do almost anything to avoid them. We must not forget that a great many illegal and often very dangerous abortions occurred before *Roe* v. *Wade* was decided. If a woman desperate for an abortion defied the criminal law, she might risk her life. If she bowed to the law, the consequences for her were grave—not just economic or social or career disadvantage, but often mortal damage to her self-respect.

The United States Constitution, as it has historically been interpreted by the Supreme Court, limits a state's power to cause substantial damage to particular citizens by constructing two constitutional tests. The first applies to all laws: the "due process" clause of the Fourteenth Amendment requires a state to act *rationally* whenever it restricts liberty. This requirement gives citizens what Justice Rehnquist, in his dissent in *Roe* v. *Wade,* called a "liberty interest." States may limit people's liberty not arbitrarily or whimsically but only for some reason, only to promote some goal or policy that states may legitimately pursue. That is a very weak restriction, however, and it has rarely proved fatal to state legislation because a state can normally find some legitimate goal that the law might be thought to serve; it can usually claim that a given restriction will promote safety or security, for example, or public convenience, or the community's health or economy. The rationality test does not permit the Supreme Court to ask whether it was necessary, or even wise, for the state to limit its citizens' liberty in order to gain the claimed advantage. Nor does it permit it to inquire whether, as a matter of psychological history, a majority of the legislators had in mind the purpose the state now cites. The test is met if the legislators could rationally believe that the laws they were passing promoted a legitimate aim.

If the Constitution protected people's liberty only in that weak way, it would hardly safeguard freedom. But it does much more. It picks out certain freedoms and makes them specific constitutional *rights* that a state cannot restrict or override unless it has a very strong reason for doing so—the Supreme Court sometimes describes this as a *compelling* reason. What counts as a sufficiently strong or compelling reason depends on the right in question. A state would need a very powerful reason indeed to justify any constraint on the political content of what an individual may say or write, for example, since the right to freedom of that kind of speech is specifically assured for all citizens in the Constitution's First Amendment. The state would presumably need to show, at least, that only by restricting such speech could it prevent what Oliver Wendell Holmes called "a clear and present danger." In *Brown* v. *Board of Education,* the Court held that the Fourteenth Amendment's equal protection clause creates a specific constitutional right against racial discrimination, and it found the various claims some states had made (including the argument that the races can be more efficiently educated when they are segregated) insufficiently persuasive or important to allow invasion of that right.

Justice Blackmun's opinion in *Roe* v. *Wade* declared that a pregnant woman has a specific constitutional right to privacy in matters of procreation, and that this general right includes a right to an abortion if she and her doctor decide upon it. He added that a state's reasons for overriding that right by making abortion a crime were not compelling during the first two trimesters of pregnancy, and he concluded that a state could not forbid abortion during that period. Justice Rehnquist, in his dissent, denied that women have any special constitutional right to control their own reproduction; he said they have only a liberty interest—only an interest protected by the much weaker rationality test. He conceded that even this interest is strong enough to make unconstitutional any statute that prohibits abortion when needed to save a mother's life, but he declared that the goals a state might serve by prohibiting abortion for other reasons, even very early in pregnancy, are legitimate, and that a state's decision to promote those goals by banning abortion would therefore not be irrational.

Much of the academic discussion about *Roe* v. *Wade* has concentrated on this particular dispute. The critics I mentioned insist that Rehnquist is right, that the Constitution, properly understood, contains no constitutional right to free choice about abortion, and that Blackmun simply invented that right and claimed to find it in the Constitution. I disagree;

I shall argue, in the next two chapters, that the Constitution does protect the right Blackmun described, and I can quickly state, here, one strong prima facie reason for thinking that it does.

The Supreme Court is a court of law, and it is therefore obliged to make its decisions consistent, so far as this is possible, with the broad constitutional traditions established and respected in its past decisions. As Justice Blackmun wrote in his opinion, several earlier Supreme Court decisions had established that a person has a specific constitutional right to make decisions about procreation for himself or herself. In the important 1965 case of *Griswold* v. *Connecticut*, for example, which I have already mentioned, the Court decided that a state may not prohibit the sale of contraceptives to married persons, and in later cases it extended that ruling to unmarried persons as well. In one of these later cases, Justice Brennan, speaking for the Court, stated the point of the past decisions this way: "If the right of privacy means anything, it is the right of the *individual,* married or single, to be free from governmental intrusion into matters so fundamentally affecting a person as the decision whether to bear or beget a child."[2]

The *Griswold* decision has apparently been accepted by the American people. It counted heavily against Judge Bork's failed nomination in 1987 that he had written that *Griswold* was wrongly decided and should be reversed, even though he qualified his opposition during the nomination hearings by suggesting that some other argument, different from that which the Supreme Court had supplied in 1965, might be found to support it. When Charles Fried, President Reagan's solicitor general, argued in another case that *Roe* v. *Wade* should be overruled, he specifically said that *Griswold* was good law and should be retained. Justice Blackmun cannot be charged with erring in treating *Griswold* as a precedent he was obliged to respect. But once one accepts that case as good law, then it follows that women do have a constitutional right to privacy that in principle includes the decision not only whether to beget children but whether to bear them. *Griswold* and the other privacy decisions can be justified only on the presumption that decisions affecting marriage and childbirth are so intimate and personal that people must in principle be allowed to make these decisions for themselves, consulting their own preferences and convictions, rather than having society impose its collective decision on them.

A decision about abortion is at least as private in that sense as any other decision the Court has protected. In one way it is more so, because it involves a woman's control not just of her sexual relations but of changes within her own body, and the Supreme Court has recognized in various ways the importance of physical integrity. Abortion cannot be distinguished from contraception by supposing that a decision about the former is less serious; on the contrary, it is more. Indeed, it may not be possible consistently to distinguish abortion, even medically, from some popular forms of contraception, because the safest and most popular contraceptives now in use—intrauterine devices and the most widely used birth-control pills—act as abortifacients; that is, they destroy fertilized ova if they fail to prevent fertilization. The Court therefore cannot logically hold that a woman's right to control her role in procreation ends with fertilization without permitting states to outlaw these contraceptives.

Justice Blackmun's legal argument in *Roe* v. *Wade* was a strong one if we assume that the *Griswold* decision was right. If a state must show a compelling reason in order to prohibit the sale or use of contraceptives because of the impact of that prohibition on people's privacy, then it must show a compelling reason for prohibiting abortion, because the impact of that prohibition is, if anything, greater. I shall therefore assume here that Blackmun's conclusion—that women have, in principle, a specific constitutional right to control their own role in procreation—was sound. (In chapters 5 and 6, I shall defend this claim further—against challenges that presume that *Griswold,* too, was wrong.) But it does not follow that *Roe* v. *Wade* was correctly decided. For perhaps states *do* have a compelling reason for restricting a woman's constitutional right to privacy in the case of abortion. There is an obvious, important difference between an abortion, which puts an end to an individual life, and forms of contraception that prevent a life from beginning at all. If that difference is legally relevant, a state might well have a compelling reason for prohibiting abortion even though it does not have one for banning at least some forms of contraception.

Many people think there is a compelling reason for prohibiting abortion and have no difficulty in stating what it is. A state must make abortion a crime, they say, in order to protect human life. That is exactly what the states that banned abortion said their reason was—in the preambles to their regulatory statutes, in their legal briefs, and in their public rhetoric. That is, moreover, what the Supreme Court justices who dissented in *Roe* v. *Wade,* or who later announced their view that the opinion was wrong, said. And it is also what justices and lawyers who *support* that decision often say. In his opinion for the Court, Justice Blackmun recognized that a state had an interest in protecting what he called "fetal life" throughout pregnancy, though he claimed that it did not give the state a compelling reason for prohibiting abortion until the third trimester.

But this premise, on which so many people rely, is dangerously ambiguous, because there are two very different aims or purposes a state might have in "protecting human life." Government may claim what I called a derivative interest in protecting human life—it may claim that a fetus has rights and interests from the moment of conception, including a right to life, and that government must protect them as much as it protects the rights and interests of anyone else subject to its dominion. Or it may claim a detached interest in protecting human life—a responsibility not just to protect its citizens' interests and rights, but to protect human life as something sacred, of intrinsic value quite apart from its personal value.

If government has both a detached and a derivative responsibility to protect human life, then its ordinary laws against murder serve them both at once—protecting the rights and interests of particular victims, and also recognizing and respecting the intrinsic value of human life. In some cases, however, as I have said, the two supposed responsibilities may conflict. People sometimes wish to kill themselves because they are in terrible pain that medicine cannot alleviate, and relatives sometimes wish to terminate the mechanical life support of a patient who is permanently unconscious. In such cases, suicide or terminating life support may be in the best interests of the person whose life ends but nevertheless seem terrible to people who believe that any deliberate killing is an insult to the intrinsic value of human life. It makes a very great difference, then, whether a government has only derivative reasons for protecting human life or whether it may legitimately claim detached reasons as well. If the latter, then government might be entitled to prevent people from ending their lives, even when these people reasonably think that they would be better off dead.

Many lawyers believe that the great constitutional debate about abortion in the United States is obviously and entirely about a state's derivative concern with abortion. They believe that the key question in *Roe* v.

Wade was whether the United States Constitution gives state legislatures the power to declare that a fetus is a person from the moment of conception, and to outlaw abortion on that ground. That is understandable, because that is the question lawyers and academic scholars have for the most part debated. I argued in the opening chapters, however, that the parallel interpretation of the *moral* argument about abortion—that it turns on whether a fetus is a person—is a serious misunderstanding. I want now to suggest that the popular view of the *constitutional* argument is defective in the same way. If the argument were just about whether states can treat a fetus as a person, the case would be an easy one, as we shall see in this chapter. They cannot. The important, difficult issue is about a state's detached, not its derivative, interests. The crucial question is whether a state can impose the majority's conception of the sacred on everyone.

IS A FETUS
A CONSTITUTIONAL PERSON?

Let us assume that pregnant women have a specific constitutional right, at least in principle, to control the use of their own bodies for reproduction. A state cannot violate that right unless it has a compelling reason for doing so. According to the popular view of what the constitutional argument is about, states that wish to prohibit abortion in order to "protect human life" are claiming, as a compelling reason, that a fetus is a person with a right to live and that they are obliged and entitled to protect that right.

At the outset of his argument in *Roe* v. *Wade*, Justice Blackmun identified a very strong form of that claim. The Fourteenth Amendment to the United States Constitution provides that no state shall deny any "person" equal protection of the law. The Supreme Court therefore had to decide, at the outset, whether a fetus, from the moment of conception, is a person within the meaning of that clause. If it had decided that a fetus is, as we might say, a "constitutional" person, then that would have been the end of the case: the Constitution itself certifies the responsibility of states to protect equally all constitutional persons.

The threshold question Blackmun had to decide is different from the question of whether a fetus has moral rights, or whether it has interests that it would be morally wrong to violate or ignore. Some people believe on theological grounds that God endows a human fetus with a rational soul at conception, and that a rational soul has a moral right to live. But most people who hold this theological view also accept that it is not relevant to constitutional interpretation, that the Constitution insists on a firm separation between state and church, and that doctrinal religious arguments do not count as legal arguments. They might therefore, without abandoning their spiritual convictions, accept that fetuses are not constitutional persons. Conversely, the legal history that so strongly influences constitutional interpretation is not directly relevant to moral questions. Justice Blackmun pointed out in his opinion in *Roe* v. *Wade*, for example, that American law had never in the past treated fetuses as constitutional persons. That is a strong argument against interpreting the Constitution to include them at the present day, but someone concerned only with the moral question would be entitled to disregard that legal history as perhaps showing only consistent and grave moral error.

Blackmun decided that a fetus is not a constitutional person. Almost all responsible lawyers, including the political and academic critics of *Roe* v. *Wade*, agree that his decision on that point was correct. The responsible critics argue that the decision was wrong because the Court should have left the states free to decide about abortion as they wished—Texas free to prohibit abortion in most circumstances and New York free to allow it in most, as it had done in the past.[3] But that position is preposterous except on the assumption that a fetus is not constitutionally entitled to equal protection. If a fetus is a constitutional person, then states not only *may* forbid abortion but in some circumstances *must* do so. The Constitution would insist that states need a compelling justification for *not* outlawing abortion, and New York's law, which permitted elective abortions in the first two trimesters even before *Roe*, would be unconstitutional. If a woman became pregnant after voluntary sexual intercourse, knowing the risks, a state would have no compelling justification for permitting her or her doctor to abort the fetus: allowing the mother to regain the freedom of her body at the expense of the fetus's life would be failing to show equal concern for the two constitutional persons.

As a number of legal scholars have pointed out, the law does not generally require people to make a sacrifice in order to save the life of another person. Someone ordinarily has no legal duty to save a stranger from drowning even if he can do so at no risk to himself and with minimal effort.[4] But abortion normally requires a physical attack on a fetus, not just a failure to aid it, and, in any case, parents are invariably made an exception to the general doctrine because they have a legal duty to care for their children. If a fetus is a person from conception, a state would have no justification for generally allowing abortion but forbidding killing infants or abandoning them in fatal circumstances.[5] The physical and emotional and economic burdens of pregnancy are intense, but so are the parallel burdens of parenthood.

Therefore, all those who say that the Supreme Court should leave the question of abortion to the states to decide as their politics dictate have in effect conceded that a fetus is not a constitutional person. The legal arguments for that near-universally accepted position are very strong. Any interpretation of the Constitution must be tested on two large and connected dimensions.[6] The first is the dimension of fit. A constitutional interpretation must be rejected if actual legal practice is wholly inconsistent with the legal principles it recommends; it must, that is, have some considerable purchase on or grounding in actual legal experience. The second is the dimension of justice. If two different views about the best interpretation of some constitutional provision both pass the test of fit—if each can claim an adequate grounding in past practice—we should prefer the one whose principles seem to us best to reflect people's moral rights and duties, because the Constitution is a statement of abstract moral ideals that each generation must reinterpret for itself.[7]

In many constitutional cases, it is difficult to decide whether some proposed interpretation fits legal practice and history well enough to qualify on the first dimension. But in *Roe* v. *Wade,* that is not difficult to decide. The contention that Justice Blackmun and everyone else rejected, that on the best interpretation a fetus is a constitutional person, is easy to dismiss because it is so dramatically contradicted by American history and practice.

When the equal protection clause was adopted, many states had liberal abortion laws, and some passed such laws later, in the years before *Roe* was decided. But no court declared that these laws violated the equal protection clause, or even that judges should regard them with suspicion or subject them to special scrutiny. Nor did any substantial number of politicians, even among those most savage in their opposition to abortion, suggest that these liberal laws were unconstitutional. It is true that during the nineteenth century liberal laws were replaced by laws that prohibited or strictly regulated abortion. The best historical evidence shows that these new laws were adopted not out of concern for fetuses, however, but in large part to protect the health of the mother and the privileges of the medical profession.[8] The structure and detail of the anti-abortion laws show, moreover, that even the strictest states rejected the idea that a fetus is a constitutional person. Even the most stringent laws did not punish abortion as severely as they did ordinary murder. The difference was not explained as the consequence of applying some general exculpatory principle to abortion—it was not said, for example, that the moral wickedness of abortion is less because abortion is in some ways like self-defense. Rather it was simply assumed that even in principle abortion is not so serious a matter as murder. Nor did states that prohibited abortion try to prevent a woman from procuring an abortion in another state, when that was possible, or abroad.

Of course, the Supreme Court sometimes upsets conventional understandings about what the Constitution requires. It did that in the *Brown* case, for example, when it held that the long-established educational system of the southern states was unconstitutional because it segregated students by race, and it did it in *Roe* v. *Wade* as well. But in each of these cases, the Court could appeal to established, more general constitutional principles that plausibly condemned the practices it held unconstitutional. It could claim, that is, that the legal history was inconsistent. In each case, moreover, substantial legal and public opinion had already been converted to the new opinion the Court endorsed. The Court could have declared a fetus a constitutional person in *Roe*, however, only by insisting that the established view, that a fetus does not have that status, was unacceptable no matter how widespread because any fetus is so plainly a person in the moral sense—is so plainly a human being with interests of its own that should be protected by rights—that no state's law should be permitted to deny this. But, as we have seen, that proposition is scarcely intelligible, and very few people believe it. Many of *Roe*'s critics, as I said, accuse the Court of having substituted moral convictions for dispassionate legal analysis. But anyone who thinks Blackmun's threshold decision wrong must himself be relying not only on a moral conviction but on a particularly odd and unpopular one.

CAN STATES MAKE A FETUS A PERSON?

The United States Constitution therefore does not declare a fetus to be a constitutional person. Now we must ask whether the Constitution leaves each state free to decide, if it wishes, that a fetus has the legal status of a person within its borders. Once again, we must take care not to become confused by the ambiguities in the word "person." There is no doubt that states can properly protect the life of a fetus in a number of different ways, and they might well declare that a fetus is a person in the course of doing so. A state may punish someone who either deliberately or recklessly injures a pregnant woman, and punish him more severely if the injury results in fetal damage or miscarriage, for no one has a constitutional right to injure any creature with impunity. Such laws need not, of course, declare or suggest that a fetus is a person; they might simply state that it is a crime to cause a miscarriage by injuring a pregnant woman, for example. But legislators might find it appealing to use the language of fetal personhood. An Illinois statute, for example, begins by declaring that a fetus is to be considered a person within Illinois borders.[9] There can be no constitutional objection to such a law so long as it makes plain, as the Illinois statute was careful to do, that it is not intended to diminish anyone's rights under the national Constitution. With that qualification, declaring a fetus a person raises no more constitutional difficulties than declaring, as every state has, that corporations are legal persons that enjoy many of the rights real people do, including the right to own property and to sue. Declaring corporations persons is a kind of shorthand for describing a complex network of rights and duties, and so long as states do not use the shorthand to curtail or diminish constitutional rights, there can be no constitutional objection.

But the suggestion that the Constitution allows states to bestow personhood on fetuses assumes more than this benign use of the language of personhood. It assumes that a state *can* curtail constitutional rights by adding new persons to the constitutional population, to the list of those whose constitutional rights are competitive with one another. The constitutional rights any citizen has are of course very much affected by who or what else is also deemed to have constitutional rights, because their rights compete or conflict with his. If a state could not only create corporations as legal persons but also endow them with a vote, it could impair the constitutional right to vote of ordinary people, because corporations' votes would dilute individuals' votes. If a state could declare trees to be persons with a constitutional right to life, it could prohibit the publication of newspapers or books in spite of the First Amendment's guarantee of free speech, which is not a license to kill. If a state could declare higher apes to be persons whose rights are competitive with the constitutional rights of ordinary people, it could prohibit its citizens from taking lifesaving medicines first tested on those animals.

Once we understand that the suggestion we are considering has these implications, we must reject it. States have no power to overrule the *national* constitutional arrangement, and if a fetus is not part of the constitutional population under that arrangement, states cannot make it one. The supremacy clause of the Constitution declares that the Constitution is the highest law of the land. If that means anything, it means that the rights the national Constitution guarantees individual American citizens cannot be repealed by the legislatures of the several states, either directly, by flat repealing legislation, or indirectly, by packing the constitutional population.[10]

It is fair to say that few critics, even the main opponents of *Roe* v. *Wade*, really believe that states have the power to make a fetus a person with competitive constitutional rights. As I pointed out earlier, even then Associate Justice Rehnquist, who dissented in that case, said that he had "little doubt" that a state could not constitutionally forbid an abortion that was necessary to save a pregnant woman's life. If a state could declare a fetus a person with a competitive right to life, then of course it could constitutionally prohibit abortion even in that case, just as it normally forbids killing one innocent person to save the life of another.

Professor John Hart Ely, of the Stanford Law School, has argued that *Roe* v. *Wade* is wrong even though a fetus is not a constitutional person because the government has the legitimate right to protect the interests of creatures who are not persons.[11] It has the power to protect the interests of dogs, for example, by forbidding and punishing cruelty to animals. But as Professor Laurence Tribe of the Harvard Law School has replied, government does not have the power to do this in ways that make the exercise of a fundamental constitutional right impossible.[12] There is an even stronger reason why Ely's argument against *Roe* v. *Wade* fails, moreover. Fetuses have no interests before approximately the point in pregnancy after which they are viable, and *Roe* v. *Wade* permits states to forbid abortion after that point, anyway.[13]

An American state, then, has no constitutional power to declare a fetus a person or to protect fetal interests at the expense of its citizens' constitutional rights. What other derivative responsibilities might it claim? Can it plausibly claim an interest in increasing the size of the population for the sake of those who are already within it and that laws against abortion serve that purpose? No, because any interest a state might have in increasing its population would give it at least as strong a reason for banning contraception as for banning abortion, and if a state's interest in increasing its population cannot justify the former, as the Supreme Court's *Griswold* decision said it could not, then it cannot justify the latter, either. In any event, no American state could plausibly claim an interest in increasing its population: it is a general assumption throughout the world that overpopulation is a more serious threat than underpopulation.

Someone might try to construct a better argument for a derivative responsibility by insisting that a society in which abortion is tolerated is one that holds human life cheap, and that in that kind of society ordinary people are more likely to be assaulted and killed. Obviously, it is a legitimate goal of society to protect people from murderous attack. But this argument is still unsatisfactory, because a state needs a *compelling* reason to justify banning abortion and therefore strong evidence that the ban is necessary. There is no evidence beyond the barest speculation that allowing the abortion of nonviable fetuses generates a culture in which people take a more callous attitude toward the slaughter of children or adults. Abortion is, in effect, freely permitted in many European countries in the first trimester of pregnancy, and these are much less violent societies than many American communities are now or were when abortion was still mostly forbidden.

It would be even harder to show that the desensitizing effect of allowing abortions is greater than other features of American society that deaden us to the horror of murder, including, for example, the death penalty, which many American states retain though almost all other civilized democracies have rejected it, or the shamefully high rate of infant mortality, which Americans seem to accept because they are unwilling to spend enough on welfare programs to reduce it, or the violent character of so many American television programs and movies. Many of the fiercest opponents of abortion accept or even enthusiastically support these much more threatening aspects of popular culture.[14]

HARD QUESTIONS

We have been considering the logical structure of *Roe* v. *Wade.* We began by reviewing Justice Blackmun's strong argument that because a pregnant woman has a constitutional right to privacy, states may not forbid abortion unless they have not merely some reason but a compelling reason for doing so. We next considered whether states do have such a compelling justification for forbidding abortion. But I limited our discussion to considering whether states have a compelling reason in virtue of a derivative responsibility to protect the rights and interests of a fetus. If a fetus were recognized in the Constitution as a person with rights—a person within the sense of the equal protection clause's declaration that "persons" must be treated as equals—then there could be no doubt that, in almost all circumstances, states do have a compelling reason to prohibit abortion—indeed, that in at least some circumstances, they *must* do so.

Justice Blackmun decided, however, that a fetus is not a person within the meaning of the national Constitution, and all the responsible opponents of his decision agree. Some lawyers have argued, however, that the national Constitution gives states the power in effect to amend the Constitution by adding fetuses to the list of those whose rights can count in fixing the constitutional rights of others, though only within the states' own borders. But there are decisive arguments against that view, and even those lawyers who have argued for it would probably reject its consequences.

So Blackmun's decision was plainly right if we understand the constitutional argument in the usual way, as an argument about whether government can treat a fetus as a person. That is only the beginning of the real constitutional argument, however. Two great questions remain. First, is the assumption I made—that women have a constitutional right to control their own role in procreation—really sound? I argued that it is, assuming that *Griswold* and the other Supreme Court decisions establishing a right to privacy are sound. But some conservative constitutional scholars challenge that whole line of decisions; they say that the "right to privacy" is just a liberal judicial invention, and that the Constitution's "framers" did not intend to create any such right. In the next chapter we shall assess this more global objection.

Second, do American states nevertheless have a compelling *detached* reason for forbidding abortion? May they outlaw abortion in order to protect the sanctity or inviolability of human life? This large question about the scope of legitimate governmental power arises, as a question of political morality, everywhere—even in nations like Great Britain that have no constitution that finally constrains what government can do. Does a decent government attempt to dictate to its citizens what intrinsic values they will recognize, and why, and how? In the United States, that is a legal question as well: it is the deepest and most important constitutional question raised by the abortion controversy. (It is also the question at the bottom of the nascent controversy about euthanasia and the right to die, as we shall see.)

These complex legal questions lead us into the great doctrinal controversies that have raged in American law schools and in American courts for many decades, about how the Constitution should be interpreted and how far judges are or should be influenced by their own personal moral convictions in deciding what it means. We must now choose between two very different conceptions of what kind of a constitution the United States really has.

5

THE
CONSTITUTIONAL
DRAMA

Lawyers who think that *Roe* v. *Wade* should be overruled make two main points. They argue, first, that the Constitution does not mention a right to abortion, and, second, that none of the statesmen and politicians who drafted and enacted the Constitution intended to grant any such right. Are these claims true? Are they relevant?

Does the United States Constitution mention a right to an abortion? Did the men who wrote it intend to create one? That depends on what we mean by "mention" and "intend." I shall argue that in the only relevant sense of those words, the answer to both questions is yes. But my argument depends not just on linguistic or historical facts but on a much more general political issue. What kind of constitution should America have?

The United States has the oldest and most stable structure of government in the world. Its Constitution insists on a republican form of government: government by the people, not a monarch or an oligarchy of nobles or mandarins. It disciplines that republican government through an intricate structure of checks and balances, first by dividing the powers of government between the national government and the several states, and then by dividing the powers of the national government among the Congress, the presidency, and the courts.

The most striking and original feature of the American Constitution, however, is the limit it places on the overall power of the governmental institutions it creates: it insists that the people as individuals retain certain fundamental rights described in the Constitution's Bill of Rights. (I mean not just the first ten amendments to the Constitution, which were adopted shortly after the nation began, but those adopted after the Civil War as well.) The First Amendment, for example, says that government may not abridge freedom of religion, speech, or the press. The Fifth Amendment says that the national government may not take life, liberty, or property without due process of law. The Fourteenth Amendment restricts the states in the same way, and then adds that the states must accord all people the equal protection of the laws. Neither the states nor the national Congress nor the president has authority to take any step that harms or insults even one individual in the ways these great clauses forbid.

We can interpret those clauses of the Bill of Rights in two very different ways, however. In effect, we can construct two very different constitutions out of them. We can interpret them, first, as abstract commands that American government respect the most fundamental principles of liberty and political decency and treat all citizens with equal concern and respect. Then we create a constitution of *principle* that lays down general, comprehensive moral standards that government must respect but that leaves it to statesmen and judges to decide what these standards mean in concrete circumstances. What the due process and equal protection clauses actually mean, on this view of the Constitution, depends on the best, most accurate understanding of liberty and equal citizenship.

Or we can interpret the Bill of Rights very differently, as expressing only the very specific, concrete expectations of the particular statesmen who wrote and voted for them. The due process and equal protection clauses would then have only the force that the particular people who voted for them would have expected them to have. If we interpret the Bill of Rights in this manner, we construct a constitution of *detail*—a collection of independent historical views and opinions unlikely to have great unity or even complete consistency.

The first of these two pictures of the Constitution is exhilarating, a stirring vision of political community. But there is an obvious difficulty: it will inevitably be controversial what the fine abstractions of the Bill of Rights actually mean when they are applied to harsh political battles. It will be controversial, for example, whether freedom of speech means that people must be free to publish or read pornography. Or whether the right to have an abortion really is a basic liberty, essential to a genuinely free society. Or whether a city government that sets aside a percentage of construction contracts for black-owned firms is treating all its residents with equal concern. Citizens will divide: a majority that wants to outlaw pornography or prohibit abortion or set aside construction contracts for black-owned firms will deny that it is violating liberty or withholding equal concern, and a resentful minority will disagree. The Supreme Court will have to decide, which means that the justices must answer intractable, profound questions of political morality that philosophers, statesmen, and citizens have debated for many centuries with no prospect of agreement. It means that the rest of us must accept the deliverances of a majority of the justices, whose insight into these great issues does not seem spectacularly special, unless we are numerous and dedicated enough to amend the Constitution, or, as is more likely, until age, death, or change produces a different Supreme Court with different convictions.

This form of government gives very great power to judges. For all practical purposes, the federal courts, and finally the Supreme Court, have the last word about what rights the Constitution affirms and protects, and what the national and state governments therefore cannot do. So some of the most important political decisions that any community must make—decisions that in most other democracies have been or would be the subject of great political struggles—have been decided for Americans by judges, rather than by elected representatives of the people.

In 1954, for example, in *Brown* v. *Board of Education,* the Supreme Court ruled that racial segregation in public schools is unconstitutional.[1] It thus declared illegal an important foundation of the social structure of a large section of the country. In the four decades since that famous case, the Court has made an enormous number of other important and well-publicized decisions. It developed an army of legal weapons against other forms of racial prejudice and discrimination. It declared prayer and religious worship in public schools illegal. It created a network of protections for those accused and convicted of crimes. And, of course, in 1973 it decided *Roe* v. *Wade.*

In each of these important decisions, a majority of the justices assumed that they were enforcing a constitution of principle, that it was up to them to decide what the abstract ideals of liberty and of equality of citizenship required when applied to the concrete controversies before them. The *Brown* decision, for example, could not have been reached by a Court aiming only to recapture the very concrete expectations of the politicians who wrote the Fourteenth Amendment, because those politicians, after enacting it, promptly segregated the public schools of the District of Columbia.

The striking Supreme Court decisions of the last few decades imposed what are widely thought to be liberal views on less-liberal majorities. But judges may also impose conservative convictions on less-conservative majorities, as the Court did in *Lochner* v. *New York* in 1905, when it struck down a state law forbidding bakeries to work their bakers more than fourteen hours a day on the ground that this infringed the economic rights of workers who wanted to work longer hours.[2] *Lochner* has long since been overruled, and lawyers cite it today only as a paradigm example of Supreme Court lunacy. But in recent years the Court has once again imposed convictions widely thought conservative on local majorities: its controversial 1989 decision in *City of Richmond* v. *J. A. Croson Co.,* which struck down Richmond's scheme reserving a percentage of municipal contracts for minority firms, had that consequence, for example.[3]

To many Americans, it seems wrong and dangerous that judges should have that kind of power. They would prefer the second vision of the Constitution I described; they would prefer that justices treated the Bill of Rights as a set of highly detailed rules, each recording the specific understandings that were widespread at given historical moments in the past. On that view, the First, Fifth, and Fourteenth Amendments guarantee citizens only what the ideas of freedom of speech or basic liberty or equal concern were commonly thought to include when those different amendments were drafted and adopted. So the Supreme Court does not have to decide whether freedom of speech, on the most appealing interpretation of that political value, protects sexually explicit literature from censorship, but only whether it would have been thought to do so in late-eighteenth-century America; not whether abortion is a fundamental right central to a genuinely free society, but only whether those who drafted and adopted the Fourteenth Amendment, after the Civil War, thought it was; not whether affirmative-action construction policies really treat citizens with equal concern, but whether the architects of the Fourteenth Amendment thought they were making such policies unconstitutional.

This picture of the Bill of Rights offers much less noble a vision than the first one I described; it makes the document only a collection of detailed separate and independent rules put together like a postage-stamp collection from different parts of American history. Indeed, it makes the point of having any bill of rights at all seem doubtful: why should Americans now be restricted in what their government can do for or to them by what very different people thought one or two centuries ago? Still, it might seem safer and also more democratic than allowing unelected judges to impose their own controversial convictions about political philosophy on the people. Some might say: history has given us a constitution that plainly limits what the majority may do. We cannot avoid that, but we can aim to make its restrictions as light and trivial as we can. Because our ancestors had on the whole a more restrictive view of liberty and equality than many lawyers and judges do now, treating the Constitution as a collection of highly detailed rules, modeled on their expectations, is likely to prove much less restrictive than treating it as a system of abstract moral principle that contemporary judges must interpret according to their own lights.

Which of these very different constitutions—the grander but perhaps more dangerous constitution of principle or the apparently safer but more mundane constitution of detail—should we aim to have? I might have asked a different question, a legal question: which kind of constitution *do* we have? The Constitution is, after all, part of American law. Suppose we apply the ordinary techniques of legal interpretation to the great clauses of the Bill of Rights: would this reveal the principled or the detailed vision? The answer, as we shall see, is relatively straightforward: ordinary legal interpretation supports the principled rather than the detailed understanding of the Constitution. It supports the noble constitution, the constitution the Supreme Court assumed we have when it made all the striking and important decisions I described.

That is a very important claim. In recent decades, many lawyers have argued the opposite. They say that the Supreme Court, in those decisions, misunderstood the Constitution, that the Constitution is actually, as a matter of strict legal analysis, a constitution of detail, that it actually leaves state legislatures free to prohibit abortion, authorize criminal investigations according to their own conceptions of proper police procedures, restrict trial safeguards for people accused of crime, and censor publications the majority finds offensive, all because those who wrote the Bill of Rights never intended to deny government these powers. They accuse advocates of the principled view—sometimes in savage terms—of ignoring legal arguments and relying only on political ones. They say, for example, that Justice Blackmun's decision in *Roe* v. *Wade* ignored strict legal argument for personal politics.

That strategy is a stunning example of attack as the best defense, and it has been remarkably successful politically. Its success can be traced, however, not to the legal arguments its proponents have marshaled— these are, as we shall see, extremely weak—but to public dissatisfaction with many of the decisions the Supreme Court reached relying on the abstract, principled view of the Constitution, particularly *Roe* v. *Wade* but also other unpopular decisions like those outlawing prayer in the public schools, and to public suspicion of judges having the power that the principled view assigns them. The public is more concerned, in other words, with the political question of what kind of a constitution we should have than with technical legal arguments about the one we do have.

I believe that popular suspicion of a principled constitution is misplaced; the American Constitution, understood as one of principle, provides a better form of government than any in which the legislative and executive branches of government are legally free to disregard fundamental principles of justice and decency. A constitution of principle, enforced by independent judges, is not undemocratic. On the contrary, it is a *precondition* of legitimate democracy that government is required to treat individual citizens as equals, and to respect their fundamental liberties and dignity. Unless those conditions are met, there can be no genuine democracy, because unless they are met, the majority has no legitimate moral title to govern.

That view of what democracy is has survived Jacobinism, majoritarianism, fascism, and communism. The eminent French historian François Furet said that the American Revolution was far more important than the French or Russian revolutions because it created the form of government that much of the rest of the democratic world, in fits and starts, has now begun to copy. We are envied for our innovation and increasingly imitated: in Paris and Bonn and Rome, in New Delhi and Strasbourg and Ottawa, even, perhaps, in the Palace of Westminster, and even, perhaps one day, in Moscow and Johannesburg. In all those places, people seem ready to accept the risk and high promise of government not by men and women, or even under law, but government under principle, the form of government we created.

American history and traditions are so interwoven with this form of government, moreover, that even if we wished, we could not now dismantle it without in effect going back to the eighteenth century and starting again. The narrow, detailed conception of our Constitution is not even an option for contemporary America, and pretending to adopt it would provide no real check on judges' power to impose their own convictions on the law, but only the dangerous illusion of such a check. Of course, there must be limits on a judge's power to interpret the Constitution according to his own political convictions. That is common ground. But we can secure genuine constraints only within the Constitution of abstract principle we have, not by pretending we have a different form of government, and only by insisting on something the principled conception makes explicit but the detailed one obscures: that judges must justify their decisions through arguments of principle and integrity, which the legal profession can criticize, and which the public, whose influence should be felt when presidents nominate judges, can sensibly assess.

As I suggested, many Americans who distrust the principled view of the Constitution and claim to support the detailed one are reacting to their dissatisfaction with Roe v. Wade. They rightly sense that if we accept the principled view, the argument for a constitutional right to abortion will seem much stronger. Many of Roe v. Wade's supporters agree, and they are attracted to a broad, principled view of the Constitution for that reason. In other words, a great number of Americans have decided what kind of constitution they want by asking what kind would benefit their side of the abortion argument; they treat that issue as a litmus test of any constitutional theory's adequacy.

The great Senate debate in 1987 about whether to confirm President Reagan's nomination of Robert Bork to the Supreme Court was in large part an attempt to discover the nominee's views about abortion, and the more recent Senate arguments about the intellectual qualifications of President Bush's two appointees—David Souter and Clarence Thomas—were about little else. Meetings of the American Bar Association have been dominated by the abortion issue, and the only significant disputes over party platforms in the 1992 election campaign were about it. We are in danger of single-issue constitutional theory, which is at least as bad as single-issue politics. It may be understandable that people approach constitutional philosophy that way. But it is also a shame. We should rather reason the other way around: we should decide what our Constitution says about abortion only after we have decided how a just society's constitution protects individual freedom and dignity.

REWRITING THE CONSTITUTION

Many of the Supreme Court's most important decisions in the decades following the Second World War pleased liberals and offended conservatives, and Republican presidents promised to appoint justices who would trim the Court's power by substituting a constitution of detail for our constitution of principle. On the whole, they were surprisingly unsuccessful, because the principled view of the Constitution has great intellectual and emotional strength, and even many of the justices who were thought conservatives when they were appointed were drawn to that view and to the decisions it supported once they were on the Court. Dwight Eisenhower, a Republican, chose two justices who became great champions of the principled view: Earl Warren, as chief justice, guided the Court to many of its most liberal decisions, and William Brennan, who served on the Court for thirty-four years, was one of the most influential liberal justices in its history. (No wonder Eisenhower said that he had made two big mistakes during his presidency, and that they were both on the Supreme Court.)

Richard Nixon appointed Harry Blackmun, who wrote the majority opinion in *Roe* v. *Wade* and remains a staunch liberal, and Nixon's choice for chief justice when Earl Warren retired, Warren Burger, joined in the *Roe* opinion and, though he was more conservative than Earl Warren, voted to protect and even extend many of the Court's decisions that conservatives most disapproved. Gerald Ford, the Republican vice president who succeeded to the presidency when Nixon resigned, appointed only one justice: John Paul Stevens, who emphatically supports *Roe* and has for many years been an articulate, imaginative liberal justice.

Ronald Reagan's and George Bush's administrations placed a high priority on appointing very conservative judges to all levels of the federal courts, and they screened judicial appointments for ideological soundness more thoroughly than any other administration ever had. They made the federal courts dramatically more conservative, and as they aimed at appointing young judges, the consequences will be long lasting. One of the five Reagan-Bush Supreme Court appointees— Antonin Scalia—has indeed become a fierce and steady advocate of a constitution of detail, and another—Clarence Thomas—has since his appointment in 1991 voted with Scalia on almost every case.

But the other three Reagan-Bush appointees—Sandra Day O'Connor, Anthony Kennedy, and David Souter—disappointed conservative expectations not just because they joined with Blackmun and Stevens in reaffirming *Roe* v. *Wade* in their joint opinion in *Planned Parenthood of Southeastern Pennsylvania* v. *Casey*, which I mentioned in chapter 1, but also because they made plain, in that opinion and in other cases, their preference for a constitution of principle. In a crucial passage, they rejected Scalia's view that the due process clause should not be used to strike down laws that were familiar and widely approved when the Fourteenth Amendment was enacted. They said that "liberty" within the meaning of that clause is not just a matter of what was thought a fundamental freedom when the clause was enacted but of what really *is* fundamental, and though they conceded that reasonable lawyers disagree over that question, they insisted that justices of the Supreme Court cannot properly escape the responsibility of making that controversial judgment for themselves.[4]

The media, commenting on the *Casey* decision, said that O'Connor, Kennedy, and Souter constituted a moderate center on the Court. That suggestion may well be exaggerated; the three justices will probably divide again, as they have in the past, over specific constitutional issues, and one or another will make decisions, as each has before, that will strike liberals as not merely moderate but very conservative. The abstract view of the Constitution is not a distinctly liberal or moderate vision, however, but a jurisprudential one, and that these three justices have endorsed that vision, though they were selected by politicians openly opposed to it, is testament to its great intellectual power.

Nevertheless, four justices now on the Supreme Court—Chief Justice Rehnquist and Justice White as well as Justices Scalia and Thomas— passionately denounce the constitution of principle as a dangerous invention.[5] We must consider the arguments for their view, and we might begin by looking more carefully at the text of the Bill of Rights. Some of the individual rights it created are quite detailed. The Third Amendment, for example, provides that Congress may not quarter soldiers in private houses in peacetime. But the rights that proved most important were written in very abstract language. The First Amendment says that Congress shall not infringe freedom of speech, shall not restrict freedom of religion, and shall not establish any religion. But it says nothing to help judges decide whether specific laws against pornography or flag burning offend freedom of speech; whether laws that draft conscientious objectors or forbid Native Americans to smoke peyote in religious ceremonies invade freedom of religion; whether laws requiring the Lord's Prayer to be recited in public schools or allowing government subsidies to parochial schools so that they can buy math books establish religion.

The most important clauses of the Fifth, Fourteenth, and other amendments are even more abstract. Both the Fifth and the Fourteenth forbid government to take life or liberty or property without "due process of law." The Supreme Court early decided that this clause was not to be understood as simply procedural, but that it imposed substantive limits on what government could do no matter what procedures it followed. But the amendments say nothing to help judges decide whether due process means that people have a right to a lawyer before the police can interrogate them, for example, or that states may not make contraception or abortion a crime. The Eighth Amendment forbids "cruel and unusual punishment," but it does not indicate whether any particular methods of executing criminals—hanging or electrocution, for example—are cruel or, indeed, whether the death penalty is itself cruel no matter what method of execution is used. The Fourteenth Amendment declares that states may deny no person "equal protection of the laws," and the Supreme Court has held that this requirement, too, is substantive and not merely procedural. But the abstract requirement of equal protection does not itself make clear whether states can segregate schools by race, or whether they must spend the same amount per pupil on public education in different school districts across the state.

Each of these great constitutional clauses is abstract in a particular way; each makes crucial use of concepts that are not legal terms of art, or taken from economics or some other branch of social science, but are drawn from ordinary moral and political use: concepts like "liberty" and "freedom" and "cruel" and "equal." Read in the most natural way, the words of the Bill of Rights do seem to create a breathtakingly abstract, principled constitution. Taken at face value, they command nothing less than that government treat everyone subject to its dominion with equal concern and respect, and that it not infringe their most basic freedoms, those liberties essential, as one prominent jurist put it, to the very idea of "ordered liberty."[6] The system of principle this striking language mandates is comprehensive because it commands both equal concern and basic liberty, which in our political culture are the two major sources of claims of individual rights. Since liberty and equality overlap in large part, each of the two major abstract clauses of the Bill of Rights—the due process and the equal protection clauses—is itself comprehensive in that same way. Particular constitutional rights that follow from the best interpretation of the equal protection clause, for example, will very likely also follow from the best interpretation of the due process clause. The Supreme Court had no difficulty in deciding that although the equal protection clause does not apply to the District of Columbia, racial segregation in the District's schools is nevertheless unconstitutional under the due process clause, which does apply to it. Indeed, it is very likely that even if there had been no First Amendment, American courts would long ago have found the freedoms of speech, press, and religion in the Fifth and Fourteenth Amendments' guarantees of basic liberty.

Many conservative lawyers, including the four present Supreme Court justices I mentioned, claim that the Bill of Rights does not mean what it seems to say. They argue that the apparently abstract clauses about free speech and due process and liberty and equality should be treated only as coded messages or shorthand statements of very concrete, detailed historical agreements. The commands of free speech and equality, in their view, protect only certain specific forms of speech and require equality only in certain very specific respects or dimensions. These revisionists hope in that way to turn the abstract, principled Bill of Rights into a document with the texture and tone of an insurance policy or a standard-form commercial lease.

In one way, as I said, this collective revisionist effort has been remarkably successful. It has achieved the Orwellian triumph, the political huckster's dream, of painting its opponents with its own shames and vices. It has persuaded many people that turning the Constitution into an out-of-date list of very limited historical agreements is really *protecting* that document, and that those who insist on stubbornly reading the Constitution to mean what it says are inventors and usurpers. Even judges who accept the broad responsibility the Constitution's language imposes on them still adopt the misleading names their revisionist opponents assign them. They call themselves "activists" or "noninterpretivists" or champions of "unenumerated rights" who wish to go "outside the four corners" of the Constitution to decide cases on a "natural law" basis.

In that important political way, the revisionist effort to narrow the Bill of Rights has been successful. But we must now consider whether it has succeeded legally, whether it has provided plausible legal arguments for construing the great abstract clauses of the Bill of Rights in a limited, detailed way. It cannot even begin to succeed in that task unless it offers what we might call a codebook—revisionists must tell us how to *de*code the great abstract constitutional phrases so that we can decide what detailed understandings are buried beneath their grand and abstract language. Revisionists say that we decode the abstract text by asking what those who wrote it or voted for it actually intended to achieve. We shall see that this suggestion is much less of an answer to our question than it might seem; it is hardly even the beginning of an answer. But let us first look at a different kind of answer some revisionists give, because it will be even easier to see that this answer, too, is unsatisfactory.

Enumerated and unenumerated rights. Revisionists insist on a distinction between two kinds of rights that the Supreme Court has recognized and enforced in the past. Some of these rights, they say, are actually mentioned, or enumerated, in the text, while others are not. They claim that the right to privacy, which the Supreme Court recognized in *Griswold* and other contraception cases and from which it derived the right to abortion in *Roe* v. *Wade,* is not actually mentioned in the text of the Constitution, and that it is therefore not a genuine constitutional right. If we allow judges to roam at will beyond the "four corners" of the Constitution, they add, we abandon all hope of limiting judicial power. That is the argument Justice White made, for example, in his majority opinion in *Bowers* v. *Hardwick,* a 1986 Supreme Court decision that refused to recognize a constitutional right of adult homosexuals to be free to engage in consensual homosexual sex. White said that since no such right is actually mentioned in the Constitution, the Court would be making it up, and he said that judge-made constitutional law was particularly suspect when it had "little or no cognizable roots in the language or design of the Constitution."[7] White, you recall, dissented in *Roe,* and so his comment in *Bowers* was presumably meant to disparage the putative right to abortion as well as that of homosexuals.

In fact, the distinction between enumerated, or mentioned, rights on the one hand, and unenumerated, or unmentioned, rights on the other makes no sense when applied to the equal protection clause, the due process clause, or the other abstract clauses of the Constitution. That distinction does make sense in some circumstances, of course. Suppose an ordinance forbids taking guns, knives, or explosives onto an airplane, and airport officials interpret the ordinance to forbid canisters of tear gas as well, on the ground that the ordinance's obvious intention was to prohibit all weapons that might be used in hijacks or other acts of terrorism. We would be right to say that gas was not actually on the list of what was banned, and to ask whether officials are really entitled to add "unenumerated" weapons to that list. The distinction we rely on— between pistols, switchblades, and hand grenades on the one hand, and tear gas on the other—depends upon a fact about the English language: neither the word "gun" nor "knife" nor "explosive" may correctly be used to refer to tear gas.

No comparable fact about the correct use of language can explain the supposed distinction between enumerated and unenumerated constitutional rights, however, because the Bill of Rights consists of broad and abstract principles of political morality, and correct application of these principles depends upon moral sense, not linguistic rules. The distinction between specific rights that are enumerated and those that are not is therefore simply irrelevant. We can see why by looking at a group of legal arguments: two that most revisionists agree support "enumerated" constitutional rights, and one they all say supports at best only an "unenumerated" right.

> 1. The equal-protection clause of the Fourteenth Amendment creates a constitutional right of equal concern and respect, from which it follows that women have a right against certain gender-based discriminations unless such discriminations are required by important state interests.[8]

2. The First Amendment, which forbids government to abridge freedom of speech, grants a right of symbolic protest, from which it follows that individuals have a right to burn the American flag.[9]
3. The due process clause of the Fourteenth Amendment protects the basic freedoms central to the very concept of "ordered liberty," including the right of privacy, from which it follows that women have a constitutional right to abortion.

None of these three arguments depends upon the meaning of words in the way that the claim "Guns include pistols but not tear gas" does. No one believes that it follows just from the meaning of the words "freedom of speech" either that states can prohibit flag burning or that they cannot. No one believes that it follows just from the meaning of the words "equal protection" that laws excluding women from certain jobs are unconstitutional or that they are not. If any of these three arguments is persuasive, it is so because the substantive moral theory it assumes is an attractive one. If the second is a good argument, for example, it is because its central claim—that the point of protecting free speech extends to the kind of protest involved in flag burning—is sound. If the third argument is successful, it is for exactly the same kind of reason: because the right to privacy and the right to abortion are indeed essential conditions of a genuinely free society. In both cases, the nerve of the argument is a moral claim; if those moral claims are accepted, the right to abortion bears no more tenuous or distant relationship to the language of the Constitution than does the right to burn a flag.

Justice White's metaphor about legal arguments having "roots" in language is opaque and mysterious; it disguises rather than dissipates obscurity. But it is safe to say that none of the three arguments claims "roots" in language in any way in which the other two do not. Some lawyers say that the third argument's conclusions about abortion are "further" from the Constitution's text than the equal-protection and free-speech claims of the other two, but this metaphor of distance is also opaque: it means or suggests nothing. Since neither a right to burn a flag nor a right against gender discrimination nor a right to abortion either follows directly from the dictionary meanings of the words in the Constitution, or is excluded by their dictionary meaning, none of these rights can be closer to or further from the text than the others.[10]

· · ·

The original intention. The distinction between enumerated and un-enumerated rights, which many revisionist lawyers have emphasized, is therefore wholly unhelpful to them. But their most important proposal, about how to read a detailed constitution into the abstract language of the historical document, is a different one. They say they believe in "originalism": that the Constitution means only what the politicians who wrote it originally intended it to mean. Judges who have to decide whether the First Amendment forbids states to make flag burning a crime, or forbids them to hold prayer in public schools, for example, should ask only the historical question: did the eighteenth-century authors of the First Amendment intend it to have those consequences? (Revisionists often use the word "framers" to describe the authors of a constitutional provision, but I shall mainly avoid the word.) If the answer is no (and revisionists believe that the answer is very likely to be no for most serious problems that arise at the tag end of the twentieth century), then the Constitution does not have that force. The effect of originalism, its backers suggest, is sharply to decrease the scope of individual constitutional rights protected by the abstract clauses, and to substitute the detailed for the principled vision of the Constitution.

Conservative Supreme Court justices have found originalism particularly useful as a defense of their views. Antonin Scalia, the most radically conservative member of the present Court, frequently writes as if the intentions of the historical sponsors of some particular clause of the Constitution are the only acceptable guide to its meaning. And the newest member of the Court, Clarence Thomas, relies on original intention whenever he can, though Thomas himself, before he joined the Court, ridiculed the original-intention test as bogus and urged conservatives to accept the constitution of principle as a plain fact and to argue for conservative moral theories as the best guide to its sound application.[11]

The most elaborate defense of the original-intention method has been provided by Robert Bork. Reagan nominated Bork to the Court as a dedicated and intense supporter of originalism, and Bork's nomination focused public attention on that view; but his attempts to explain and defend it in his nomination hearings were not generally regarded as convincing.[12] In the book he wrote after his nomination was defeated, Bork tried to amplify and improve his defense. He described originalism as something so fundamental and self-evident that only tricksters could fail to accept and obey it. "Of course," he said, "the judge is bound to apply the law as those who made the law wanted him to. That is the common, everyday view of what law is. I stress the point only because that commonsense view is hotly, extensively and eruditely denied by constitutional sophisticates, particularly those who teach the subject in the law schools."[13] But having begun in that confident way, Bork's discussion of originalism was so full of qualifications, exceptions, and obscurities that originalism soon began to look hardly commonsensical or self-evident at all.

The truth is that there are grave intellectual difficulties in that view, some of them much discussed in the literature, and we should know what they are so that we can identify the challenges Bork's defense was obliged to meet. There is, first, the difficulty of deciding who the Constitution's authors actually were. Several of the first ten amendments were extensively discussed and revised in the course of their drafting and adoption at the end of the eighteenth century. So were the amendments adopted late in the nineteenth. Whose intentions should today's judges consult—the intentions of the congressmen who debated and recommended the amendments, of the state legislators who ratified them, or of the public whose wishes these politicians were supposed to be enforcing? How about all the hundreds of thousands of national and state legislators and private citizens who might have campaigned to amend the Constitution, over the centuries, had they understood it differently? Do they not count as well? What about the Supreme Court and lower-court judges who have been interpreting the Constitution from the time it was enacted to the present day? Since their decisions are precedents, they also "made the law." Why do their intentions not count?

Suppose that we somehow decide whose intentions count. Suppose we decide (for example, though it is hard to see on what ground) that only the original legislative sponsors of a particular constitutional clause or amendment count as its authors, so that only their intentions are important in determining what the clause means. What do we mean by their *intentions*? We must, for a start, observe an obvious distinction that is inexplicably ignored in many discussions of originalism: the distinction between what people mean to say, and what they expect (or hope or wish or fear) will be the *result* of their saying it. Originalism is sometimes explained as the view that the Constitution says only what those who wrote it meant it to say. That commonsensical statement is indeed roughly, if not absolutely, true. But originalists claim something very different and more controversial: that the Constitution must be understood to mean only what its authors expected would be the result of their having written what they did. Only this claim could possibly convert the Constitution from the abstract statement of principle it manifestly is to the concrete, detailed document revisionists prefer.

Everyone is familiar with the general distinction between what people mean to say and what they expect or hope will happen as a result of their having said it. People often say "Don't bother" when they hope the person they are speaking to will ignore what they have said and will indeed bother. The distinction is especially important when people give orders or make requests in language that is normally understood as abstract or in some other way requiring judgment.

Suppose you offer to go out to buy sandwiches for lunch, and I ask you, in the hearing of my wife, to buy me something "healthy." I might mean what I appear to have said: that I want a sandwich that is, in fact, a healthy one. If you believe that that is indeed what I meant, you will have to rely on your own judgment. You will not buy me a hot pastrami sandwich even if you know how much I crave pastrami or unaccountably believe it to be good for me. Nor, when you do not bring back what I wanted, could I accuse you of having misunderstood or disobeyed me, no matter how much I had hoped against hope that you would think hot pastrami healthy. But there are other possibilities. Suppose that when I spoke I winked at you or pulled a face my wife could not see or otherwise suggested that you should ignore the literal meaning of my words. I would then have actually meant to ask for an *un*healthy lunch, no doubt with hot pastrami on my mind, and if you then brought back a piece of fruit and a yogurt I could rightly accuse you of not doing what I had asked. Now suppose something different: that I speak a language that resembles but is not exactly English, and that in my language there is a word that I pronounce "healthy" but that means "rich and fatty and briny." Then, if you brought back yogurt and fruit, it would be because you had indeed misunderstood me, though perhaps blamelessly.

Now consider one last possibility. Suppose that I speak English, that I mean by "healthy" what you mean by it, that I believe hot pastrami actually to be healthy, and that in telling you to bring me something healthy, I really meant that you should bring me a hot pastrami sandwich—I was just speaking in code, or shorthand. That is all conceivable, but it would be very odd, and it is hard to imagine what evidence you might have to suppose it. Why shouldn't I have just asked for hot pastrami? Or explicitly asked (in case there was no hot pastrami) for a sandwich you knew I considered healthy, whether or not you agreed? If I really am a competent English speaker, why did I use the language so badly in trying to say what I meant?

The late-eighteenth-century authors of the Eighth Amendment (as we have defined them) declared that "cruel and unusual punishments" are unconstitutional. What did they intend to say? We can identify the same four possibilities. First, they intended to say what the words naturally suggest: whatever punishments are cruel and unusual are unconstitutional. Second, they were, in effect, winking: they were sadists who were really calling for cruelty in punishment. Third, their language, though very like the English we now speak, was actually different from it in that the word "cruel" then meant what we mean by "costly"; they actually intended to say that *expensive* and unusual punishments were unconstitutional. Fourth, they meant to say that punishments that they (or most people) then thought cruel and unusual were unconstitutional.

Which of these possibilities correctly describes what those federal politicians meant to say when they voted for the Eighth Amendment? That depends, of course, on historical facts, but there can be no real doubt as to which description is the most accurate, in the case of either the Eighth Amendment or any of the other amendments in the Bill of Rights. There is no evidence whatsoever that the politicians who enacted these amendments were so deceitful or so linguistically incompetent, or spoke a language so different from contemporary English, that any of the last three of these possibilities is plausible. If they had meant to enact their own convictions about cruel and unusual punishments— or about free speech or due process—they could and would have found language suited to that purpose.

Of course, many of these eighteenth-century politicians seriously disagreed with contemporary ideas about which punishments are cruel, or what process is due. For example, most of them did not think that public floggings were cruel; these horrible spectacles were actually commonplace then. But *that* is no evidence that they meant to say that only the punishments they believed cruel and unusual were to be unconstitutional, any more than my believing hot pastrami healthy proves that I meant to ask for a hot pastrami sandwich when I said I wanted a healthy one. We can only assume that the Constitution's authors meant to say what they did say.

Moreover, we have very strong positive evidence for this assumption. The very best evidence is that the authors chose to use such abstract language. They also made plain in many other ways that they wanted government officials who interpreted their Constitution to disregard their own opinions about what effects it would have in specific cases; the parties to the original Constitutional Convention in Philadelphia directed that all their work papers be burned so that their detailed opinions would never be known.

As I said, originalism would be neither controversial nor important if it merely directed judges to interpret the Constitution in accordance with what its authors meant to say. Judges would still have to decide what the abstract principles the authors plainly meant to lay down mean in controversial cases. Originalism appears to be a useful and important thesis because it tells judges to pay attention not to what the constitutional authors meant to *say,* but to what these authors intended to *achieve* by saying what they did. But this is also, on a second look, totally unhelpful, because it begs the question of *which* of the authors' intentions judges should make decisive.

Suppose that my mother, now dead for many years, told me when I was young never to do anything unfair in business, and that I am eager to keep faith with her instruction. Suppose I know that she herself, managing her own business, drove small competitors to the wall by undercutting them and then raising prices when they were gone, a practice common in her day and widely thought fair. Suppose I myself, like most people today, find this an unfair business practice. What shall I do? How would it help if someone told me that I should give full effect to her intentions as well as to what she actually said? She had at least *two* relevant convictions: the first was her desire that her son should do nothing that really is unfair in the conduct of his business; the second was her belief that ruining competitors by temporarily driving prices below cost is not unfair. I now find that I cannot both satisfy the desire and accept the belief, and so I cannot reach a decision simply by resolving to follow her convictions. I must decide *which* of my mother's convictions—the more abstract or the more detailed—is the right one to follow.

This is not a problem of discovering what her "true" intentions were, of course, since both the convictions were genuine. Nor is it a problem of discovering which would have been more important to her—which, as someone might put it, she would have abandoned first. Her moral views were not discrete preferences that might conflict, like wanting both a new car and a summer vacation. Her moral views were interdependent: she would not object to my undercutting my competitors only because she did not consider undercutting unfair; if she had become persuaded that it was—as she might very well have been had she lived longer and encountered a different business climate—then she would no longer have wanted or expected me to do so. So I must choose between two senses of doing what she wanted. I may obey her abstract wish, which necessarily means deciding for myself whether destructive price cutting is unfair, because there is no other way I *can* obey her abstract wish. Or I may defer to her concrete belief and rely on her own dated judgment. There seems no doubt as to which would best respect her authority and wishes: I must respect her general desire that I not act unfairly. It would be misleading to say that she intended to "delegate" to me the decision about what was unfair. That misses the point: her intention can accurately be described only as the intention that I do what is in fact fair, not what I think fair, even though, of course, I can only carry out her intention by acting on my own convictions.

Similarly, we must assume that the intentions of the authors of the Constitution were honorable rather than cynical. They intended to commit the nation to abstract principles of political morality about free speech and due process and proper punishment and equality. They themselves had various concrete, detailed opinions about the correct application of these abstract principles to particular issues. Today's judges may think that the Constitution's authors were mistaken in some of these concrete opinions, and that they did not reach correct conclusions about the effect of their own principles. Today's judges may believe, in other words, that the authors' abstract and concrete convictions were in conflict; if so they, the judges, must decide themselves which to follow. Originalism's advice—follow the "framers'" convictions—is plainly no help in making that decision.[14]

To summarize, those who made the Constitution had abstract intentions and more detailed convictions. They intended a great constitutional adventure: that the United States be governed according to the correct understanding of what genuine liberty requires and of how government shows equal concern for all its citizens. They had their own understanding of the concrete implications of these abstract ideals. Originalism argues that judges should attend to the authors' more concrete convictions rather than to their more abstract ideals. It offers no serious argument for that choice. But even if we accept it, we encounter another, fatal problem. Even the more concrete convictions can be stated at different levels of abstraction or concreteness, and originalism is empty unless it can stipulate which level to choose and show why its stipulation is not arbitrary.

The enduring problem of racial injustice offers the best example of the enormous difficulty originalists face in answering that challenge. In 1954, in the *Brown* decision, the Supreme Court held that the equal protection clause of the Fourteenth Amendment forbids states to segregate public schools by race. More recently, the Court has decided that the same clause forbids certain kinds of affirmative-action programs: in 1989 it held, as we saw, that the city of Richmond's setting aside 30 percent of government construction contracts for minority-owned firms was a violation of the clause. In other cases, the Court has decided that in principle the clause protects women against gender discrimination as well.[15] But it has refused to extend the protection of the clause to homosexuals; in 1986, in the *Bowers* case I mentioned, it held Georgia's anti-sodomy law constitutional in spite of the argument of homosexual groups that the law discriminated against them on the basis of their sexual orientation.

Were these various cases correctly decided? Let us try to answer that question as originalism recommends. We test the decisions against the assumption that cases arising under the equal protection clause must be decided in the way that the congressmen who adopted the Fourteenth Amendment after the Civil War would have expected or wanted. We therefore consult intellectual historians of the Reconstruction; we read everything we can find by way of the debates and drafting records and reports in Congress; we forage in public records and private diaries and annotated notebooks. And we conclude as follows:

The authors of the equal protection clause believed, as a matter of abstract political principle, that people should all be equal in the eye of the law and the state. They were convinced that certain specific forms of official discrimination against recently freed black citizens were morally wrong for that reason, and they adopted the amendment mainly to prevent certain states from discriminating against blacks in those ways. They agreed, for example, that it would be morally wrong for a state to create certain special remedies for breach of contract and make these remedies available to white plaintiffs but not black ones. They assumed that the equal protection clause would prohibit that form of discrimination.

They also shared certain opinions about which forms of official discrimination were not wrong and would not be prohibited by the clause. They shared the view, for example, that racial segregation of public schools did not violate the clause. (In fact, as I said, many of them voted to segregate the schools of the District of Columbia.) None of them even considered the possibility that state institutions would one day adopt affirmative-action racial quotas designed to repair the damages of past segregation. Therefore, none of them had any opinion, one way or the other, about whether such quotas would violate the clause.

Some of them thought that women were unjustly treated by laws that discriminated in favor of men, but most did not, and assumed that the gender-based distinctions then common were not outlawed by the clause. Most thought that homosexual acts were grossly immoral, and would have been mystified by any suggestion that prohibitions on such acts constituted an unjustified form of discrimination.

Now, in light of these opinions held by the authors of the equal protection clause, what does the clause mean today? There are four different answers that we might give to that question.

1. The clause has the effect of condemning all the cases of discrimination, and only those cases, that the authors collectively expected it to condemn. It forbids discriminating against blacks by denying them standard remedies for breach of contract, but it does not forbid racially segregated schools, or affirmative-action quotas that disadvantage whites, or discrimination against women or homosexuals.

2. The clause forbids any serious discrimination against blacks. Judges must decide for themselves whether school segregation is a serious form of discrimination. Since the clause establishes only

black equality, however, judges may not use it to strike down affirmative-action quotas or laws discriminating against women or homosexuals.

3. The clause forbids any serious racial discrimination. Even though its authors never imagined the possibility of affirmative-action programs, the clause they wrote may prohibit them. Judges must decide for themselves whether it does, and must therefore decide whether such programs are serious violations of equality. But they cannot properly extend the clause to protect women or homosexuals, because that would be to extend the clause to cover gender and sexual orientation rather than just racial equality.

4. The clause establishes a general principle of equality that affirms genuine equal citizenship for all Americans. So if we believe that school segregation, affirmative-action quota systems, and laws that disadvantage people because of their sex or sexual orientation are all violations of equal citizenship, because each of these fails to treat some group of citizens with equal concern, the equal protection clause condemns them all, in spite of what its authors themselves may have thought or would have approved.

We cannot choose among these four "readings" of the Fourteenth Amendment simply by telling ourselves that we must be faithful to the authors' own convictions or beliefs. The four readings represent not different theories about what the authors' views were but different ways of structuring the same views, with very different consequences. How are we to choose among them?

The first reading is a reductive one. It supposes that we respect the authority of the Constitution's authors by deciding issues as we believe they would have decided them in our shoes, today, if they had lived so long and by some bizarre miracle had changed none of their political or moral opinions in the meantime. This reductive thesis entails that the Supreme Court's landmark decision in *Brown* was a flat mistake, because we know that the authors of the equal protection clause did not believe that it outlawed explicit racial segregation in public schools. The first reading would entail that the affirmative-action and gender-discrimination decisions I mentioned were wrong, and a great many other famous Supreme Court decisions as well. Indeed, much of what is simply taken for granted in contemporary constitutional law—that the Eighth

Amendment outlaws public floggings, for example—would be plain error.

The Supreme Court has never taken the reductive view seriously. The Bill of Rights would not have survived if it had, except as an antiquated piece of memorabilia of no practical consequence. No serious constitutional theorist—not even Bork and Scalia, who claim to be devout originalists—takes this position. (Scalia doubts that any judge would accept public floggings as constitutional, even though he agrees that strict reductionism would require that.[16]) But the most powerful argument against the reductive reading is the near-universal acceptance of the *Brown* decision outlawing racial segregation in public schools. Bork himself recognizes that no constitutional method is acceptable that would make that decision impossible.

So let us set the unloved and unsupported reductive reading aside. Each of the three remaining readings concedes—insists—that justices must exercise their own political judgment about equality. Two judges who both accept the same reading may nonetheless reach very different decisions about what the clause forbids if they have different political or moral opinions about what counts as significant and unjustifiable discrimination. But the three accounts are progressively more abstract, and progressively assign judges more and more responsibility for judgment. If someone accepts originalism but rejects the first, reductive account of what it means for the equal protection clause, can he stop short of accepting the fourth, most abstract account?

We may now return to Bork's attempted defense of originalism. He discusses the Supreme Court's decisions about race, and the meaning of the equal protection clause, at several points in his book, and makes almost exactly these distinctions among different levels of abstraction at which that clause might be construed. But when he comes to state which level originalism recommends, he wavers. He rejects the first, reductive account. At some points he seems to accept the third account and at other places the second. He never accepts the fourth, because in his view the Constitution gives no protection to homosexuals. But his explanation of why he rejects the first account offers no reason for not accepting the fourth; on the contrary, it seems to mandate it.

When he explains why the *Brown* decision was the right one, for example, he says that the people he calls "the ratifiers" of the equal protection clause intended to establish a principle of equality, and that they were simply wrong to imagine that equality would not condemn racial segregation. So the ratifiers had inconsistent views, and judges must follow the more abstract of these—the *principle* they enacted—rather than the ratifiers' own specific views about what that principle required. It does not matter what the ratifiers thought about the particular problem of racial segregation in schools, Bork says, or whether or not they disagreed with one another, because a judge is concerned with principle and not with specific intentions.

> In short, all that a judge committed to original understanding requires is that the text, structure and history of the Constitution provide him not with a conclusion but with a major premise. That major premise is a principle or stated value that the ratifiers wanted to protect against hostile legislation or executive action. The judge must then see whether that principle or value is threatened by the statute or action challenged in the case before him. The answer to that question provides his minor premise, and the conclusion follows. It does not follow without difficulty, and two judges equally devoted to the original purpose may disagree about the reach or application of the principle at stake and so arrive at different results, but that in no way distinguishes the task from the difficulties of applying any other legal writing.[17]

This amazing passage could have been written by almost any of the people Bork takes to be his intellectual enemies. For his analysis comes to this: the Constitution enacts abstract principles that judges must interpret, as best they can, according to their own lights. Bork does say that the principle the judge applies must be one that the "ratifiers wanted," but once he abandons the reductive interpretation of what they wanted, and once he accepts that the principle they wanted might have condemned their own specific views (as in the case of segregation), then he has nothing left to which he can tether an opinion about what they wanted except the exceedingly abstract language they used.

If it does not matter that the authors of the Fourteenth Amendment and their public thought segregation was constitutional, then why should it matter whether they thought affirmative-action quotas were constitutional? And if we know that they meant to enact a general principle of equality, then why should it matter that they still lacked the sensibility or experience to see that women as well as blacks might be the victims of unequal, discriminatory practices? Why shouldn't we say that just as they were mistaken in thinking that school segregation was not a violation of racial equality, they were also mistaken in thinking (if they did) that race was the only ground for unfair discrimination in American society? And if we take that step, how can we resist the further conclusion that the "major premise" of principle they adopted—that the states must not be guilty of prejudice or discrimination—applies also to prejudice against homosexuals, whatever they themselves might have thought about that?

Bork does not think that the equal protection clause applies to gender discrimination or to discrimination against homosexuals. But that must be because though he is personally convinced that racial segregation is a piece of unjustified discrimination, he does not believe that laws that discriminate against women or homosexuals are so seriously unjust. For once he abandons the reductive strategy that limits the force of the equal protection clause to its authors' own specific convictions, then he has no other means of checking the abstract language. He is in a kind of free-fall, in which originalism can mean anything and the only check on his judgment is his own political instinct.

Where do we stand now? The most natural interpretation of the Bill of Rights seems to give judges great and frightening power, and it is understandable that constitutional lawyers, particularly those upset by past Supreme Court decisions, should try to tame the Bill of Rights, to change it from a system of principle to what I called a postage-stamp collection. But these efforts fail and are bound to fail because the text and history of the Bill of Rights will not accept that transformation. The revisionist efforts are bound to fail, moreover, in a paradoxical and disastrous way. The ideas on which they are based—that there is a distinction between "enumerated" and "unenumerated" constitutional rights, and that the intentions of a group of original authors can define a concrete constitutional interpretation—are spurious. Judges who purport to rely on these ideas must actually be deciding on very different and hidden grounds. The effort to limit judicial power ends by allowing judges the undisciplined power of the arbitrary. The idea that the Constitution cannot mean what it says ends in the unwelcome conclusion that it means nothing at all.

Scalia's bitter separate opinion in *Casey,* denouncing the majority for reaffirming *Roe* v. *Wade,* illustrates this point. In explaining why the Constitution does not guarantee a right to an abortion, he appealed to both of the revisionist devices we have been exploring. There is no such right, he said, "because of two simple facts: (1) The Constitution says absolutely nothing about it, and (2) the long-standing traditions of American society have permitted it to be legally proscribed."[18]

Scalia's flat assertion that the Constitution says nothing about abortion begs the question, of course. The Fourteenth Amendment does explicitly forbid states to abridge liberty without due process of law, and the question is whether laws prohibiting abortion do exactly that. If they do, as the majority in *Casey* claimed, then the Constitution does say something about abortion: it forbids states to prohibit it. Scalia's entire argument therefore depends on his assertion that because a majority of states had outlawed abortion before the Fourteenth Amendment was adopted, it would be wrong to interpret the due process clause as denying them the power to do so now. But Scalia, who accepts the *Brown* decision, knows that segregated education was widespread when the Fourteenth Amendment was adopted and was apparently approved by most of the politicians who adopted it. How can he distinguish between these two historical practices? He insists that racial classifications are different from prohibitions on abortion because the former are "contradicted by a *text*"—the equal protection clause. But the text of that clause does not explicitly condemn separate public facilities for different races or racial segregation of schools, both of which existed generally when the clause was adopted. Nothing in Scalia's opinion explains why he does not treat the racially discriminatory practices that flourished when the Fourteenth Amendment was adopted as fixing the content of that amendment rather than being condemned by it, or why he takes a different view of the practices that outlawed abortion.

CONSTITUTIONAL INTEGRITY

Originalism cannot save us from judicial power; on the contrary, its arbitrary distinctions intensify that power. What is to be done? First, the public can and should refuse any longer to accept bogus arguments about original intention and unenumerated rights. We can look forward to the day when a judge would be as embarrassed to appeal to those concepts as a scientist would be to appeal to phlogiston or bodily humors or ghosts. Even more important, we can begin to take our actual Constitution seriously, as those many nations now hoping to imitate us have already done. The Constitution insists that our judges do their best collectively to construct, reinspect, and revise, generation by generation, the skeleton of freedom and equality of concern that its great clauses, in their majestic abstraction, command. We must abandon the pointless search for mechanical or semantic constraints and seek genuine constraints in the only place where they can be found: in good argument.

We must accept that honest lawyers and judges and scholars will inevitably disagree, sometimes profoundly, about what equal concern for all citizens requires, about which rights are central to liberty and which only peripheral, and about dozens of other inescapable constitutional moral issues. We must acknowledge, in the political process of nominating and confirming federal judges, what is already evident to anyone who looks: that constitutional adjudicators cannot be neutral about these great questions, and that the Senate should refuse to confirm nominees whose convictions are too idiosyncratic or who refuse honestly to disclose what their convictions are. Most people now agree that the second stage of the Thomas confirmation hearings of 1991 was tawdry, but the first stage was intellectually disastrous, because both candidate and senators conspired to pretend that philosophy had nothing to do with judging, and that a nominee should be allowed to duck questions by saying that as a judge he would abandon past convictions the way a runner sheds clothing.[19]

The process of nomination and confirmation is an important part of the system of checks through which the Constitution disciplines the imposing power it assigns to judges. So, at least theoretically, is the power the people retain to amend the Constitution if they believe the Court's decisions are intolerable, or to impeach particular justices. But these extreme remedies are impractical, and the main engines for disciplining judges are intellectual rather than political or legal.

The American community as a whole, and not just its lawyers and professors, must hold judges to intellectual standards. We must insist that they make as good arguments as they can, and we must then ask ourselves whether their arguments are good enough. Of course, there is no formula to guarantee that judges will not be swayed by bad argument in complex or novel or crucial constitutional cases, or even in easy ones. No formula can protect us from another judicial decision as bad as *Lochner* or *Bowers*. The stench of those decisions does not rise from any failure of the justices to obey some rule of judging, from any mechanical vice. After a near century of treating *Lochner* as the paradigm of a bad judicial decision, no one has in fact produced a sound mechanical test that it failed.

The vice of bad decisions is bad argument and bad conviction; all we can do about those bad decisions is to point out how and where the arguments were bad or the convictions unacceptable. Nor should we fall into the trap that has snared so many law professors: the fallacious claim that because no mechanical formula exists for distinguishing good decisions from bad ones, and because lawyers and judges are bound to disagree in a complex or hard case, then no one argument is better than another and legal reasoning is a waste of time.[20] We must insist, instead, on a general principle of genuine power: the idea, instinct in the concept of law itself, that whatever their views of justice and fairness, judges must also accept an independent and superior constraint of *integrity* in the decisions they make.[21]

Integrity in law has several dimensions. First, it insists that judicial decision be a matter of principle, not compromise or strategy or political accommodation. That apparent banality is often ignored: the Supreme Court's present position on the politically sensitive issue of affirmative action, for example, cannot be justified on any coherent set of principles, even very conservative ones.[22] Second, as Justices O'Connor, Kennedy, and Souter emphasized in their *Casey* opinion, integrity holds vertically: a judge who claims that a particular liberty is fundamental must show that his claim is consistent with principles embedded in Supreme Court precedent and with the main structures of our constitutional arrangement. Third, integrity holds horizontally: a judge who adopts a principle in one case must give full weight to it in other cases he decides or endorses, even in apparently unrelated fields of law.

Of course, not even the most scrupulous attention to integrity, by all judges in all courts, will produce uniform judicial decisions, or guarantee decisions you approve, or protect you from those you hate. Nothing can do that. The point of integrity is principle, not uniformity: we are governed most profoundly not by an ad hoc list of detailed rules but by an ideal, and controversy is therefore at the heart of our story. But the discipline of integrity is nevertheless formidable. In the next chapter, we test its force, because we return to the most controversial constitutional issue of our day.

6

ABORTION
IN COURT:
PART II

In chapter 4, I said that the difficult constitutional question in *Roe* v.
Wade was not whether states are permitted under the Constitution
to treat a fetus as a constitutional person. They plainly are not. I set
out two other, much more difficult questions that our reformulation of
the moral argument about abortion helps us to identify as the central
issues in the constitutional debate. First, do women have a constitutional
right of procreative autonomy—a right to control their own role in
procreation unless the state has a compelling reason for denying them
that control? Second, do states have this compelling reason not because
a fetus is a person but because of a detached responsibility to protect the
sanctity of human life considered as an intrinsic value?

Most of the lawyers who think *Roe* v. *Wade* was wrong have directed
their arguments to the first of these questions. They say that women do
not have a constitutionally protected right to procreative autonomy
because no such right is mentioned in the text and because none of the
"framers" of the Constitution intended women to have such a right. I
have tried to show that these objections are misplaced because the
constitutional provisions that command liberty and equality are abstract.
The key legal question is whether the best interpretation of these
abstract provisions, respecting the requirements of integrity I described,
supports this right of procreative autonomy. If it does, then in the

pertinent sense the Constitution *does* "mention" such a right, and those who created the Constitution *did* "intend" it.

The second question, too, is a matter of interpretation. On the best interpretation of the abstract provisions of the Bill of Rights, does government have the detached power to protect intrinsic values as well as the derivative power to protect particular people? Some people believe that government should not have this detached power at all, that government can properly act only to protect the rights or interests of particular people or creatures, not intrinsic values, which it must leave to individual conscience. (That was apparently the position of John Stuart Mill.) But this restricted view of the powers the United States Constitution allows government is ruled out by the constraints of integrity, because too much of American political practice assumes the contrary.

Neither cultural achievements nor animal species nor future human beings are creatures with rights or interests. But no one doubts that government may treat art and culture as having intrinsic value, or that government may act to protect the environment, endangered animal species, and the quality of life of future generations. Government may properly levy taxes that will be used to support museums, for example; it can forbid people to destroy their own buildings if it deems these to be of historical architectural value; it can prohibit manufacturing practices that threaten endangered species or injure future generations. Why should government not have the power to enforce a much more passionate conviction—that abortion is a desecration of the inherent value that attaches to every human life?

It is not true that an individual woman's decision to have an abortion affects only herself (or only herself and the fetus's father), for individual decisions inevitably affect shared collective values. Part of the sense of the sacred is a sense of taboo, and it is surely harder to maintain a taboo against abortion, and to raise one's children to respect it, in a community where others not only reject it but violate it openly, especially if they receive official financial or moral support.

So if, on the best understanding of the Constitution's abstract provisions, American states lack the power to forbid abortion, then this must be because of something specific about abortion or reproduction; it is not because states may not legislate to protect intrinsic values at all. I distinguished two issues—whether a woman has a right to procreative autonomy and whether states have a compelling interest in protecting the intrinsic value of human life. Our discussion has now brought them together as two sides of the same issue. Is there something special about procreation and abortion so that, though government may regulate people's behavior in other ways in order to protect intrinsic values, pregnant women have a right that government not forbid them to terminate their pregnancies?

The question so described lies at the intersection of two sometimes competing traditions, both of which are part of America's political heritage. The first is the tradition of personal freedom. The second assigns government responsibility for guarding the public moral space in which all citizens live. A good part of constitutional law consists in reconciling these two ideas. What is the appropriate balance in the case of abortion?

Both the majority and dissenting opinions in *Roe* v. *Wade* said that a state has an interest in "protecting human life." We have now assigned a particular sense to that ambiguous claim: it means that any political community has a legitimate concern in protecting the *sanctity* or *inviolability* of human life by requiring its members to acknowledge the intrinsic value of human life in their individual decisions. But this is still ambiguous. It might describe either of two goals, and the distinction between them is extremely important.

One is the goal of responsibility. A state might aim that its citizens treat decisions about abortion as matters of moral importance; that they recognize that fundamental intrinsic values are at stake in such decisions and decide reflectively, not out of immediate convenience but out of examined conviction. The second is the goal of conformity. A state might aim that its citizens obey rules and practices that the majority believes best express and protect the sanctity of life, that women abort, if ever, only in circumstances in which a majority thinks abortion appropriate or, at least, permissible.

These goals of responsibility and conformity are not only different but antagonistic. If we aim at responsibility, we must leave citizens free, in the end, to decide as they think right, because that is what moral responsibility entails. But if we aim at conformity, we demand instead that citizens act in a way that might be contrary to their own moral convictions; this discourages rather than encourages them to develop their own sense of when and why life is sacred.

The traditional way of understanding the abortion controversy, which we have now rejected, submerges the distinction between these two goals. If a fetus is a person, then of course the state's dominant goal must be to protect it, just as it protects all other people. And the state must therefore subordinate any interest it has in developing its citizens' sense of moral responsibility to its interest that they act on a specific moral conclusion: that killing people is wrong.

But when we shift the state's interest, as we have, to protecting an intrinsic value, then the opposition between the two goals moves into the foreground. The sanctity of life is a highly controversial, *contestable* value. It is controversial, for example, whether abortion or childbirth best serves the intrinsic value of life when a fetus is deformed, or when having a child would seriously depress a woman's chance to make something valuable of her own life. Does a state protect a contestable value best by encouraging people to accept it *as* contestable, understanding that they are responsible for deciding for themselves what it means? Or does the state protect a contestable value best by itself deciding, through the political process, which interpretation is the right one, and then forcing everyone to conform? The goal of responsibility justifies the first choice, the goal of conformity the second. A state cannot pursue both goals at the same time.

RESPONSIBILITY

I can think of no reason why government should not aim that its citizens treat decisions about human life and death as matters of serious moral importance. So in my view, the United States Constitution does allow state governments to pursue the goal of responsibility—but only in ways that respect the crucial difference between advancing that goal and wholly or partly coercing a final decision. May a state require a woman contemplating abortion to wait twenty-four hours before having the procedure? May it require that she be given information explaining the gravity of a decision to abort? May it require a pregnant teenage woman to consult with her parents, or with some other adult? Or a married woman to inform her husband, if she can? Must the government help to pay for abortion services for those too poor to pay themselves if it helps to pay for childbirth?

Since many constitutional lawyers think that the only issue in *Roe* v. *Wade* was whether states may treat a fetus as a person, they do not distinguish between the goals of coercion and responsibility; they have therefore assumed that if *Roe* v. *Wade* is right, and states may not coerce women by forbidding abortion altogether, it directly follows that states must include abortion in their medical aid programs and that they may not require that women delay abortion or consult with others or be given information. That explains why many lawyers thought that the Supreme Court's decisions in the years following *Roe*, which did allow states to discriminate in financial support and to regulate abortion in these various ways, amounted to a partial overruling or undermining of *Roe*.

The Court has been consistent in upholding financial discrimination. In 1977, in *Maher* v. *Roe*,[1] it ruled that a state may refuse to give financial aid for nontherapeutic abortions even if it does help to pay for childbirth; and in 1980, in *Harris* v. *McRae*, as I said, the Court upheld the constitutionality of the Hyde amendment, which prohibits federal medical welfare funds to be used for even medically needed abortions. But the Court has changed its mind, to some degree, about regulating abortion in ways short of prohibiting it. In 1986, for example, in *Thornburgh* v. *American College of Obstetricians and Gynecologists*, the Court held unconstitutional a variety of state laws that imposed fixed waiting periods for women seeking abortion or required doctors to furnish them with specified information, including information about fetal development and alternatives to abortion.[2] But in 1989, in *Webster* v. *Reproductive Services Incorporation of Missouri*, after President Reagan had replaced three members of the *Roe* majority with his own choices, the Court upheld a variety of very severe restrictions on abortion.[3] Many lawyers said that *Webster* was a partial overruling of *Roe*, and when the Supreme Court announced that in 1992 it would review the lower-court decision in *Planned Parenthood of Southeastern Pennsylvania* v. *Casey*, which had upheld restrictions of the kind that had been held unconstitutional in *Thornburgh*, most commentators expected that the Court's *Casey* decision would further undermine *Roe*.

But when we understand *Roe* as I have suggested—as about inherent value and not about personhood—then we see that *Casey* dealt primarily with issues not resolved by *Roe*. It is perfectly consistent to insist that states have no power to impose on their citizens a particular view of how and why life is sacred, and yet also to insist that states do have the power to encourage their citizens to treat the question of abortion seriously. The joint opinion of Justices O'Connor, Kennedy, and Souter in *Casey* made that distinction clear: the three justices affirmed *Roe*'s rule that states may not prohibit abortion but nevertheless affirmed a state's legitimate interest in encouraging responsibility. "What is at stake is the woman's right to make the ultimate decision, not a right to be insulated from all others in doing so,"[4] they said, and therefore "states are free to enact laws to provide a reasonable framework for a woman to make a decision that has such profound and lasting meaning."[5] A state may reasonably think, they added, that a woman considering abortion should at least be aware of arguments against it that others in the community believe important, so that "even in the earliest stages of pregnancy, the State may enact rules and regulations designed to encourage her to know that there are philosophic and social arguments of great weight that can be brought to bear in favor of continuing the pregnancy."[6]

But courts must be careful not to allow a state to disguise what is actually a coercive rule as a rule merely encouraging responsibility. The joint opinion adopted the following test: a state regulation is unconstitutional, even if it does not purport to prohibit abortion, if either its purpose or effect is to create an "undue burden" on a woman who chooses abortion by posing "substantial obstacles" to that choice.[7] The line between a regulation that imposes such an obstacle and one that only makes an abortion somewhat more expensive or inconvenient, which the joint opinion declared permissible, is plainly difficult to draw in many cases. A majority of the Court in *Casey* ruled that requiring a married woman to notify her husband before an abortion does unduly burden her decision, because many women fear physical, psychological, and economic intimidation.[8] A different majority also held, however, that Pennsylvania's mandatory twenty-four-hour delay between the doctor's furnishing the patient with prescribed information and the time of the abortion had not been shown to impose an undue burden.[9]

The Court may well have been wrong not to declare these latter restrictions unconstitutional as well, and later in this chapter I shall argue that it was. Nevertheless, it is a serious mistake to say, as some "pro-choice" groups did immediately after the *Casey* decision, that because the Court upheld almost all the Pennsylvania restrictions, it in effect overruled *Roe* v. *Wade* and sent women back to the days of illegal back-street abortions. It is both politically and intellectually crucial to recognize the distinction between even onerous restrictions on abortion, which might perhaps be thought to serve the goal of responsibility, and outright prohibition of it, which could be justified only by appeal to the goal of coercion, even if the line between the two is sometimes blurred.

COERCION

Complex as the issues about responsibility are, the heart of the national debate remains the question of coercion. Do the states of the United States have the power to decide for everyone that abortion insults the intrinsic value of human life and to prohibit it on that ground? In *Casey,* four justices said that they still aim to reverse *Roe* and declare that states do have that power. Are they right, as a matter of American constitutional law? Should any state or nation have that power, as a matter of justice and decent government?

As I said, government sometimes acts properly when it coerces people in order to protect certain intrinsic values: when it collects taxes to finance national museums or when it imposes conservation measures to protect endangered animal species, for example. Why is abortion different? Why can a state not forbid abortion on the same ground: that the majority of its citizens thinks that aborting a fetus, except, perhaps, when the mother's own life is at stake, is an intolerable insult to the inherent value of human life? There are two central and connected reasons why prohibiting abortion is a very different matter.

First, in the case of abortion, the effect of coercion on particular people—pregnant women—is far greater. Making abortion criminal may destroy a woman's life. Protecting art or historic buildings or endangered animal species or future generations is rarely as damaging to particular people, and might well be unconstitutional if it were. Second, our convictions about how and why human life has intrinsic importance, from which we draw our views about abortion, are much more fundamental to our overall moral personalities than our convictions about culture or about endangered species, even though these too concern intrinsic values. Our beliefs about human life are decisive in forming our opinions about *all* life-and-death matters—abortion, suicide, euthanasia, the death penalty, and conscientious objection to war. Indeed, their power is even greater than this, because our opinions about how and why our *own* lives have intrinsic value influence every major decision we make about how we live.[10] Very few people's opinions about conserving the artifacts of a culture or saving endangered species are as foundational to their moral personality, as interwoven with the structural choices of their lives.

These interconnections are most evident in the lives of people who are religious in traditional ways. The connection between their faith and their opinions about abortion is not contingent but constitutive—the latter are shadows of religious beliefs about why human life itself is important, and these beliefs are at work in every aspect of their lives. Most people who are not religious also have general, instinctive convictions about whether, why, and how any human life has intrinsic value. No one can lead even a mildly reflective life without revealing such convictions, and they surface, for almost everyone, at the same critical moments in life—in opinions and decisions about children, death, and war, for example. An atheist may have convictions about the point or meaning of human life that are just as pervasive, just as foundational to his moral personality, as those of a devout Catholic, Jew, Muslim, Hindu, or Buddhist. An atheist's system of beliefs may have, in the words of a famous Supreme Court opinion, "a place in the life of its possessor parallel to that filled by the orthodox belief in God."[11] We may describe most people's beliefs about the inherent value of human life—beliefs deployed in their opinions about abortion—as *essentially* religious beliefs. (Later, I shall defend that description as a matter of constitutional interpretation.)

It is true that many people assume that no belief is religious in character unless it presupposes belief in a personal deity. But many established religions—some forms of Buddhism and Hinduism, for example—include no commitment to such a supreme being. Once we set aside the idea that every religious belief presupposes a god, it is doubtful that we can discover any defining feature that all, but only, religious beliefs have. How then shall we classify a belief as religious? In a less rigid way: by asking whether it is sufficiently similar in content to plainly religious beliefs.[12] On that test, the belief that the value of human life transcends its value for the creature whose life it is—that human life is impersonally and objectively valuable—is a religious belief, even when it is held by people who do not believe in God. It is, in fact, one of the most fundamental purposes of traditional religions to make that claim to their faithful, and to embody it in some vision or narrative that makes the belief seem intelligible and persuasive. Religion in that way responds to the most terrifying feature of human life: that we have lives to lead, and death to face, with no apparent reason to believe that our living, still less how we live, makes any genuine difference at all.

The existential question—does human life have any intrinsic or objective importance?—has been raised in many ways. People ask about the "meaning" or "point" of life, for example. But however it is put, this foundational question cannot be answered by showing that living in a given recommended way—observing some specified moral code, for example, or following a given theory of justice—will make people safer, freer, happier, or more prosperous, or that it will help them to fulfill or realize their human nature. The existential question is deeper, because it asks why any of this matters.

In this way, beliefs about the intrinsic importance of human life may be distinguished from more secular convictions about morality, fairness, and justice. The latter address themselves to the issue of how competing interests of people should be served or adjusted or compromised; they rarely reflect a distinctive view about why human interests have objective intrinsic importance, or even whether they do.[13] People with very different views about the ultimate meaning of life can agree about justice, and people with much the same views about the former issue can disagree dramatically about the latter. Of course, many people worry about fairness and justice because they believe that it is intrinsically important how a human life goes.[14] But their views about what justice requires are not, for that reason, themselves views about why or in what way that is important.

Religions try to answer the deeper existential question by connecting individual human lives to some impersonal value. They declare that all human lives (or, for more parochial religions, the lives of believers) have intrinsic importance because they benefit from some source of value beyond subjective human experience: the love of a creator or redeemer, for example; or nature, believed to impart normative importance to everything it creates; or a natural order understood in some other but equally transcendental way. Some members of each of these religious groups believe that because human life has intrinsic importance, abortion is always, or almost always, wrong. Others reach a contrary conclusion: that abortion is sometimes necessary in order truly to respect life's inherent value, which depends on the intrinsic importance of human creative investment, including the acts and decisions through which people shape their own lives. In both cases, the belief affirms an essentially religious idea, that the importance of human life transcends subjective experience.

The two ways in which abortion is special, even among issues that involve claims about inherent value, suggest a formulation of the abstract right of privacy on which the *Roe* decision relied that is somewhat different from the conventional formulation. Americans have a constitutional right that government not infringe certain personal liberties when it acts to safeguard an intrinsic value. A state may not curtail liberty, in order to protect an intrinsic value, when the effect on one group of citizens would be special and grave, when the community is seriously divided about what respect for that value requires, and when people's opinions about the nature of that value reflect essentially religious convictions that are fundamental to moral personality.[15] It bears repeating that if a fetus were a constitutional person from the moment of conception, this principle would not guarantee a right to abortion. The principle is limited to cases in which the state claims an authority to protect an inherent value, not the rights and interests of another person. But once we accept that a fetus is not a constitutional person and shift the ground of constitutional inquiry to the different question of whether a state may forbid abortion in order to respect the intrinsic value of human life, then the principle of privacy plainly does apply, because political decisions about procreation then meet the tests that it provides.

Judicial decisions that have applied that general principle of privacy to reproduction, contraception, and abortion have been collected, through the common-law method of adjudication, into a distinct, more concrete principle that we may call the principle of procreative autonomy. It provides the best available justification for the Supreme Court's decisions about contraception. In one of these cases, in a remark I have already quoted, Justice Brennan, speaking for the Court, said, "If the right of privacy means anything, it is the right of the *individual*, married or single, to be free from governmental intrusion into matters so fundamentally affecting a person as the decision whether to bear or beget a child."

The principle of procreative autonomy elaborates on Justice Brennan's remark. It explains the sense in which individual procreative decisions are, as he said, fundamental. Many political decisions, including economic ones, have serious and special impact on some individuals. Procreative decisions are fundamental in a different way; the moral issues on which they hinge are religious in the broad sense I defined, touching the ultimate purpose and value of human life itself. The state's power to prohibit contraception can plausibly be defended only on the assumption that government has the general power to dictate to all citizens what respect for the inherent value of human life requires: that it requires, for example, that people not make love except with the intention to procreate.

The Supreme Court, in denying the state the specific power to make contraception criminal, presupposed the more general principle of procreative autonomy I am defending. That is important, as I have said, because almost no one believes that the Court's contraception decisions should now be overruled. The law's integrity demands that the principles necessary to support an authoritative set of judicial decisions must be accepted in other contexts as well. It might seem an appealing political compromise to apply the principle of procreative autonomy to contraception, which almost no one now thinks states can forbid, but not to abortion, which powerful constituencies violently oppose. But the point of integrity—the point of law itself—is exactly to rule out political compromises of that kind. We must be one nation of principle: our Constitution must represent conviction, not the tactical strategies of justices eager to satisfy as many political constituencies as possible.

Integrity does not, of course, require that judges respect principles embedded in past decisions that they and others regard as *mistakes*. It permits the Supreme Court to declare, as it has several times in the past, that a given decision or string of decisions was in error, because the principles underlying it are inconsistent with more fundamental principles embedded in the Constitution's structure and history. The Court cannot declare everything in the past a mistake; that would destroy integrity under the pretext of serving it. It must exercise its power to disregard past decisions modestly, and it must exercise it in good faith.

It cannot ignore principles underlying past decisions it purports to approve, decisions it would ratify if asked to do so, decisions almost no one, not even among the sternest critics of the Court's past performance, now disapproves of or regards as mistakes. The contraception cases fall into that category, and it would be both dangerous and offensive for the Court cynically to ignore the principles these cases presupposed in any decision it reaches about abortion.

So integrity demands general recognition of the principle of procreative autonomy, and therefore of the right of women to decide for themselves not only whether to conceive but whether to bear a child. If you remain in doubt—if you are not yet convinced that *Roe* was right on the most basic issues—then consider the possibility that in some state a majority of voters might come to think that it shows *disrespect* for the sanctity of life to continue a pregnancy in some circumstances—in cases of fetal deformity, for example. If a majority has the power to impose its own views about the sanctity of life on everyone, then the state could *require* someone to abort, even if that were against her own religious or ethical convictions, at least if abortion had become physically as safe as, for example, the vaccinations and inoculations we now expect our governments to require.

Of course, if we centered the abortion controversy on the question of whether a fetus is a person with a right to live, then one state's having the right to forbid abortion would not mean that another had the right to require it. But that *does* follow once we recognize that the constitutional question at stake is whether a state can impose on everyone an official interpretation of the inherent value of life. It would be intolerable for a state to require an abortion to prevent the birth of a deformed child. In the United States, no one doubts that such a requirement would be unconstitutional. But the reason why—because it denies a pregnant woman's right to decide for herself what the sanctity of life requires her to do about her own pregnancy—applies with exactly equal force in the other direction. A state just as seriously insults the dignity of a pregnant woman when it forces her to the opposite choice. That the choice is approved by a majority is no better justification in the one case than in the other.

TEXTUAL HOMES

The general structure of the Bill of Rights is such that any moral right as fundamental as the right of procreative autonomy is very likely to have a safe home in its text. Indeed, we should expect to see a principle of that foundational nature protected not just by one but by several constitutional provisions, since these overlap in the way I have described.

The right of procreative autonomy follows from any competent interpretation of the due process clause and of the Supreme Court's past decisions applying it. I have described the very powerful arguments supporting that view, but I shall now add a different and further textual basis for that right. The First Amendment prohibits government from establishing any religion, and it guarantees all citizens the free exercise of their own religion. The Fourteenth Amendment, which incorporates the First Amendment, imposes the same prohibition and same responsibility on the states. These provisions also guarantee the right of procreative autonomy. (One present Supreme Court justice—Justice Stevens—has repeatedly endorsed this defense of the right, and much of the rhetoric of the three-justice joint opinion in *Casey*, as we shall see, is at least suggestive of it.) The First Amendment defense of the right to an abortion is more complex than the due process defense, and it is less easily demonstrated on grounds of precedent alone. But it is a natural defense, and it illuminates an important dimension of the national debate about abortion. It also illustrates both the power and the constraining force of the ideal of legal integrity.

Locating the abortion controversy in the First Amendment will seem natural to people who instinctively perceive that the controversy is at bottom a religious one. Some critics might fear, however, that I am trying to revive an old argument now rejected even by some of those who once subscribed to it. This argument holds that because the morality of abortion is a matter of controversy among religious groups—because abortion is considered sinful by some orthodox religions, conspicuously the Roman Catholic church, but permissible by others—the separation of church and state means that government must leave the subject of abortion alone.

That would indeed be a very bad argument if states were permitted to treat a fetus as a person with rights and interests competitive with the rights of a pregnant woman, for the most important responsibility of government, as I said, is to identify the sometimes competing rights and interests of people for whom it is responsible, and to decide how these rights may best be accommodated and these interests best served. Government has no reason to abdicate that responsibility just because or when organized religion also takes an interest in those matters. Religious bodies and groups were among the strongest campaigners against slavery, and they have for centuries sought social justice, the eradication of suffering and disease, and a vast variety of other humanitarian goals. If the distinction between church and state barred government from taking up those causes as well, the doctrine would paralyze government altogether.

But the issue of whether a fetus is a person with rights and interests of its own has already been decided in the United States by secular government in the only way it can be decided under the American constitutional system. Now we are considering a different constitutional issue: whether states may nevertheless prohibit abortion in order to endorse a controversial view about what respect for the intrinsic value of human life requires. That is not an issue about who has rights, or how people's competing interests should be balanced and protected. If states are forbidden to prohibit conduct just on the ground that it insults the intrinsic value of human life, they are not thereby disabled from pursuing their normal responsibilities. On the contrary, it is one of government's most fundamental duties, recognized throughout Western democracies since the eighteenth century, to ensure that people have a right to live in accordance with their own religious convictions. So the reasons for rejecting the bad argument I described are not arguments against my suggestion that the First Amendment forbids states to force people to conform to an official view about what the sanctity of human life requires.

It is controversial how the clauses of the Constitution that guarantee the "free exercise" of religion and forbid the "establishment" of a religion should be interpreted, and the Supreme Court's rulings on these matters are markedly unclear.[16] But any satisfactory interpretation of these clauses must cover two issues. First, it must fill out the phrase "free exercise" by explaining the features that make a conviction a religious belief rather than a nonreligious moral principle or a personal preference. Second, it must interpret "establishment" by explaining the difference between secular and religious aims of government. Difficult cases arise when a government, for the secular purpose of serving and protecting other people's ordinary interests, restricts or penalizes conduct that is required by genuinely religious convictions.[17] Such cases require courts to decide how far the constitutional right of free exercise keeps the government from adopting policies it believes would increase the general secular welfare of the community. It is a very different matter, however, when the government supports one side of an argument about an essentially religious issue. Legislation for this purpose that substantially impaired anyone's religious freedom would violate both of the First Amendment's religion clauses at once.

Of course, if a fetus were a constitutional person, with interests government is obliged and entitled to protect, then legislation outlawing abortion would fall into the first of these categories, even though many people's convictions permitting or requiring abortion are genuinely religious. The laws would plainly be constitutional because the right of free exercise of religion does not include permission to kill a person; it does not extend, for example, to human sacrifice in religious ritual. But a fetus is not a constitutional person. If people's convictions about what the inherent value of human life requires are religious convictions, a government's demand for conformity would be imposing a collective religion, and the case would fall into the second category.

What makes a belief religious for purposes of the First Amendment? The great majority of eighteenth-century statesmen who wrote and ratified the First Amendment may well have assumed that every religious conviction presupposes a belief in a personal god. But the Supreme Court has apparently decided that this restriction is unacceptable as part of a constitutional definition of religion; in 1965, in *United States* v. *Seeger*, it held that a man who opposed all war on general ethical principles but did not believe in God was entitled to an exemption from military service under a statute limiting the grounds for claiming exemption to religious ones; the Court cited, among other reasons, the fact that not all the major religions represented in the United States presuppose such a being.[18] Once the idea of religion is separated from the idea of a god, however, courts that accept the constraints of integrity face great difficulty in distinguishing between religious and other kinds of conviction. There are two possibilities: a conviction can be deemed religious because of its content—because it speaks to concerns that the community identifies as distinctly religious—or because it has very great subjective importance to the person who holds it, as orthodox religious convictions do for devout believers.

In *Seeger*, the Court suggested that a scruple is religious if it has "a place in the life of its possessor parallel to that filled by the orthodox belief in God of one who clearly qualifies for the exemption." That statement, taken by itself, is ambiguous. It might mean that a conviction is religious if it answers the same questions that orthodox religion answers for a believer, which is a test of content, or that it is religious if it is embraced as fervently as orthodox religion is embraced by a devout believer, which is a test of subjective importance. The opinion as a whole is indecisive about which of these two meanings, or which combination of them, the Court intended, and the ambiguity has damaged the development of constitutional law in this area. In any case, however, a subjective-importance test is plainly inadequate by itself to distinguish religious from other forms of conviction, or indeed from intensely felt preferences. Even very devout people often consider their plainly nonreligious affiliations, like patriotism, as equally or even more important to them. Some test of content is at least necessary, and I believe is sufficient.

I argued earlier that a belief in the objective and intrinsic importance of human life has a distinctly religious content. Convictions that endorse the objective importance of human life speak to the same issues—about the place of an individual human life in an impersonal and infinite universe—as orthodox religious beliefs do for those who hold them. Several of the theologians the Court cited in *Seeger* made this point. The Court called the following statement from the schema of a recent ecumenical council, for example, "a most significant declaration on religion": "Men expect from their various religions answers to the riddles of the human condition: What is man? What is the meaning and purpose of our lives?"[19]

I can think of no plausible account of the content that a belief must have in order to be deemed religious that would rule out convictions about why and how human life has intrinsic objective importance, except the abandoned notion that religious belief must presuppose a god. It is, of course, essential that any test of religious content distinguish between religious beliefs on the one hand and nonreligious political or moral convictions on the other. But we have already seen how the belief in life's intrinsic objective importance (and other beliefs that interpret and follow directly from that belief) differs from opinions about political fairness or the just distribution of economic or other resources.

We can see the distinction at work in the Supreme Court's disposition of the conscientious-objector cases. In *Seeger,* the Court presumed that the Constitution would not allow Congress to discriminate against nonconventional religions by exempting from military service men whose opposition to all war was based on theistic religion but refusing to exempt men whose opposition to all war was grounded in a nontheistic belief. On the other hand, in 1971, in *Gillette* v. *United States,* the Court upheld Congress's refusal to grant exemption to men who opposed not all war but only some wars, even to those whose convictions condemning a particular war were supported by their religion. Though the Court offered various practical grounds for the distinction, they were unpersuasive; its decision can adequately be justified only by arguing that though a flat opposition to all war is based on the conviction that human life as such is sacred, which is a distinctly religious conviction, selective opposition is at least normally based on considerations of justice or policy that permit killing in some cases but not others, and that are not themselves religious in content even when they are endorsed by a religious group. As the Court said,

A virtually limitless variety of beliefs are subsumable under the rubric, "objection to a particular war." All the factors that might go into nonconscientious dissent from policy, also might appear as the concrete basis of an objection that has roots as well in conscience and religion. Indeed, over the realm of possible situations, opposition to a particular war may more likely be political and nonconscientious, than otherwise.[20]

So the popular sense that the abortion issue is fundamentally a religious one, and some lawyers' sense that it therefore lies outside the proper limits of state action, are at bottom sound, though for reasons somewhat more complex than is often supposed. They rest on a natural—indeed, irresistible—understanding of the First Amendment: that a state has no business prescribing what people should think about the ultimate point and value of human life, about why life has intrinsic importance, and about how that value is respected or dishonored in different circumstances. Of course, not every woman who decides to have an abortion broods first about why and how human life is sacred. Many who do not nevertheless act out of convictions that, as I suggested in chapter 3, presuppose views about that essentially religious issue, and a government that makes abortion a crime denies the free exercise of religion as much to such women as to women who do self-consciously draw their views about abortion from religious faith. Some women, it is true, choose abortion unreflectively, or yield to fear or the pressures of others or act for some other reason that cannot be traced to even submerged views about the sanctity of life. The First Amendment guarantees their right to decide as well, even though it is arguable that coercion would not infringe the free exercise of religion in their case, because any government that prohibits abortion commits itself to a controversial interpretation of the sanctity of life and therefore limits liberty by commanding one essentially religious position over others, which the First Amendment forbids. Of course, these are also reasons why coercion about abortion offends the due process and the equal protection clauses of the Constitution as well: it would be odd if the best interpretation of constitutional liberty and equality did not insist that people have an equal right to follow their own conscience in profoundly spiritual matters.

Consider, now, the following objection. If my view of the scope of the free-exercise-of-religion clause were correct, someone might say, the government could not forbid an aesthete to alter the exterior of his landmark house, or make a libertarian, who thinks economic liberty the most important right, pay taxes.[21] This objection would be powerful if my argument used a test of subjective importance to identify religious convictions, because on such a test the aesthete's or libertarian's convictions might well be religious. But my argument rejected that test: I said that convictions about the intrinsic value of human life are religious on a test of content, not of subjective importance. A law forbidding people from tearing down landmark houses does not raise essentially religious issues, no matter how much some people would prefer to build modern masterpieces on the sites of old homes, because it does not presuppose any particular conception of why and how human life is sacred, or take a position on any other historically religious matter.[22]

Even more plainly, my argument does not justify exempting Milton

Friedman from paying tax on the ground of his free-market faith; government collects taxes in order to serve its citizens' various secular interests, not to declare or support a particular view about any essentially religious matter. True, some people resist paying taxes for reasons that do implicate their convictions about the intrinsic value of human life—refusing to help finance war, for example. In such cases, compulsory taxation does plausibly impair the free exercise of religion. But the problem falls into the first of the two categories I distinguished, and the appropriate balancing sustains the tax, given that the infringement of free exercise is limited and the importance of uniform taxation is great.

I conclude that the right to procreative autonomy, from which a right of choice about abortion flows, is well grounded in the First Amendment. And it would be remarkable if so basic a right did not figure in the best interpretation of constitutional liberty and equality as well. It would be remarkable, that is, if lawyers who accepted the right of procreative autonomy did not also think that right fundamental to the concept of ordered liberty and thus protected by the due process clause, or to be part of what the government's equal concern for all citizens requires and so protected by the equal protection clause. It is hardly an embarrassment that lawyers defending a right to abortion have disagreed about which clause to emphasize. Some constitutional lawyers have an odd taste for neatness: they want rights mapped uniquely onto constitutional clauses with no overlap, as if redundancy were a constitutional vice. Once we understand, however, that the Bill of Rights is not a list of concrete, detailed remedies drawn up by parsimonious draftsmen but a commitment to an abstract ideal of just government, that taste makes no sense—any more than would the proposition that freedom of religion is not also liberty, or that protecting freedom for everyone has nothing to do with equality.

The right of procreative autonomy has an important place not only in the structure of the American Constitution but in Western political culture more generally. The most important feature of that culture is a belief in individual human dignity: that people have the moral right—and the moral responsibility—to confront the most fundamental questions about the meaning and value of their own lives for themselves, answering to their own consciences and convictions. That assumption was the engine of emancipation and of racial equality, for example. The

most powerful arguments against slavery before the Civil War, and for
equal protection after it, were framed in the language of dignity: for both
religious and secular abolitionists, the cruelest aspect of slavery was its
failure to recognize a slave's right to decide central issues of value for
himself. Indeed, the most basic premise of Western democracy—that
government should be republican rather than despotic—embodies a
commitment to that conception of dignity. The principle of procreative
autonomy, in a broad sense, is embedded in any genuinely democratic
culture.

I want to guard, however, against an interpretation of this principle
that I would disown. My argument does not suppose that people either
are or should be indifferent, as individuals or as members of a political
community, to the decisions about abortion that their friends or neigh-
bors or fellow citizens or fellow human beings make. On the contrary,
the argument emphasizes several reasons why people should not be
indifferent. Individual choices together create a moral environment that
inevitably influences what others can do. So a person's concern for his
or her own life, and for that of children and friends, gives a reason for
worrying about how even strangers treat the inherent value of human
life. Moreover, our concern that people lead good lives is not naturally
limited to our concern for our own life and the lives of our family, nor
should it be. We want others, even strangers, not to lead what we regard
as blighted lives, ruined by terrible acts of desecration.

But the most powerful reason we have for wanting others to respect
the intrinsic value of human life—in the way we think that value
demands respect—is not concern for our own or other people's interests
at all, but just concern for the value itself. If people did *not* think it
transcendently important that human lives not be wasted by abortion,
then they would not have the kind of commitment my argument assumes most people do have. So of course people who think that almost
all abortion is immoral must take a passionate interest in the issue; and
liberals who count such people as deranged busybodies are insensitive
as well as wrong.

Nevertheless, we must insist on religious tolerance in this area as in
others about which people once cared just as passionately and in the
same way, and once thought sufficiently important to wage not just
sit-ins but wars. Tolerance is a cost we must pay for our adventure in
liberty. We are committed, by our love of liberty and dignity, to live in

communities in which no group is thought clever or spiritual or numerous enough to decide essentially religious matters for everyone else. If we have genuine concern for the lives others lead, we will also accept that no life is a good one lived against the grain of conviction, that it does not help someone else's life but spoils it to force values upon him he cannot accept but can only bow before out of fear or prudence.

ROE V. *WADE* REVISITED

Let us now take a fresh look at the great and controversial decision in *Roe* v. *Wade*. It did three things. First, it reaffirmed a pregnant woman's constitutional right of procreative autonomy, and declared that states do not have the power simply to forbid abortion on any terms they wish. Second, it recognized that states nevertheless do have a legitimate interest in regulating abortion. Third, it constructed a detailed régime for balancing that right and that interest: it declared, roughly, that states may not forbid abortion for any reason in the first trimester of pregnancy, that they may regulate abortion in the second trimester only out of concern for the health of the mother, and, finally, that they may outlaw abortion altogether when the fetus has become a viable being, that is, in the third trimester of pregnancy. We must inspect those three decisions against the background of our argument so far.

Our argument confirms *Roe's* first holding. The crucial issue in the constitutional controversy is not whether a fetus is a person within the meaning of the Constitution, but whether states have a legitimate power to dictate how their citizens must respect the inherent value of life. Since any competent interpretation of the Constitution must recognize a principle of procreative autonomy, states do not have the power simply to forbid abortion altogether.

Roe was also right on the second score. States do have a legitimate interest in regulating decisions its citizens make about abortion. It was mysterious, in *Roe* and other judicial decisions, what that interest was, but we have identified it as the legitimate interest in maintaining a moral environment in which decisions about life and death are taken seriously and treated as matters of moral gravity.

Was *Roe* right on the third score? Does the trimester scheme it set forth permit states to further their legitimate interests while adequately protecting a pregnant woman's right of autonomy? That scheme has been criticized as arbitrary and overly rigid, even by lawyers who agree that the Texas statute *Roe* struck down, which prohibited abortions except to save the life of the mother, was unconstitutional. Why is the point of fetal viability the crucial one? We may put that question in two ways. First, why should fetal viability mark the earliest time at which a state is entitled to prohibit abortion? If it can prohibit abortion then, why not earlier, as many citizens plainly wish? Second, why should fetal viability mark the end of a pregnant woman's right to protection? If a state may not prohibit abortion before that point, then why may it do so after?

I begin with the second form of the question. What happens at the point of fetal viability to make the right of procreative autonomy less powerful or effective? Two answers present themselves. First, at about the time of fetal viability but not much before, the brain may have developed sufficiently so that a primitive form of fetal sentience is possible.[23] A fetus might then sensibly be said to have interests of its own. This does not mean, I must emphasize, that a state may declare a fetus a person at that point. The question of who is a constitutional person must be decided nationally, as I argued. But a state may nevertheless act to protect the interests even of creatures—animals, for example—who are not constitutional persons, so long as it respects people's constitutional rights in doing so. So at the point of fetal viability, the state may claim a legitimate interest that is independent of its interest in enforcing its conception of the sanctity of life.

Second, before the moment of fetal viability arrives, a pregnant woman has usually had ample opportunity to reflect upon and decide whether she believes it best and right to continue her pregnancy or to terminate it. Only a tiny number of abortions are performed during the third trimester—only about .01 percent, and even fewer if we exclude emergency abortions undertaken to save the mother's life. It is true that some women—most of them very young—are unaware of their pregnancies until they are nearly at term, but this is very rare. In almost all cases, a woman knows she is pregnant in good time to make a reflective decision before the fetus is viable. This suggests that a state does not unduly burden most women's right to choose if it insists that they decide before that point, and it also suggests an important reason why a state might properly so insist.

It is an almost universal conviction that abortion becomes steadily more problematic morally as a fetus develops toward infanthood, as the difference between pregnancy and infancy becomes more a matter of the baby's location than of its development. This widespread conviction seems odd so long as we believe that whether abortion is wrong depends only on whether a fetus is a person from the moment of conception. But the belief is compelling once we see that abortion is wrong, when it is, because it insults the sanctity of human life. The insult to that value is greater when the life destroyed is further advanced—when the creative natural and human investment in it is greater. The rare woman who has had a genuine opportunity to abort early in her pregnancy, when in almost everyone's view the insult is much less, but who decides on abortion only near the end may well be indifferent to the moral and social meaning of her act. Society has a right, if its members so decide, to protect its culture from that kind of indifference, so long as the means it chooses do not infringe the rights of pregnant women to a choice. Many people think society has not only a right but an important responsibility to act in that way.

Taken together, these two answers provide, I believe, a persuasive explanation of why government is entitled to prohibit abortion, subject to certain exceptions, after the sixth month of pregnancy. But do they answer the question asked from the other direction? Why may the government not prohibit abortion earlier? A fetus's central nervous system is not sufficiently developed before approximately that point to allow any form of sentience, but must that be decisive? Wouldn't women have a sufficient opportunity to exercise their right of autonomy if they were forbidden abortion after just five months? Four? Three?

Justice Blackmun chose a point in pregnancy that he thought plainly late enough to give women a fair chance to exercise their right, in normal circumstances, and that was also salient, as I just said, for two other reasons: viability seems, on the best developmental evidence, the earliest time at which a fetus might be thought to have interests of its own, and it is also the point at which its natural development is so far along that deliberately waiting until after that point seems contemptuous of the inherent value of human life. These three factors together indicated fetal viability as the most appropriate point at which a state could properly assert its derivative interests in protecting a fetus's interests, and its own detached interest in responsibility. True, Blackmun might have chosen a somewhat earlier point in pregnancy for that purpose. Though an earlier time would not have been as appropriate, it might have been acceptable if it was still late enough to give pregnant women enough time to exercise their rights to terminate an unwanted pregnancy, and if realistic exceptions were allowed for women who did not know that they were pregnant. But though a somewhat different scheme from the one Blackmun designed might have been acceptable, that is hardly an argument for overruling his scheme now. So important a decision should not be overruled, after nearly twenty years, unless it was clearly wrong, and his decision was certainly not clearly wrong.

This was one reason the crucial three-justice opinion in *Casey* cited in 1992 for reaffirming *Roe:* it said that too many people had come to rely on the decision to permit overruling it now. But the joint opinion also made a compelling argument that *Roe*'s "central holding" was correct— indeed, it made a more powerful argument for the right of procreative autonomy than Blackmun had made in 1973, and that argument matched, in several important respects, the argument we have been exploring in this book.[24] Though the three justices did not mention the idea of the sacred, much of what they said appealed to that concept: they said, for example, that people oppose abortion because they believe it inconsistent with the proper "reverence for the wonder of creation."[25] They declared that states cannot impose an official view about abortion because "at the heart of liberty is the right to define one's own concept of existence, of meaning, of the universe, and of the mystery of human life." Any society committed to liberty, they insisted, will leave such decisions to individual conscience because "beliefs about such matters could not define the attributes of personhood were they formed under the compulsion of the State." The opinion was studded with religious allusions, mentioning not only reverence for creation and the mystery of life, but also the "spiritual imperatives" of women. This is further evidence of the striking overlap between the First Amendment and the due process clause on which the opinion explicitly relied: the arguments the opinion gave for its due process claim would have supported the freedom of religion argument I have described as well.

The *Casey* decision was important because it made plainer than ever before how central the abortion issue is to the very idea of freedom. Not just for America, but for any nation dedicated to liberty, the question of how far government may legitimately impose collective judgments about spiritual matters on individual citizens is absolutely crucial. It is hardly surprising that American law leaves women freer to follow their own conscience than do the laws of many other nations, for the Bill of Rights places more emphasis on individual liberty, especially in matters touching conscience and the sacred, than does any other constitution. *Roe* v. *Wade* is not yet wholly safe: if a single new justice is appointed who believes it should be overruled, it will fall. That would be a bleak day in American constitutional history, for it would mean that American citizens were no longer secure in their freedom to follow their own reflective convictions in the most personal, conscience-driven, and religious decisions many of them will ever make.

TOMORROW'S ARGUMENTS

The Supreme Court's decision in *Casey* made that bleak day much less likely in the near future, however: though *Roe* does hang on the vote of a single Supreme Court justice, it now seems more likely than not to survive. President Clinton has indicated he will appoint only justices who support that decision if any vacancies occur during his administration, and *Casey* may well seem, at least in retrospect, to mark the point after which most lawyers assumed that some constitutional right to abortion would remain in the United States. The most serious legal arguments in the next few years will probably be disputes about whether some regulation serves the permissible state goal of responsibility or the illegitimate one of coercion. Some of these arguments would be forestalled by the Freedom of Choice Act now pending in Congress, which was designed to protect women's right to abortion if *Roe* had been overruled, but which will be pressed by its sponsors anyway in order to try to prevent states from regulating abortion in some of the ways that *Casey* permits. Even if that act passes, however, some states will try to adopt regulations it has not anticipated or forbidden, and the Supreme Court will have to decide whether these are legitimate regulations improving responsibility or illegitimate ones attempting coercion. As I said, the three-justice opinion in *Casey* proposed that the decisive test be whether the purpose or effect of the regulation is to create an "undue burden" on a woman who chooses abortion by posing "substantial obstacles" to that choice.

The Court will almost certainly have to refine this test, because states will adopt a variety of restrictions falling short of outright prohibition of abortion and the Court will have to decide which are constitutional and which are not. "Undue burden" is another abstraction, like "due process" and "equal protection," and it will take judgment and moral sense to apply. Since a woman's right to procreative autonomy is fundamental, we must regard a constraint as undue if it makes the exercise of that right all but impossible for some women, as the three-justice opinion held Pennsylvania's spousal notification requirement did. But even a restraint that does not make abortion practically impossible for anyone, but makes it sufficiently more expensive or difficult that it will deter some women from having an abortion that they, on reflection, want, imposes an "undue" burden if it seems, on balance, *designed* to have that consequence. Of course, it makes little sense for judges to ask about the motives that the various individual legislators of a given state had in mind in voting for some statute. The question of whether a statute has a given purpose is a question of interpretation not of empirical psychology: it is a matter of judging whether, given what the statute does, and what those who proposed and defended it said in official statements before and during its passage, it makes interpretive sense to attribute that purpose to it.[26]

Judges deciding whether some regulation of abortion has a coercive purpose must take three things into account: the degree to which the restriction could reasonably be expected to make a woman's deliberation about abortion more reflective and responsible, the risk that it will prevent some women who have responsibly decided on abortion from acting on that decision, and the possibility that the expected improvement in the responsibility of decisions about abortion could have been achieved in some different way with less coercive consequences. In that light, the decision in *Casey*, upholding Pennsylvania's version of a mandatory waiting period, seems open to challenge. Perhaps some Pennsylvania women will think again about abortion during a mandatory waiting period, but it seems doubtful that many will. Waiting periods are plainly desirable before some decisions—buying a gun, for example, or choosing doctor-assisted suicide where it is legal. But most women seeking abortion will already have reflected at length over the step they are taking—some will have agonized over it—and a single day's waiting period is unlikely to make their consideration of the issues significantly deeper. There are certainly much better methods to encourage women to reflect about abortion and understand its moral gravity—providing financial aid to poor mothers so that pregnant women can choose between childbirth and abortion on grounds other than financial necessity, for example.

On the other hand, mandatory waiting periods do mean that many women, particularly poor ones, who have reflected very deeply on their own sense of what respect for the sanctity of life requires and decided on an abortion will be deterred from having it. If women who live at a considerable distance from an abortion clinic, as many do in rural areas, are made to wait for twenty-four hours after their first visit to the clinic, they will have to make two possibly expensive trips rather than one, explain two trips to those they may not wish to know about the abortion, and endure the gauntlet of "pro-life" protesters outside the clinic twice. That requirement might indeed prevent some women who want an abortion from having one. Moreover, Pennsylvania could have achieved substantially the same result, in encouraging women to reflect before an abortion, in a way that did not have that consequence: it could, for example, have allowed doctors to give the required information on the telephone a day before the scheduled abortion.

The Pennsylvania rule seems, therefore, to fail the test that three of the justices who upheld that rule—Justices O'Connor, Kennedy, and Souter—had themselves laid down, and it is important to notice that these justices conceded that possibility. They said they found the argument that the rule would deter many women "troubling"; they emphasized that the district court had not actually made a finding that the mandatory waiting period imposed "substantial obstacles," and suggested that they might well respect such a finding in a later case. (But in December 1992, the Court declined to review a lower-court decision upholding a Mississippi twenty-four-hour waiting period requirement.[27])

Do the *Casey* opinions suggest a reason for reexamining the Supreme Court's long-standing decision that a government which provides general and comprehensive health care for the poor may nevertheless deny them funds for even therapeutic abortion? It is true, as the Court has declared, that there is a great difference between forbidding abortion and refusing to pay its costs. No one has a constitutional right that government contribute to the costs of any particular medical procedure—government may constitutionally decide to help pay the costs of renal dialysis but not heart transplants, for example, or to exclude psychiatric care from an otherwise comprehensive medical-care program. Such decisions, whether made rightly or wrongly, are part of government's responsibility to allocate its funds in accordance with collective policy decisions of priority. But federal and state regulations excluding abortion from general health-care programs are a different matter, because they are designed to affect the choices people make as well as who pays for them. As the Supreme Court itself said, in the decision in which it held the policy constitutional, "The Hyde amendment, like the Connecticut welfare regulation . . . by means of unequal subsidization of abortion and other medical services, encourages alternative activity deemed to be in the public interest."[28]

The Court rejected the argument that this official attempt to induce people to follow socially approved views about abortion counts as favoring one set of religious values over others. But it conceived that argument as the bad argument I described earlier: it said that government is not disabled from punishing theft just because Judeo-Christian religions also condemn it. The Court did not consider the very different argument I have been making in this chapter: that because opinions about abortion rest on differing interpretations of a shared belief in the sanctity of human life, they are themselves essentially religious beliefs. If so, then government's deciding to withhold funds for medically necessary abortions on the ground that such abortions are not "in the public interest" is tantamount to establishing one interpretation of the sanctity of life as the official creed of the community, and that raises a much more serious First Amendment issue than the Court recognized. Though, as I said, the *Casey* joint opinion did not explicitly refer to religion or to the First Amendment, it did declare that people's views about abortion depend on their convictions about the "concept of existence, of meaning, of the universe, and of the mystery of human life," and that "beliefs about such matters could not define the attributes of personhood were they formed under the compulsion of the State."

Particularly in an age when government is necessarily involved in the financing of medical care, and when many women who believe abortion crucially important to them will be unable to obtain a safe abortion without financial help, withholding that help, for the purpose of inducing women to "alternate activity," seems enough like compulsion to suggest that past Supreme Court decisions upholding the Hyde amendment and similar state laws should now be reconsidered. It might be objected that if government supports abortion financially, it uses funds collected in taxes from those who believe that abortion insults life's sanctity and so denies them the free exercise of *their* essentially religious beliefs. Or that refusing to pay for abortions is the only way that government can remain neutral on the issue. But financing medical treatment for people whose religious practices some taxpayers find offensive no more denies those taxpayers religious freedom than does using municipal fire trucks to put out a fire in a church they also disapprove, and it would be ludicrous to interpret a policy of financial aid for all medical care during pregnancy, which includes abortion as well as childbirth, as showing any bias toward the former. True, the Court's position about financing abortions is a long-standing one, and that argues in favor of not disturbing it now. But *Casey* signaled not only a new endorsement of *Roe* v. *Wade* but a change in the Court's understanding of why *Roe* was right, and constitutional integrity may now require a fresh look at many of the decisions that were taken before that new understanding was realized.

On his second day in office, President Clinton, expressing his determination that health-care decisions be removed from the political debate about abortion, reversed a variety of policies the Reagan–Bush administrations had adopted. Clinton repealed the "gag rule" that forbade certain personnel at federally supported clinics to counsel about or even mention abortion; he lifted restrictions on federally funded research into the medical use of fetal tissue; he allowed abortions to be performed at overseas military hospitals; and he ended restrictions on the use of United Nations contributions for abortion counseling.[29] But other legal issues will continue to be of great practical importance to women contemplating an abortion. For several years, federal judges have granted injunctions against members of "Operation Rescue" and other anti-abortion groups who use violence to intimidate women entering abortion clinics. These judges relied on an 1871 federal law, called the Ku Klux Klan law, which prohibits conspiracies to deprive "any person or class of persons" of equal protection of the laws. The Supreme Court has long interpreted that language to forbid conspiracies driven by what the Court called a "class-based, invidiously discriminatory animus," but in

January 1993, in *Bray* v. *Alexandria Women's Health Clinic*, the Court decided by a six-to-three vote that the law did not apply to organized abortion-clinic violence because, as Justice Scalia put it, there are "common and respectable" reasons for opposing abortion that do not include any hatred for women as a class.[30] That is certainly true, but it is also true that violent anti-abortion groups are moved by an "invidiously discriminatory animus" toward a specific group of women, not for their race or gender, but for their essentially religious or spiritual convictions, and any plausible interpretation of the principles justifying the place of the Ku Klux Klan law in contemporary federalism would hold that kind of discrimination to be within the spirit of the law.

Some justices worried that applying the law to this case would mean that a single, Reconstruction-era statute was now being used to transfer to the federal government jurisdiction over vast areas of the criminal and civil law traditionally reserved to the states. But such a concern seems unduly timid about the Supreme Court's ability to draw a line between an organized, nationwide campaign of violence directed against people for their constitutionally protected convictions, which should be a matter of national concern under any defensible view of federalism, and the rest of state civil or criminal law. It is hard to imagine conspiracies like Operation Rescue being organized against any other controversial and essentially religious conviction. But if any were—if a similar national operation used violence to try to stop life support being withdrawn from persistently vegetative patients, for example—then the Ku Klux Klan law interpreted as I have suggested would properly apply, again with no implication that federal law was usurping large provinces of law traditionally left to the states. The Bush administration had joined Operation Rescue in asking the Court to reach the decision it did. But Representative Charles E. Schumer and Senator Edward Kennedy have both announced that they will now sponsor new legislation giving federal officials power to respond to such violence.[31]

We should notice, finally, that one of the most important decisions affecting abortion in America in the next several years will be a commercial rather than a legal one. A French company—Roussel Uclaf—has developed an abortion pill it calls RU-486, which, though it requires medical procedures in a proper facility at some stage, is less expensive and more confidential than surgical abortion in a hospital or clinic. The pill has been marketed in France, Great Britain, and Sweden, and has been taken by over 100,000 women. Roussel Uclaf, which is owned by a German firm, Hoechst A.G., has not attempted to sell the drug in other countries, including Germany, because it is afraid of angering anti-abortion groups, and it has so far declined to apply to the Food and Drug Administration for permission to sell it in the United States. (Though Americans are usually allowed to import small quantities of medicine bought abroad, even though not cleared for sale in the United States, Bush's Justice Department refused to allow a woman to import RU-486 in 1992.[32] On his second day, Clinton also ordered a review of that decision.[33]) Clinton has said that he will invite Roussel to apply for such permission, which could be granted quickly because the drug has been so thoroughly tested in Europe, and the Commissioner of Food and Drugs, Dr. David A. Kessler, has indicated that he would welcome an application.[34] But the company has not yet decided whether it will risk demonstrations and boycott of its group's other products by selling the drug in the United States. A woman's opportunity to have a safe and inexpensive abortion depends on more than the government and the Supreme Court.

7

DYING AND
LIVING

Abortion is a waste of the start of human life. Death intervenes before life in earnest has even begun. Now we turn to decisions that people must make about death at the other end of life, after life in earnest has ended. We shall find that the same issues recur, that the mortal questions we ask about the two edges of life have much in common.

Every day, rational people all over the world plead to be allowed to die. Sometimes they plead for others to kill them. Some of them are dying already, many in great pain, like Lillian Boyes, a seventy-year-old Englishwoman who was dying from a terrible form of rheumatoid arthritis so painful that even the most powerful painkillers left her in agony, screaming when her son touched her hand with his finger. Some of them want to die because they are unwilling to live in the only way left open to them, like Patricia Diane Trumbull, a forty-five-year-old New Yorker suffering from leukemia who refused chemotherapy and bone-marrow transplants, even though she was told the treatment would give her a one-in-four chance of surviving, because she knew the ravages of the treatment and did not think the odds good enough to endure it. Or Janet Adkins, a fifty-four-year-old Oregonian who knew she was in the early stages of Alzheimer's disease and wanted to die while she was still able to arrange it. Sometimes relatives plead for a family member to be allowed to die because the patient herself is in a permanent vegetative state, like Nancy Cruzan, whose cerebral cortex was destroyed by lack of oxygen after an accident, and whose life support was finally terminated in 1990, after she had lived for seven years as a vegetable, and after her parents had been to the Supreme Court and back.

Doctors command technology that can keep people alive—sometimes for weeks, sometimes for years—who are near death or horribly crippled, intubated, disfigured by experimental operations, in pain or sedated into near oblivion, connected to dozens of machines that do most of their living for them, explored by dozens of doctors none of whom they would recognize, and for whom they are not so much patients as battlegrounds. We all dread that. We also dread—some of us dread it more—life as an unthinking yet scrupulously tended vegetable. More and more of us now realize the importance of making decisions in advance about whether we want to be treated that way. Every state in the United States now recognizes some form of advance directive: either "living wills"—documents stipulating that specified medical procedures should not be used to keep the signer alive in certain specified circumstances, or "health-care proxies"—documents appointing someone else to make life-and-death decisions for the signer when he no longer can. And we all know we may have to make such decisions—as relatives or friends or doctors—for others who have signed no living wills or proxies. (In spite of recent publicity, very few people have signed living wills. One poll in 1991 reported that 87 percent of those interviewed believed a doctor should be either required or permitted to withdraw life support if the patient had signed a living will so requesting, but another reported that only 17 percent of those interviewed have actually signed one; many people do not know how to find and execute the right form or are too superstitious or squeamish to sign a document requesting death.[1])

These are individual decisions, but voters also have political decisions to make. The community must decide how far to permit its members to choose death. The draft statute that Californians rejected in 1992 declared, "The right to choose to eliminate pain and suffering, and to die with dignity at the time and place of our own choosing when we are terminally ill is an integral part of our right to control our own destinies," and it set out a "directive" that a terminally ill patient might sign requesting "aid-in-dying" at a time and place of his choice when two physicians certified that death would occur anyway within six months. The draft statute required that any such directive be witnessed by two people, neither of whom was related to the signer or could benefit from his death or was his doctor, and it provided that the directive could be revoked at any time either verbally or in writing. Though this statute and a similar Washington State statute proposed in 1991 were rejected in referendums, groups pressing for such legislation, like the Hemlock Society, believe it inevitable that the law will move in that direction. A recent nationwide poll commissioned by the Boston *Globe* and Harvard School of Public Health showed 64 percent in favor of some form of legalized euthanasia.[2]

In most European countries, the law now makes no statutory provision for legally effective living wills or health-care proxies, though in 1992 a bill was introduced into the British Parliament that would allow people to decline in advance certain forms of heroic medical treatment. No Western country formally permits doctors (or anyone else) to kill patients even at their own request.[3] In The Netherlands, however, for several years an informal consensus that included public prosecutors and the judiciary allowed doctors to kill such patients provided that doctors followed guidelines sanctioned by judicial practice. In 1993, the Dutch parliament ratified that practice in a law that stopped short of making euthanasia legal but declared that doctors would not be prosecuted if they followed procedures and restrictions the law set out. Though 80 percent of Dutch people support the right to die, and the Dutch practice is approved and has been warmly defended by many Dutch and foreign doctors and commentators, it has also been heavily criticized.[4]

Lawyers and judges also have decisions to make. Do Americans have a *constitutional* right to die? In Nancy Cruzan's case, the United States Supreme Court seemed to recognize, at least in principle, that states must honor living wills. But what about a patient who has not made such a will, and whose relatives or doctors now think that it is in his best interests to die? What powers does a state have over that decision? And what is the boundary between what someone can request, for himself or others, and what the state may refuse? People can require, through living wills, that they not be kept alive through machines. But they cannot require, as the law now stands, that they be killed. Where is the line to be drawn between not being kept alive and being killed? Can a state prohibit doctors from giving their patients morphine, which stops their pain, in doses that will probably kill them?

Each of these personal, political, and legal decisions has hundreds of facets. Some are medical and some sociological. Suppose a law like the California draft statute I described does pass in an American state. What are the risks that people will ask to be killed after a misdiagnosis? Or that they will die before new treatments are discovered or developed that would have saved their lives if they had waited? (The California draft directive declared that the patient signing it knew of that theoretical possibility and wanted to die anyway.) How far can these risks be reduced by medical review boards, waiting periods, or other devices? What would be the social consequences of such a law? What would be the effect on people's regard for doctors, or for doctors' sense of their vocation? Would a profession that helps people to die, even though with the best motives, grow more careless or less zealous about saving lives? Would legally sanctioned killing make the community as a whole more callous about death? Would it have as great or greater an effect, in that direction, as capital punishment does?

These and similar questions are now much discussed in newspapers, medical journals, and symposia of what are called "medical ethicists." But there are also philosophical and moral questions to consider, and these are even more important and difficult. It is obviously important to think about who should make life-or-death decisions, with what safeguards and formal requirements, and whether and how the decisions, once made, should be reviewed by others. But it is also important to think about an even more fundamental matter: which decision is the *right* one to make, no matter who makes it?

That paramount question is sometimes thought to lie in the exclusive province of religion. But it must also be asked by people who are not religious, or by those whose religion gives no answer they believe suited to the contemporary world. It is also a political question, moreover. We cannot think intelligently about the legal and political issues—about who should make what choices, what constitutions should permit, and what nations and states should do—unless we have a better shared understanding, not necessarily about the meaning of death but at least about what kind of question we are asking. How should we think about when and how to die?

In January 1993, the *American Journal of Public Health* published an important survey indicating how deeply divided our culture is about those questions, and how recalcitrant to change our medical institutions are, even in the face of shifting convictions.[5] Fourteen hundred doctors and nurses at five major hospitals were asked about their treatment of terminally ill patients: fully 70 percent of the resident doctors said that they themselves *overtreated* such patients, against their own conscience, and against what they knew to be the patients' interests and wishes. Four times as many of those surveyed thought that doctors overtreated dying patients as that they undertreated them, and 81 percent said they agreed that "the most common form of narcotic abuse in caring for dying patients is undertreatment of pain." These amazing responses may simply show appalling institutional inertia, or they may reveal how much doctors fear legal responsibility, or community or professional disapproval. But they underline how urgently we need a franker public discussion of death than we have yet had.

People must decide about their own death, or someone else's, in three main kinds of situations.

Conscious and competent. Suicide is no longer a crime in the United States, Britain, and most other Western countries, and the increasing power of new medical technology has plainly increased people's interest in that way of controlling the time and manner of one's own death. In 1991, *Final Exit,* a detailed suicide manual written by the president of the Hemlock Society, which describes ways even a very ill patient can kill himself, rose in a week to the top of *The New York Times* best-seller list for how-to books, leaping over sex manuals and treatises on how to make money quickly. AIDS has contributed to heightened public interest in suicide, as it has to so many other changes in American attitudes toward illness and death. Brian Smith, who is in charge of an AIDS counseling program in San Francisco, says that most AIDS victims talk about taking their own lives. Many of them begin to squirrel away potentially lethal pills as soon as they are diagnosed. Smith says that such patients think: "I won't have the next fifty years the way I was planning to, at least I can control my death."[6]

But many very sick or handicapped people, though fully conscious, are unable to commit suicide unaided. Under American law, except in special circumstances, people in full command of their mental faculties can refuse medical treatment even though they will die without it. But it does not follow that once they have been connected to life-sustaining equipment they have a legal right to have the equipment disconnected when they request, because that involves the assistance of others in their death, and the law of most states and most Western countries prohibits people to assist in another's suicide. Many doctors have nevertheless been willing quietly to terminate mechanical life support when begged to do so by people who are dying.

In an important Canadian decision in January 1992, a Quebec judge, Mr. Justice Dufour, ruled that people have the right to demand that life support be removed, even when they are not dying, if they find life intolerable in the circumstances in which they must live it. Nancy B., a twenty-five-year-old victim of a rare neurological disease called Guillain-Barre syndrome and paralyzed from the neck down, asked the judge to order her doctor to turn off the respirator that kept her alive. Her doctor said that she could go on living on a respirator for many years, but she wanted to die. "The only thing I have is television and looking at the walls. It's enough. It's been two and a half years that I've been on this thing, and I think I've done my share."[7] The judge said he would be very happy if Nancy B. changed her mind, but that he understood her and would grant her request. The respirator was withdrawn, and Nancy B. died in February 1992.

But the laws of all Western countries (except, in practice, The Netherlands) still prohibit doctors or others from directly killing people at their own request, by injecting an immediately lethal poison, for example. So the law produces the apparently irrational result that people can choose to die lingering deaths by refusing to eat, by refusing treatment that keeps them alive, or by being disconnected from respirators and suffocating, but they cannot choose a quick, painless death that their doctors could easily provide.[8] Many people, including many doctors, think that this distinction is not irrational but, on the contrary, essential. They think that doctors should in no circumstances be killers. But to many other people, that principle seems cruelly abstract.

Nigel Cox had been Lillian Boyes's doctor for thirteen years and they had had a close personal relationship; he had promised her that she would not suffer, but the painkilling medication he had counted on failed, and she begged him to kill her. He injected her with a lethal dose of potassium chloride, and she died within minutes. He scrupulously reported the injection in her medical records, and a Catholic nurse who discovered the report informed hospital authorities. He was tried for attempted murder because the body had been cremated and there was no evidence that the injection had actually killed her. Though his lawyer argued that he had given her potassium chloride only to relieve her suffering, the jury disagreed—the drug has no analgesic effect—and by a vote of eleven to one found him guilty. The judge—Mr. Justice Ognall—sentenced Dr. Cox to a year in jail, but suspended the sentence. The judge said that the doctor had allowed his professional duty to be overridden by compassion for a dying patient who had become an admired and cherished friend. "What you did," the judge told him, "was not only criminal, it was a total betrayal of your unequivocal duty as a physician." It was widely expected that in view of his conviction, Dr. Cox would not be permitted to practice medicine again. But though the General Medical Council reprimanded him, saying that what he did was wrong and that the law should not be changed to permit it, the board did not bar him from practicing. His employer, the Wessex Regional Health Authority, permitted him to return to his duties at the Royal Hampshire County Hospital in Winchester, but only on condition that he accept supervision of his work by a more senior doctor. Some British organizations expressed dismay at what they took to be the leniency of these official bodies. Jack Scarisbrook, chairman of the pressure group Life, said, "It is contrary to all the finest ethics of the medical profession and is very dangerous in relation to the trust we all ought to be able to put in our doctors." But other groups were outraged that Dr. Cox had even been convicted of a crime, and a campaign to legalize euthanasia in such cases has been launched.[9]

In 1991, in the United States, a similar case was treated rather differently by the public and the medical profession. Patricia Trumbull's doctor, Timothy Quill of Rochester, New York, reported in *The New England Journal of Medicine* that at Trumbull's prompting he had prescribed enough barbiturate pills to kill her and told her how many to take for that purpose. When she was ready, she took the pills and died on her sofa. A New York State prosecutor asked a grand jury to consider whether Dr. Quill should be prosecuted for assisting suicide, a crime which carries a five-to-fifteen-year sentence in New York. The grand jury decided that he should not be.[10] The New York State Health Department then asked its Board for Professional Medical Conduct to consider whether Dr. Quill's license should be revoked or whether he should be censured. The board decided unanimously that "no charge of misconduct was warranted."[11]

The board was particularly concerned to distinguish what Dr. Quill had done from the much-publicized acts of Jack Kevorkian, a Detroit doctor whom the press has nicknamed Dr. Death. Dr. Kevorkian has constructed a variety of suicide machines, which he writes about and describes on television, and at least nine people have used his machines to kill themselves. He installed one of these machines in the back of his Volkswagen van; it allows patients to kill themselves by pressing a button that injects poison through a needle that the doctor has inserted into a vein. (Michigan, which was one of a minority of American states having no law forbidding assisting suicide, enacted such a law in 1992 for a limited period, in hopes of preventing Dr. Kevorkian from making any further use of his machines in that state. The law took effect in March of 1993, and at least one person, a fifty-three-year-old victim of bone cancer, used a Kevorkian machine to kill himself after the law was passed but before the deadline.) Dr. Quill, the board said, acted differently, because he did not know whether his patient would take the lethal dose or not. But that distinction is unimpressive, because Dr. Quill did know what his patient intended to do. The important distinction between the two doctors, as both the board and Dr. Quill pointed out, is that Dr. Kevorkian knew each of his patients for only a short time, while the long and close professional relationship between Dr. Quill and Patricia Trumbull (like the relationship between Dr. Cox and Lillian Boyes) had allowed him much more insight into her situation and needs.

Unconscious. Doctors are often forced to decide whether to continue life support for someone who is unconscious and dying—someone in severe cardiac failure, for example. Almost every hospital has developed a policy—some formal and some informal—about when to resuscitate someone whose chances of surviving for more than days are negligible and who will spend those hours or days semiconscious at best. Some patients ask—either by signing living wills or simply by pleading with doctors and hospital staff—not to be revived if they fall into such a state. But others, on the contrary, insist that everything possible be done to keep them alive as long as possible, and relatives often take the same view. For example, a seventy-six-year-old widow who never left an intensive care unit after her open-heart operation endured crisis after crisis and steadily refused her consent not to be resuscitated after the next one. Finally she suffered respiratory arrest on her ventilator. Her daughter refused to consent to a no-resuscitation order even then; she said that the family had a tradition of "fighting to the bitter end," as they had in the case of the patient's aunt and husband. "Even our cat got transfusions when it was dying," the daughter said.[12]

Many unconscious patients are not about to die, however. Some accidents and diseases leave their victims either in comas or in what doctors call a persistent vegetative state.[13] In either case they are unconscious—though many patients in a persistent vegetative state have open, moving eyes—and the higher centers of their brains have been permanently damaged in a way that rules out any return to consciousness. They are capable of no sensation and no thought.[14] They must be groomed, and turned, which is difficult because they are often in spasm. But if they are fed and given water, through tubes, they can live indefinitely. A specialist has estimated that there are between five thousand and ten thousand people in that condition in the United States now. The cost of maintaining each of them varies from state to state and institution to institution: it has been estimated as ranging from about two thousand to ten thousand dollars a month.

The relatives of a patient in a vegetative state often treat him as still alive: they visit him, often daily, and sometimes talk to him though he cannot hear. But sometimes, when they are certain that recovery is impossible, they ask that his feeding and hydration tubes be withdrawn and other forms of life support terminated, even when he has not signed a living will. Nancy Cruzan's parents told a Missouri judge that she had several times, over the years, expressed a wish not to be kept alive in such circumstances. The judge agreed, and consented to the tubes being removed. But the lawyer who had been appointed by the court to represent Nancy Cruzan felt it his responsibility to appeal that decision, and the Missouri Supreme Court held that Missouri law did not permit life support to be halted unless there was "clear and convincing" evidence that the patient had formed that wish. It said that if Nancy Cruzan had executed a formal living will, that would have provided the necessary proof, but that the informal, casual statements her family and friends remembered did not.

Nancy Cruzan's parents appealed to the United States Supreme Court, which upheld the Missouri court's decision: it said that Missouri was entitled to insist on clear and convincing evidence—a living will or some other formal document—before permitting hospitals to withdraw life support. But, as I said, a majority of the justices, for the first time, recognized that competent people do have a constitutional right to direct that life support be withheld from them if they become permanently vegetative. States may, the Court said, impose very strenuous requirements on the form that an advance directive must take. But they must give effect to advance directives in some form. Several states revised their laws after the *Cruzan* decision, and every state has now made provision for honoring living wills, health-care proxies, or, in most states, both. In 1990, Congress adopted a law requiring all hospitals supported by federal funds to inform any entering patient—even a candidate for a bunion removal—of his state's law about advance directives, and of the formalities he must follow if he wants to be sure he is not kept alive if he becomes a vegetable during his stay.

British law about the rights of unconscious patients has recently been clarified. In April of 1989, Anthony Bland was caught in a stampede at the Hillsborough, England, football stadium; his lungs were crushed and his brain deprived of oxygen so long that he fell into a permanent vegetative state from which he never recovered. In 1992, his parents petitioned the courts to declare that it would be lawful for doctors to remove life support and allow him to die. The trial judge said it would be, because that was in the patient's interests. The Court of Appeals affirmed; Lord Justice Hoffmann, in a strikingly philosophical opinion with which the other justices on the panel agreed, said, "from what we have learned of Anthony Bland from those closest to him, that forced as we are to choose, we think it more likely that in his present state he would choose to die than to live," and that even though respect for the sanctity of life might argue in favor of keeping him alive, respect for the competing principle of self-determination justified the law permitting him to die. The House of Lords affirmed the Court of Appeal's decision, but most of the opinions that made up its judgment emphasized, not the patient's self-determination, but the fact that continuing treatment was not in his best interests.[15] (I shall discuss the importance of distinguishing these two issues—the autonomy of a patient and that patient's best interests—shortly.)

But not everyone takes the view that Nancy Cruzan's and Anthony Bland's parents did about whether their relatives in a persistent vegetative state should be allowed to die. In 1989, Helga Wanglie, an active woman of eighty-five, broke her hip and suffered several cardiopulmo-nary arrests during the course of her treatment; she suffered severe anoxia in 1990 and fell into a persistent vegetative state. In 1991, the Hennepin County Medical Center in Minnesota, where Mrs. Wanglie was being treated, suggested that her respirator should be turned off and that she be allowed to die, on the ground that further treatment was futile and inappropriate. (The hospital had no direct financial interest in ceasing treatment; the enormous cost—estimated at $500,000—was borne by a health-care plan that said that cost should not be a considera-tion in the decision.) But Mr. Wanglie refused his consent; he said that he believed that life should be continued as long as possible, no matter in what conditions, and though he had earlier said that he had never discussed the matter with his wife he later remembered that he had, and that she shared his views. On July 1, 1991, Judge Patricia Belois denied the hospital's request; she said that it had offered no reason to doubt that Mr. Wanglie was a competent guardian of his wife's interests. She died four days later, still attached to the respirator.[16]

Conscious but incompetent. Recent studies suggest that between roughly one-quarter and one-half of all people over the age of eighty-five—a growing segment of the whole population—are seriously demented, and that the leading cause of that dementia is Alzheimer's disease.[17] In the advanced stages of this progressive disease, victims have lost all memory and sense of continuity of self, and are incompetent to attend to any of their own needs or functions. Janet Adkins was in the early stages of the disease—she could still beat her thirty-year-old son at tennis but could no longer keep score—and she knew what was coming. She read about Dr. Kevorkian's poison-injecting machine, and she telephoned him. They agreed that they would meet in Michigan, where he dined with her and her husband and videotaped an interview with her. She satisfied him that she was still in sound mind, that she had reflected on the matter, and that she wished to die. Two days later, she and Dr. Kevorkian entered the back of his van; he inserted the needle and explained what she had to do. Janet Adkins pressed the button and died.

Mrs. Adkins was competent when she made her decision to die. In the late stages of Alzheimer's disease, no such decision is possible. Late-stage victims often behave in a way that suggests a paranoid fear of being harmed. If we can attribute any relevant desire to them, it would be a desire to live rather than to die. Should competent people have the power to specify what kind of medical treatment they receive if they ever become wholly incompetent in that way? Should they have the power to direct that they should not be kept alive by routine treatment—surgery if they develop cancer, antibiotics if they develop pneumonia? Should they have the power to direct that they should actually be killed? That last suggestion might seem preposterous: how can we permit anyone to arrange in advance to be killed years later, when he may then give every sign of wanting to live? But it is a sobering thought that if Mrs. Adkins had had that power, she could have enjoyed years of additional useful life, confident that she would not be allowed to reach the condition she dreaded.

THREE MORTAL ISSUES

These decisions about death, in the circumstances we have been discussing, have implications for three distinct moral and political issues, and these, as we shall see, are often confused.

Autonomy. People who believe that competent patients should be permitted to arrange their own deaths, with the assistance of willing doctors if they wish, often appeal to the principle of autonomy. They say that it is crucial to people's right to make central decisions for themselves that they should be allowed to end their lives when they wish, at least if their decision is not plainly irrational. But some opponents of euthanasia also appeal to autonomy: they worry that if euthanasia were legal people would be killed who really wanted to stay alive. Of course, any remotely acceptable law permitting euthanasia for competent people would insist that they not be killed unless they have clearly asked to die. But someone who is terminally ill, and whose care is expensive or burdensome, or whose situation is agonizing for relatives and friends, may well feel guilty about the money and attention being devoted to him. Such a person is especially vulnerable to pressure: he might prefer that a doctor not even raise the question of whether he would like to consider dying with medical assistance; he might prefer that the question never arise, or that he not even have the right to request death.[18] Many of the people who voted against the Washington and California referendums were worried about putting sick people in that position, and some critics of the Dutch scheme claim that in that country the elderly are beginning to look upon doctors as their enemies.

People also worry about protecting autonomy, though in a different way and for different reasons, when the patient is unconscious, as Nancy Cruzan was. We can respect the autonomy of someone who has become unconscious only by asking what he would have decided himself, under appropriate conditions, before he became incompetent. That may seem easy when the patient has signed a living will dictating what is to be done in such circumstances, or when he has made his wishes known in a less formal but nevertheless emphatic way—for example, by repeatedly telling relatives. Yet even in such cases, there is no guarantee that he did not change his mind sometime after the last formal or informal declaration, or that he wouldn't have changed his mind if he had thought about the matter again.

If someone had not indicated his wishes, formally or informally, then of course it is possible that he never considered the matter at all, and had no view either way. In such a case, relatives might ask whether he would have wanted to be allowed to die or to be killed if he *had* thought about it. That is a very tricky judgment; everything depends on the setting one imagines. Are we asking what he would have thought after reading a specific novel or hearing a specific argument? Or in the absence of any discussion or argument? In a good mood? Or depressed? Still, people do think they can sensibly judge what some friend or relative would have wanted. Their opinion is usually based on their sense of what would be most consistent with his personality as a whole. The daughter of the widow in intensive care I mentioned said, with great confidence, that her nearly dead mother would want everything done to keep her alive as long as possible. The daughter's reason was not a remembered conversation or even an imagined one, but a family tradition that she insisted her mother shared: a tradition of fighting every other kind of battle to the end. Even when Mr. Wanglie said he had had no conversation with his wife about the matter, he was confident that she would have wanted to continue; he, too, was relying on his sense of her personality and values. Nancy Cruzan's parents and friends may well have relied more on a similar sense, in reaching their view that she would not have wanted to be kept alive, than on the conversations they testified about. They talked about her vivacity and her sense of the importance of activity and engagement; they thought that a person like that would particularly despise living as a manicured vegetable.

These familiar appeals to the patient's whole personality, offered to show that life support either should or should not be terminated, are usually presented as showing what the patient would have decided himself. So understood, they aim to protect the patient's autonomy. But we should notice that they can also be understood differently: as arguments about what would be in the patient's best interests. In that case, they appeal to the idea that it is better for someone to live a life that is structured by a theme, even through its end. They argue, for example, that because a patient has been a fighter even against hopeless odds all her life, it is better for her that she fight death to the absolute end, even when unconscious. Or that because Nancy Cruzan had prided herself on self-reliance, it is better for her that her life end when that is no longer possible.

When we understand the appeal to personality in that way, we will not be troubled by the difficulty I mentioned: that our judgment depends on the setting in which we imagine someone to be thinking about whether to live or die. We can judge which decision would be consistent with his personality without imagining him thinking about it at all. But the underlying idea—that what happens to someone after he has become permanently unconscious can be good or bad for *him*—may seem mysterious. We shall shortly return to it.

In the third kind of case I distinguished—a patient who is conscious but seriously demented or mentally incompetent—much more difficult questions arise about autonomy. In such cases, two autonomies are in play: the autonomy of the demented patient and the autonomy of the person who became demented. These two autonomies can conflict, and the resulting problems are complex and difficult.

Best interests. Many people are opposed to euthanasia on paternalistic grounds. They think that even when people have deliberately and self-consciously chosen to die—when we know that is their genuine wish—it is nevertheless *bad* for them to die. Almost all of us take that view in at least some cases. Almost all of us would think it terrible, for example, for an otherwise healthy young man to kill himself when he is in a depression that might well be temporary or that might respond to medical or other forms of treatment. Even if he has reflected on the matter and still wants to die, we believe that he has made a mistake, and that dying is against his interests. We might think it right to try to prevent his suicide even if that means committing him to an institution, or violating his autonomy in other ways. Our grounds are paternalistic: we think that he does not know his own interests and that we know what is good for him better than he does.

It might seem ridiculous to take the same view about someone in the last stages of a painful and terminal disease. How could Lillian Boyes, the rheumatoid-arthritis patient dying slowly and in great pain, have been making a mistake about her own interests when she decided to die at once? But a great many people do think that it would be against their interests to die even if they were in great pain that could not be relieved; they would want to continue living as long as they could still think or understand, no matter through what suffering. Some people want to stay alive as long as they can no matter in *what* condition. They cling desperately to any kind of life, as the widow in intensive care did when she was still periodically conscious and as her daughter did, for her, when she was not. When a lower Missouri court finally decided, after all, that Nancy Cruzan's parents had produced enough evidence of her wishes, and the Missouri officials, perhaps for political reasons, decided not to appeal back to higher courts, the tubes that kept her alive were withdrawn. Several of the nurses who had cared for her protested and wept—out of sympathy for her, they said. We cannot understand the public debate over euthanasia unless we make sense of these attitudes.

We must also be able to make sense of the opposite attitude: that people who are permanently unconscious are better off dead. How could death be better for someone who has no sense whatever of the condition he is in? Why take the trouble to sign a living will for these circumstances? Why shouldn't Nancy Cruzan, for example, have thought it would be a matter of *indifference* to her whether she continued alive as a vegetable or not, that it couldn't matter less to *her*? Why should her parents have gone to such inordinate trouble—bringing endless lawsuits and appeals—to change her state from all but dead to actually, technically dead?

Many people who sign living wills say they are acting for the sake of others: they want to save relatives the expense of keeping them pointlessly alive, or they want the money that the community would spend caring for them to be used for others who may have real lives to lead. But Nancy Cruzan's relatives bore none of the cost of keeping her alive.

Missouri paid it all, and its voters had decided that the expense was worthwhile, that the policy of keeping people alive as long as possible served what they believed to be an important value. (Do we have any reason to think that Missouri voters would increase public funds for infant care, for example, if more of its residents signed living wills?) Cruzan's parents, it is true, wanted her to be allowed to die. But they wanted this for *her* sake, not theirs. They did not bring their expensive and draining lawsuit for their own sake. They felt that she would be better off dead, and that is what seems, on a second look, so mysterious. In another, later Missouri case, a judge made the same decision about another young woman in a vegetative state: he said that he was required to decide what was in *her* best interests, and that it was in her best interests to die at once. Though lawyers argued both sides of that issue, and the case was a protracted one involving judicial decisions at several levels, no one challenged the view that the central question was whether it could responsibly be thought to be in the best interests of a perma- nently vegetative patient to die.[19] (In January 1993, the new attorney general of Missouri asked the courts to dismiss the case, allowing the patient's family to decide whether she should continue to have life support. His decision changed official policy in Missouri.)

So there are mysteries on both sides. Why do we care so much, one way or the other, about dying when there is nothing to live for but also no pain or suffering that death will stop? Why aren't more of us simply indifferent about what happens to us, or to those we love, in that circumstance?

Sanctity. We must distinguish, from the issues of autonomy and best interests, a third issue. Is euthanasia wrong—even when the patient desires death, and even when death is in his best interests—because it invariably violates the intrinsic value and sanctity of human life? Some of the political groups that opposed the euthanasia initiatives in Wash- ington and California sensed a connection between permissiveness about euthanasia and a liberal attitude toward abortion, and they cited it as part of their ground for opposing the initiatives. I referred to that connection myself in discussing the distinction between two different grounds for opposing abortion—that it is against the interests of the fetus, and that it violates the intrinsic value of human life. As I pointed out, Justices Rehnquist and Scalia in the *Cruzan* case both embraced the parallel distinction about euthanasia: they said that Missouri had the right to adopt strict rules about euthanasia, even if these rules acted against the autonomy and the best interests of patients, in order to protect human life itself.

This distinction—between the intrinsic value of life and its personal value for the patient—explains why so many people think that euthanasia is wrong in *all* circumstances. They think that a person should bear the pain, or be cared for unconscious, until his life ends naturally—by which they mean other than through a human decision to end it—because they believe that deliberately ending a human life denies its inherent, cosmic value. People who say that suicide and euthanasia are against God's will take that view. John Locke, the seventeenth-century British philosopher who had a great influence over the drafters of the American Constitution, opposed suicide on such a ground: he said that a human life is the property not of the person living that life, who is just a tenant, but of God, so that suicide is a kind of theft or embezzlement. That claim can be detached from the images of property in which Locke couched it: euthanasia, like abortion, can be seen as an insult to God's gift of life.

The conviction that human life is sacred probably provides the most powerful emotional basis for resisting euthanasia in the different forms and contexts we have been distinguishing. The Roman Catholic church is the sternest, most vigilant, and no doubt most effective opponent of euthanasia, as it is of abortion. (Indeed, as I have said, the stress some prominent Catholics place on the consistency of the church's views on these two subjects is itself an argument that its opposition to abortion does not depend on the assumption that a fetus is a person with rights and interests.) Many other religious groups are also firm in their campaign against any legalization of euthanasia, though in the summer of 1991, one major denomination, the General Assembly of the Church of Christ, formally accepted the legitimacy of suicide for the terminally ill.[20]

One of my main claims throughout this book has been that there is a secular as well as a religious interpretation of the idea that human life is sacred. Atheists, too, may feel instinctively that suicide and euthanasia are problematic because human life has intrinsic value. These two facts—that religious groups divide about euthanasia, and that sanctity has a secular dimension—suggest that the conviction that human life is sacred may turn out to provide a crucial argument *for* rather than against euthanasia.

THE CRUZAN CASE

We have now distinguished three different moral issues pertinent to questions about suicide and euthanasia: we should be concerned, in answering those questions, about the patients' autonomy, about their best interests, and about the intrinsic value of their lives. The interplay among these three—and the dangers of confusing them—are very well illustrated by Chief Justice Rehnquist's opinion for the majority in the Supreme Court's decision of Nancy Cruzan's case. All three goals figured in his opinion, but they were not carefully distinguished, and the weaknesses in his argument would have been more evident had they been.

Missouri, as I said, forbade doctors to terminate life support unless there is "clear and convincing" proof, in the shape of a formal document, of what the patient had previously decided. In his dissenting opinion, Justice Brennan said that this Missouri rule did not respect people's autonomy because it forced a vegetable life on people who dreaded it and had said so but who had not signed living wills, as very few people have. Only an even-handed rule, Brennan said, that requires officials to decide whether on balance it is more likely than not that the patient would have wanted to die adequately protects autonomy.

Justice Rehnquist disagreed. He said the Missouri rule was well calculated to protect people's autonomy. But his argument actually revealed, and turned on, an important assumption not about autonomy but about the best interests of people who have fallen into a permanent vegetative state. He conceded that Missouri's rule might often lead to the "mistaken" result of keeping alive a patient who had decided he wanted to die if permanently unconscious. But, he said, the rule prevents mistakes in the opposite direction: it ensures that people would continue to live who in fact wanted to, even if they had made chance statements to the contrary. The latter mistake is much more serious than the former, he thought, because death is irrevocable. If someone continues living, he said, even though as a vegetable, and then later, more conclusive evidence is discovered indicating that he would have preferred to die, he can be allowed to die then, and little is lost. But if he is allowed to die immediately, and the opposite evidence is discovered, then that is a true tragedy, because the mistake cannot be corrected.

This curious argument obviously depends on a hidden assumption about what is in fact in such a patient's interests. Rehnquist assumes that no serious harm is done in keeping alive someone who would have wanted to die; without that assumption, his premise—that caution lies on the side of not terminating life support—is plainly invalid. If we were to assume (as a great many people do) that it is very harmful for someone to live on for years in a vegetative state, his argument fails. (The possibility that adequate evidence of a wish to die might be discovered later—that parents and friends had overlooked something as convincing as a living will, for example—is remote. Even if, by some freak happenstance, such evidence did turn up, the patient would still have suffered the significant damage of living for years in a state he was desperate to avoid.)

Something like Rehnquist's assumption is shared by people who argue that doctors should never be allowed to disconnect life-support systems because there is always *some* chance, however remote, of a miraculous recovery. Obviously, medical procedures should be de-signed to minimize the likelihood that a patient will be allowed to die when there is any realistic medical ground at all for supposing that he might return to consciousness and competence. But the common view that even the faintest theoretical chance of a recovery justifies keeping human vegetables alive indefinitely presupposes, as Rehnquist's argu-ment did, that staying alive indefinitely cannot itself be against the patient's interests. If we accept the possibility that it may be, then we can no longer rely on a bare mathematical possibility of recovery as an excuse for not doing what the patient himself probably wanted. Another familiar argument against legalizing euthanasia for conscious people—that old people are vulnerable and can sometimes be pressured into asking to die—makes the same mistake: it fails to recognize that forcing people to live who genuinely want to die causes serious damage to them. So does the even more familiar "slippery slope" argument: that legaliz-ing euthanasia even in carefully limited cases makes it more likely that it will later be legalized in other, more doubtful, cases as well, and that the process may end in Nazi eugenics. That argument also loses its bite once we understand that legalizing *no* euthanasia is itself harmful to many people; then we realize that doing our best to draw and maintain a defensible line, acknowledging and trying to guard against the risk that others will draw the line differently in the future, is better than abandoning those people altogether. There are dangers both in legalizing and refusing to legalize; the rival dangers must be balanced, and neither should be ignored.

Rehnquist had a further argument justifying Missouri's strict burden of proof, an argument that does not depend on any hidden assumption about what is in the best interests of any patient. He said that the Missouri rule was justified even if it worked against Nancy Cruzan's interests because Missouri has a right to preserve human life. That argument assumes that a state has a detached interest in preserving human life, whatever the patient's own interests might be; it assumes that a state may require that people be kept alive out of respect for the intrinsic value or sanctity of life.

That argument, if sound, would justify Missouri's refusing to honor any evidence of the patient's past wish not to be kept alive, even a flawlessly executed living will. Justice Scalia said as much, even more dramatically, in his concurring opinion: a state has the constitutional power to prohibit suicide in any circumstance, he said, even for someone dying in terrible pain who would plainly be better off dead, because it has the power to protect human life for its own sake. A state need not honor a living will if it has decided that allowing people to die is an insult to life's sanctity.

Justice Scalia was apparently mistaken in his judgment about the effect of the Court's decision in the *Cruzan* case. Most commentators have concluded, after studying all the opinions the various justices wrote in the case, that its effect was to affirm some constitutional right to die, even though the actual ruling upheld the power of a state to impose severe restrictions on the way in which that right must be exercised. Still, Rehnquist's assumption—that a state may properly act to protect human life for its own sake—was an important part of his opinion, in which two other justices joined. So all three of the distinct issues in the euthanasia controversy—the autonomy of the patient, the patient's best interests, and the independent and perhaps competing inherent value of human life itself—played an important though somewhat confused part in the Supreme Court's decision of this historic case.

DEATH AND LIFE

It is a platitude that we live our whole lives in the shadow of death; it is also true that we die in the shadow of our whole lives. Death's central horror is oblivion—the terrifying, absolute dying of the light. But oblivion is not all there is to death; if it were, people would not worry so much about whether their technical, biological lives continue after they have become unconscious and the void has begun, after the light is already dead forever. Death has dominion because it is not only the start of nothing but the end of everything, and how we think and talk about dying—the emphasis we put on dying with "dignity"—shows how important it is that life ends *appropriately,* that death keeps faith with the way we want to have lived.

We cannot understand what death means to people—why some would rather be dead than existing permanently sedated or incompetent, why others would want to "fight on" even in terrible pain or even when they are unconscious and cannot savor the fight; why so few people think that whether they live or die once they fall permanently unconscious does not matter to them at all—we cannot understand any of this, or much else that people feel about death, unless we turn away from death for a while and back to life.

In almost every case, someone who is permanently unconscious or incompetent was not born into that condition: the tragedy lies at the end of a life that someone has led in earnest. When we ask what would be best for him, we are not judging only his future and ignoring his past. We worry about the effect of his life's last stage on the character of his life as a whole, as we might worry about the effect of a play's last scene or a poem's last stanza on the entire creative work. That is the familiar but mysterious worry we must now try to analyze.

So far as we know, Socrates was the first philosopher to make prominent the question of how to live well. But both before and after him, philosophers, moralists, priests, prophets, novelists, psychiatrists, poets, and busybodies have also speculated about the circumstances and signs of a good life, about what makes one life successful or meaningful or enviable and another impoverished or wasted or pointless. Those wise and foolish people have given very different answers. Socrates said that a good life consists in self-knowledge, Aristotle that it consists in the perfection of skill and talent, the Catholic philosophers that it consists in devotion and the love of God, Hume in the satisfaction of what one genuinely and naturally wants, Bentham in as much pleasure as possible. Others have taken a more negative view of the idea of a good life. Skeptics say that the very idea that one life could really be any better than another is sanctimonious nonsense.

Few of us are skeptical in that way, but most of us have only ramshackle ideas, not philosophical theories, about what kinds of lives are good ones. We almost all think material comfort well worth having. Dedicated ascetics aside, and all else equal, we consider a life of pain or poverty much worse than a comfortable one, and many people's picture of the most satisfactory life for them includes very great wealth. But even for them, material comfort is only part of the story. For many people, for example, achievement also plays an important part. We want (as people often say) to *do* something with our lives, to leave the world a better place for our having been in it. There are grand forms of that ambition: people aim to invent or discover something marvelous, write great music or poetry or philosophy, liberate a nation or make one just. There are less grand forms: many people want nothing more than to play their part well in a cooperative enterprise like a family or a farm or a team, to have contributed to something important rather than to have done it all themselves. Some people think "experience" an important component in a good life: they want to have traveled, perhaps to exotic places, to have lived in different ways, to have tried everything. Others take pride in almost the opposite: in rootedness, in belonging to a place, and to national or ethnic or religious traditions into which they believe they have been born, traditions of faith or humor or food or culture. Almost everyone thinks family and friends are an important part of a good life: that a life without special and intense concerns for particular people would lack something crucial.

Most of these different ideas about a good life we hold intuitively and in the background; we do not reexamine them except in moments of special crisis or drama. But these background ideas are always there, guiding decisions and choices that may seem to us automatic, and accounting for at least some part of the exhilaration or boredom or shame or sadness we find ourselves feeling, from time to time, about the way our lives are going. It is absolutely crucial to notice, however, that these various opinions and convictions, however inarticulate or submerged, are *critical* in the sense that they concern what makes a life successful rather than unsuccessful—when someone has made something of his life, not just wasted it. They are not, that is, opinions only about how to make life pleasant or enjoyable minute by minute, day by day.

I want to capture that difference by pointing out a distinction between two kinds of reasons people have for wanting their lives to go one way rather than another. First, everyone has what I shall call *experiential* interests. We all do things because we like the experience of doing them: playing softball, perhaps, or cooking or eating well, or watching football, or seeing *Casablanca* for the twelfth time, or walking in the woods in October, or listening to *The Marriage of Figaro*, or sailing fast just off the wind, or just working hard at something. Pleasures like these are essential to a good life—a life with nothing that is marvelous only because of how it feels would be not pure but preposterous. But the value of these experiences, judged one by one, depends precisely on the fact that we do find them pleasurable or exciting *as experiences*. People who do not enjoy an activity I do—who are bored by my enthusiasm for televised football, for example—are not making a *mistake;* their lives are not worse for not sharing my tastes. My own life would not be worse, or defective in some way, if I found watching football as unpleasant as my wife does. Football—and working hard and eating well—seem good to me, add something to my life, because and when they feel good.

Of course, a great many things are bad as experiences, too: pain, nausea, and listening to most politicians. We take pains to avoid these experiences, and sometimes we dread them. But we do not disapprove of people, if there are any, who don't much mind dental pain or listening to politicians. Nor are these the kinds of experiences, at least within limits, that make a life as a whole worse. My life is not a worse life to have lived—I have nothing to regret, still less to take shame in—because I have suffered in the dentist's chair. That is shown, among other ways, by the fact that our attitude toward these forms of suffering is dramatically time sensitive: we are indifferent about pain we suffer in the dentist's chair once the pain is past.

But most people think that they also have what I shall call *critical* interests: interests that it does make their life genuinely better to satisfy, interests they would be mistaken, and genuinely worse off, if they did not recognize. Convictions about what helps to make a life good on the whole are convictions about those more important interests. They represent critical judgments rather than just experiential preferences. Most people enjoy and want close friendships because they believe that such friendships are good, that people *should* want them. I have many opinions about what is good for me in that critical sense. I feel that it is important that I have a close relationship with my children, for example, that I manage some success in my work, and—what I despair of achieving—that I secure some grasp, even if only desperately minimal, of the state of advanced science of my era. I do think my life would have been worse had I never understood the importance of being close to my children, for example, if I had not suffered pain at estrangements from them. Having a close relationship with my children is not important just because I happen to want the experience; on the contrary, I believe a life without wanting it would be a much worse one.[21]

I do not mean that experiential interests are characteristically frivolous or critical interests inevitably profound. There is nothing frivolous about Mozart or particularly profound about my laughable attempts to understand cosmology. Nor am I trying to contrast supposedly elite, reflective, philosophical lives with more ordinary or mundane ones. I mean to identify what is elite, in the sense of aspirational, within most lives. Nor am I saying that people who do not consciously reflect on how their lives are going as a whole, who just get on with living, taking things as they come, are defective or not living well. Lives like that can be extremely attractive, even enviable, and they are plainly preferable to lives ruined by detailed planning and constant trial-balance-sheet assessments of progress. I do believe, however, that even people whose lives feel unplanned are nevertheless often guided by a sense of the general style of life they think appropriate, of what choices strike them as not only good at the moment but in character for them.

We need the distinction between experiential and critical interests to understand many of our convictions about how people should be treated. We need it, for example, to explain why we think that mind-changing drugs or other forms of brainwashing that produce long-lasting pleasure and contentment are not in their victims' interests: we mean they are not in their *critical* interests. Understanding the difference between experiential and critical interests is also essential to understanding a certain kind of tragedy, in life as well as in fiction. It is tragic when someone looks back on his life, near the end, and finds it wasted, empty of any real significance, with nothing in which he can take any pride at all. The classic literary exposition of that sense of waste is Tolstoy's account of the death of Ivan Ilyich.

> Worse than his physical sufferings were his mental sufferings, which were his chief torture. . . . "What if in reality my whole life has been wrong?" It occurred to him that what had appeared utterly impossible the night before—that he had not lived his life as he should have done—might after all be true. It struck him that those scarcely detected inclinations of his to fight against what the most highly placed people regarded as good, those scarcely noticeable impulses which he had immediately suppressed, might have been the real thing and all the rest false. And his professional duties, and his ordering of his life, and his family, and all his social and official interests might all have been false. He tried to defend it all to himself. And suddenly he realized the weakness of what he was defending. There was nothing to defend. "But if that is so," he said to himself, "and I am leaving this life with the consciousness that I have lost all that was given me and there's no putting it right— what then?"[22]

We cannot explain that terrible kind of regret if we think, as some philosophers have, that the only interests people have are experiential ones. The converted hedonist, or man of property and power, who enjoyed his life fully day by day may now regret the enjoyment, too. He may say that his pleasure was superficial or thin or incomplete. But that is a critical judgment made now, in retrospect, from the perspective of his new convictions, not a new discovery about the actual felt quality of the experiences he had then.

It is not at all puzzling why we all care about our experiential interests. Nothing is more natural than any animal's desire to put itself in the way of pleasure and out of the way of pain. If lying in the sun or listening to music gives us great pleasure, and dental drills and electrical shocks and nausea are very disagreeable, then it is hardly surprising that we seek out the former and try to avoid the latter. But it might seem puzzling why people should also care about their critical interests or even have the concept of such interests. Why should Ivan Ilyich, who in the past had exactly what gave him pleasure, despair at the end of his life that he has made a mistake, that he should have chosen a radically different kind of life? Why should some people—saints and some artists—deliberately choose lives of discomfort, even poverty, in order to do something they regard as more valuable than simple enjoyment? Why should people care about not "wasting" their lives? Why should they care about anything except having as good a time as possible?

Jeremy Bentham and other utilitarian philosophers denied that people ever do care about anything else. Bentham might have said that Ivan Ilyich was really worried that he might have had even more pleasure than he did if he had devoted himself less to profit and status. But that is a very poor account of the regret people feel when they think they have led the wrong kind of life. They feel not that they could have had a more enjoyable time leading a different life but that having a good time is not, after all, as important as they thought. They want, suddenly, to have made something, or contributed to something, or helped someone, or been closer to more people, not just because these were missed opportunities for more pleasure but because they are important in themselves. And even people who do regret missed opportunities for pleasure do so as *critical* hedonists: they believe that the experience of pleasure is a kind of achievement.

Can we explain critical interests? I do not mean a Darwinian theory that explains, if any evolutionary account can explain, why the species developed the beliefs that some lives are more worth living than others and that it is a matter for regret when the wrong life has been lived, even if it was a pleasant one. Nor do I mean a biological account that explains how people are genetically disposed to these ideas, or a social-scientific one that shows how these ideas are carried in or restricted by culture. We need an *intellectual* explanation of critical interests, so that we may better understand these ideas from the inside, understand introspectively how they connect with other large beliefs we have about life and death and why human life has intrinsic value.

Is it merely a brute fact that some of us happen to want friendship or achievement for its own sake, not just as a pleasurable experience? That we sometimes change our minds about what we want for its own sake, and then regret our previous choices? That flat account greatly understates the psychological complexity of the matter, viewed from the inside, because it leaves mysterious why we should be *puzzled* about what kind of life is best for us. And puzzled we often are.

Think of someone—yourself, if you can—facing an important self-defining decision. If you are a woman with a chance to begin a demanding career that intrigues you, but only by sacrificing time with your young children, which choice do you make? Or, if you are a law-school graduate with an offer from an established firm, do you reject it for a less challenging offer that is more likely—but by no means certain—to lead to a political career later? Or, if you are a Jew, should you abandon your comfortable life in Los Angeles and emigrate to Israel to identify yourself firmly with that nation's fate?

People do not make momentous decisions like these by trying to predict how much pleasure each choice might bring them. We sometimes say that we discover our own identities through such decisions. But we do not mean that we discover how we have already been wired, as, we might say, a computer "discovers" its own programming. We can search our past for clues about what satisfies us or makes us happy, but life-shaping decisions are also occasions for imaginative fantasy and, above all, for commitment. People are often deeply uncertain about which decision is right: we shift and change before we settle, if we ever do, into the comfort of firm conviction. Some of us believe that each person's nature is fixed by biology or society, that whatever ambitions we have are built into us by genetics or culture. But even so, our built-in ambitions are more complex and abstract than merely to lead one particular kind of life or another. We have the abstract ambition to lead a *good* life, and we worry, some of us all our lives, about what that is.

People think it important not just that their life contain a variety of the right experiences, achievements, and connections, but that it have a structure that expresses a coherent choice among these—for some, that it display a steady, self-defining commitment to a vision of character or achievement that the life as a whole, seen as an integral creative narrative, illustrates and expresses. Of course, this ideal of integrity does not itself define a way to live: it presupposes substantive convictions. No one who thinks his life has been based on mistake will take comfort from seeing that it was based on only one mistake. But integrity nevertheless has great independent importance in life as it does in art and science. We admire the person who does it his way, even if that is very much not our way. Integrity is closely connected to dignity, moreover: we think that someone who acts out of character, for gain or to avoid trouble, has insufficient respect for himself.[23]

Recognizing the independent importance of integrity helps us to understand much that would otherwise be puzzling in the idea of critical interests. When we reflect about what makes a person's life good, we are torn between what seem to be antagonistic beliefs. On the one hand, a person's critical interests seem very much to depend on his personality. The commitment someone makes to a given conception of virtue or achievement—to his Jewish roots, for example—is part of what makes a life organized around that commitment right for him. But that appealing idea is hard to reconcile with an even more fundamental conviction we also have—that a person's thinking a given choice right for him does not make it so, that the sometimes agonized process of decision is a process of judgment, not just choice, that it may go wrong, that one may be *mistaken* about what is really important in life. That belief is indispensable to the basic distinction between critical and experiential interests, and to the challenge and tragedy most people feel. It is at the very foundation of our ethical lives.

The first of these two ideas—that our critical interests are personal— seems to pull us toward the annihilating idea that critical interests are only subjective, only matters of how we feel. The second seems to pull us toward the equally unacceptable idea that everyone's critical interests are the same, over all history, that there is only one truly best way for anyone to live. The remedy is to embrace neither of these extreme positions but instead to remind ourselves of how it feels to believe that a given life is the right one. We feel this not as a discovery of a timeless formula, good for all times and places, but as a direct response to our own specific circumstances of place, culture, and capacity. The response, however, includes conviction: it is important both that we find a life *good* and that we *find* it good. Integrity plays two parts in this story: it is the mark of conviction, of commitment, not just past choice; it also reflects investment, the idea that the value of a life lies in part *in* its integrity, so that its having already been established as one kind of life argues, though of course far from conclusively, that it should go on being that kind of life.

As I said, some philosophers are deeply skeptical about the whole idea that people have critical interests, that there is any inherent difference between a "good" or a "bad" life beyond how pleasant or enjoyable it is. They say that there is nothing for people to be agonized about, that Ivan Ilyich was silly or demented, that the illusion of critical interests is just what the Oxford biologist Richard Dawkins has called religion—a computer virus passed from one human brain to another down many centuries[24]—that from the point of view of the universe, it makes no difference whatsoever how people live. My purpose, here as throughout this book, is not to defend the various ethical or religious convictions I am describing from skeptical attacks of this sort but to observe how widespread and powerful these convictions are, and how pervasive an influence they have over our various moral and political beliefs, including those about abortion and euthanasia.

But it might be helpful to distinguish two forms the skeptical attack takes, because the difference is important. The first we might call an external form. It purports to criticize the way people think about their lives on the basis of some general philosophical position about metaphysics or the ultimate nature of reality. The British philosopher John Mackie, for example, said that there could not be objective values in the universe, because they would be such "queer" kinds of entities.[25] That form of skepticism is disengaged from the human enterprise it criticizes: it bases its criticism on an a priori and wholly general assumption about the kinds of entity or truth or knowledge that are metaphysically possible. It aims to change not how we lead our lives but the philosophical claims we make. External skepticism always fails, in my view, because it cannot characterize the external claims it criticizes, except in uncashable metaphors about "queer" entities and the like.[26] But in any case, external skepticism is unthreatening, because we can embrace it, if we wish, and continue to live and feel as we have before.

The second kind of skepticism—internal skepticism—is a very different matter. It is the disabling substantive skepticism of the person who is suddenly gripped by the implications, as he thinks, of discovering that there is no God; or of someone like Goncharov's gray hero, Oblomov, who suddenly sees no point in anything, no reason to leave his bed; or of most of us, sometime, in the black hours, when the idea that it is important how we live—when anyway we will soon be dead— suddenly seems irretrievably preposterous. This skepticism is dangerous exactly because it plays the same structuring role for people in its grip, except in a draining, negative way, that positive convictions play for those who embrace them.

The philosophical standing of internal skepticism is no different from that of the positive convictions it challenges; it, too, claims authority only on the basis of what we cannot but think when we ask the questions it answers. If it is true, it is true in exactly the same way, and with no more independent foundation in an objective world, than the positive opinions it mocks. That is why it is so dangerous. There is no answer to internal skepticism once it has taken hold except to test it again by measuring the conviction it finally brings. Most people then find that it has loosened its grip.[27]

DEATH'S MEANING

We have explored the complex idea of critical interests because we cannot think about whether death is in someone's best interests unless we understand this dimension of the interests people have. It would be easy to decide whether it was in the best interests of Lillian Boyes or Nancy Cruzan or Janet Adkins to live or die if we had only their experiential interests in mind. Lillian Boyes had only pain to look forward to, and no pleasurable experiences that could possibly compensate for its experiential horror, so it was plainly in her interests, measured that way, to die as soon as possible. Nancy Cruzan would never have any experience, good or bad, again, so her experiential interests would not be affected by a decision either way. Janet Adkins probably had more to gain in pleasant experience by living on until a natural death—she would have remained capable of simple pleasures for several years, and many demented people do not suffer at all—so she was wrong to kill herself when she did if her experiential life was all that mattered.

Several opinions in the House of Lords decision in the *Bland* case I mentioned simply assumed that only experiential interests can matter, at least legally, and therefore had no difficulty in deciding that it could be neither in *nor* against Anthony Bland's interests that his life support be discontinued. Lord Mustill, for example, considered and rejected the argument that it was against Bland's interests that his body was full of tubes to no point or that his family's happy recollections of him were being replaced by horrific ones or that his situation was causing them great misery; that cannot be so, Mustill said, because "he does not know what is happening to his body and cannot be affronted by it; he does not know of his family's continuing sorrow. . . . The distressing truth which must not be shirked is that [discontinuing life support] is not in the best interests of Anthony Bland, for he has no best interests of any kind."[28]

If we accept this view that only experiential interests count, we can make no sense of the widespread, near universal, view I described: that decisions like those we have been reviewing are often personally problematic and racking. We agonize about these decisions, for ourselves when we are contemplating living wills, or for relatives and friends, only or mainly because we take our and their critical interests into account. We must therefore begin by asking: how does it matter to the critical success of our whole life how we die? We should distinguish between two different ways that it might matter: because death is the far boundary of life, and every part of our life, including the very last, is important; and because death is special, a peculiarly significant event in the narrative of our lives, like the final scene of a play, with everything about it intensified, under a special spotlight. In the first sense, when we die is important because of what will happen to us if we die later; in the second, how we die matters because it is how we *die*.

Let us begin with the first, less theatrical, of these ideas. Sometimes people want to live on, even though in pain or dreadfully crippled, in order to do something they believe important to have done. They want to finish a job, for example, or to learn something they have always wanted to know. Gareth Evans, a brilliant philosopher who died of cancer at the age of thirty-four, struggled to work on his unfinished manuscript as long as medicine could keep him in a condition in which he could work at all.[29] Many people want to live on, as long as they can, for a more general reason: so long as they have any sense at all, they think, just being alive is *something*. Though Philip Roth had persuaded his eighty-six-year-old father to sign a living will, he hesitated when his father was dying and the doctors asked whether Roth wanted him put on a respirator. Roth thought, "How could I take it on myself to decide that my father should be finished with life, life which is ours to know just once?"[30]

On the other hand, people often think they have strong reasons of a comparable kind for *not* staying alive. The badness of the experiences that lie ahead is one: terrible pain or constant nausea or the horror of intubation or the confusions of sedation. When Roth thought about the misery to come, he whispered, "Dad, I'm going to have to let you go." But people's reasons for wanting to die include critical reasons as well; many people, as I said, think it undignified or bad in some other way to live under certain conditions, however they might feel if they feel at all. Many people do not want to be remembered living in those circumstances; others think it degrading to be wholly dependent, or to be the object of continuing anguish. These feelings are often expressed as a distaste for causing trouble, pain, or expense to others, but the aversion is not fully captured in that other-regarding preference. It may be just as strong when the burden of physical care is imposed on professionals whose career is precisely in providing such care, and when the financial burden falls on a public eager to bear it. At least part of what people fear about dependence is its impact not on those responsible for their care, but on their own dignity.

I must emphasize that this is *not* a belief that every kind of dependent life under severe handicaps is not worth living. That belief is disproved not only by dramatic examples, like the brilliant life of Stephen Hawking, the almost wholly paralyzed cosmologist, but by the millions of ordinary people throughout the world who lead engaged, valuable lives in spite of appalling handicaps and dependencies. It is, however, plausible, and to many people compelling, that total dependence is in itself a very bad thing, quite apart from the pain or discomfort it often but not invariably entails. Total or near-total dependence with nothing positive to redeem it may seem not only to add nothing to the overall quality of a life but to take something important from it. That seems especially true when there is no possibility even of understanding that care has been given, or of being grateful for it. Sunny von Bulow still lies wholly unconscious in a hospital room in Manhattan; every day she is turned and groomed by people willing and paid to do it. She will never respond in any way to that care. It would not have been odd for her to think, before she fell into her coma, that this kind of pointless solicitude was insulting, itself an affront to her dignity.

When patients remain conscious, their sense of integrity and of the coherence of their lives crucially affects their judgment about whether it is in their best interests to continue to live. Athletes, or others whose physical activity was at the center of their self-conception, are more likely to find a paraplegic's life intolerable. When Nancy B., the Canadian woman who won the right to have her respirator turned off, said that all she had in her life was television, she was saying not that watching television was painful, but that a wholly passive life, which watching television had come to symbolize, was worse than none. For such people, a life without the power of motion is unacceptable, not for reasons explicable in experiential terms, but because it is stunningly inadequate to the conception of self around which their own lives have so far been constructed. Adding decades of immobility to a life formerly organized around action will for them leave a narrative wreck, with no structure or sense, a life worse than one that ends when its activity ends.

Others will have radically different senses of self, of what has been critically important to their own lives. Many people, for example, would want to live on, almost no matter how horrible their circumstances, so long as they were able to read, or understand if read to them, the next day's newspaper. They would want to hear as many chapters as possible of the many thousands of stories about science and culture and politics and society that they had been following all their lives. People who embrace that newspaper test have assumed, and cannot easily disown, that part of the point of living is to know and care how things are turning out.

So people's views about how to live color their convictions about when to die, and the impact is intensified when it engages the second way in which people think death is important. There is no doubt that most people treat the manner of their deaths as of special, symbolic importance: they want their deaths, if possible, to express and in that way vividly to confirm the values they believe most important to their lives. That ancient hope is a recurrent theme of Shakespearean drama. (Siward, for example, learning that Macbeth has killed Young Siward at Dunsinane in that poor boy's first battle, says: "Had I as many sons as I have hairs, I would not wish them to a fairer death.") When the great British political columnist Peter Jenkins realized on his deathbed that any conversation might be his last, he insisted on talking, though his nurses warned him not to, and on talking about political philosophy and the latest threats to free speech.

The idea of a good (or less bad) death is not exhausted by how one dies—whether in battle or in bed—but includes timing as well. It explains the premium people often put on living to "see" some particular event, after which the idea of their own death seems less tragic to them. A woman dying of cancer, whose life can be prolonged though only in great pain, might think she had good reason to live until the birth of an expected grandchild, or a long-awaited graduation, or some other family milestone. The aim of living not just until, but actually for, an event has very great expressive power. It confirms, in a fashion much exploited by novelists and dramatists, the critical importance of the values it identifies to the patient's sense of his own integrity, to the special character of his life. If his has been a life rooted in family, if he has counted, as among the high peaks of his life, family holidays and congresses and celebrations, then stretching his life to include one more such event does not merely add to a long list of occasions and successes. Treating the next one as salient for death confirms the importance of them all.

Many people have a parallel reason for wanting to die if an unconscious, vegetable life were all that remained. For some, this is an understandable worry about how they will be remembered. But for most, it is a more abstract and self-directed concern that their death, whatever else it is like, express their conviction that life has had value because of what life made it possible for them to do and feel. They are horrified that their death might express, instead, the opposite idea, which they detest as a perversion: that mere biological life—just hanging on—has independent value. Nietzsche said, "In a certain state it is indecent to live longer. To go on vegetating in cowardly dependence on physicians and machinations, after the meaning of life, the right to life, has been lost, that ought to prompt a profound contempt in society." He said he wanted "to die proudly when it is no longer possible to live proudly."[31] That concern might make no sense for unconscious patients in a world where everyone treated the onset of permanent unconsciousness as itself the event of death, the final curtain after which nothing else is part of the story. But in such a world, no one would be kept alive in permanent unconsciousness anyway. No one would need worry, as many people in our world do, that others will feed or care for his vegetating body with what he believes the ultimate insult: the conviction that they do it for *him*.

The relatives I mentioned, who visit permanently unconscious patients regularly, and feel uncomfortable or anxious when they cannot, do not necessarily have that conviction. They come because they cannot bear not to see and touch someone they love so long as that is possible and not bad for him, and because they think that closing the final door before he is biologically dead and buried or cremated—before they can *mourn* him—would be a terrible betrayal, a declaration of indifference rather than the intense concern they still feel. There is no contradiction, but great force and sense, in the views of parents who fight, in court if necessary, to have life support terminated but who will not leave their child's side until it is. But some people do believe—as Mr. Wanglie believed about his wife—that it *is* in a patient's best interests to be kept alive as long as possible, even in an unconscious state. For such people, contemplating themselves in that position, integrity delivers a very different command. The struggle to stay alive, no matter how hopeless or how thin the life, expresses a virtue central to *their* lives, the virtue of defiance in the face of inevitable death. It is not just a matter of taste on which people happen to divide, as they divide about surfing or soccer. None of us wants to end our lives out of character.

Now we can better answer the question of why people think what they do about death, and why they differ so dramatically. Whether it is in someone's best interests that his life end in one way rather than another depends on so much else that is special about him—about the shape and character of his life and his own sense of his integrity and critical interests—that no uniform collective decision can possibly hope to serve everyone even decently. So we have that reason of beneficence, as well as reasons of autonomy, why the state should not impose some uniform, general view by way of sovereign law but should encourage people to make provision for their future care themselves, as best they can, and why if they have made no provision the law should so far as possible leave decisions in the hands of their relatives or other people close to them whose sense of their best interests—shaped by intimate knowledge of everything that makes up where their best interests lie—is likely to be much sounder than some universal, theoretical, abstract judgment born in the stony halls where interest groups maneuver and political deals are done.

SANCTITY AND SELF-INTEREST

Let us turn now to what I said was a separate issue: how far euthanasia in its various forms—suicide, assisting suicide, or withholding medical treatment or life support—may be wrong even if it *is* in a patient's best interests. In discussing abortion, I defended a particular understanding of the sanctity of life: that once a human life has begun, it is a waste—an inherently bad event—when the investment in that life is wasted. I distinguished between two different dimensions of the investment in a human life that a decision for death might be thought to waste—what I called the natural and the human dimensions—and I used that distinction to construct a distinctly conservative view about abortion: that the natural investment in a human life is dominantly more important than the human investment, and that choosing premature death is therefore the greatest possible insult to life's sacred value. We can use the same distinction to construct a distinctly conservative view about euthanasia. If we adopt the view congenial to many religious traditions, that nature's investment in a human life has been frustrated whenever someone dies who could be kept technically alive longer, then any human intervention—injecting a lethal drug into someone dying of a painful cancer or withdrawing life support from a person in a persistent vegetative state— cheats nature, and if the natural investment, understood in that way, dominates the sanctity of life, then euthanasia always insults that value. That argument, I believe, forms the most powerful basis for the strong conservative opposition to all forms of euthanasia throughout the world. It is not, of course, the only argument: people worry about practical and administrative issues, and they are terrified lest they license the death of someone who might have been restored to a genuine life. But the instinct that deliberate death is a savage insult to the instrinsic value of life, even when it is in the patient's interest, is the deepest, most important part of the conservative revulsion against euthanasia. Justices Rehnquist and Scalia, as we saw, both relied on that instinct in their decisions in the *Cruzan* case.

The instinct is central to many religious traditions. In its most straightforward formulation, as we saw, the appeal to the sanctity of life uses the image of property: a person's life belongs not to him but to God. But some religious leaders and scholars have put the point more formally: by distinguishing, as I have, between the question of when keeping someone alive is good for him and when it is good because it respects a value he embodies. Richard Neuhaus, for example, in an influential article in *Commentary*, aligned himself with critics of "rational quality-of-life measurement" who contend "that the question whether life is good for the person gets things backwards." "The argument of the critics," he said, "is that life is a good *of* the person."[32] An article on Jewish views of euthanasia said, "According to Jewish law, life is to be preserved, even at great cost. Each moment of human life is considered to be intrinsically sacred. Preserving life supersedes living the 'good life.'"[33]

We know, however, that the idea that human life is sacred or inviolable is both more complex, and more open to different and competing interpretations, than its religious use sometimes acknowledges, and we can construct other interpretations of that idea that ground more liberal attitudes toward euthanasia. Even people who accept the dominance of the natural investment in life (and who hold very conservative views about abortion for that reason) may nevertheless disagree that euthanasia inevitably frustrates nature. They may plausibly believe that prolonging the life of a patient who is riddled with disease or no longer conscious does nothing to help realize the natural wonder of a human life, that nature's purposes are not served when plastic, suction, and chemistry keep a heart beating in a lifeless, mindless body, a heart that nature, on its own, would have stilled.

That is a less conservative view because it denies that biological death always cheats nature. But suppose we also deny that the natural contribution to life is dominant, and insist that the human contribution is important as well, and that it, too, should not be frustrated or wasted. Then we will have a much stronger reason for denying that euthanasia always insults the sanctity of life: we will then insist that sometimes euthanasia *supports* that value. In order to see this, we must now elaborate—and qualify—a distinction that I have emphasized throughout this book: the distinction between the question of what acts or events are in some creature's interests and the question of what acts or events respect the sanctity of that creature's life. The idea I introduced in this chapter—that people have critical as well as experiential interests—complicates that distinction.

Anyone who believes in the sanctity of human life believes that once a human life has begun it matters, intrinsically, that that life go well, that the investment it represents be realized rather than frustrated. Someone's convictions about his own critical interests are opinions about what it means for his *own* human life to go well, and these convictions can therefore best be understood as a special application of his general commitment to the sanctity of life. He is eager to make something of his own life, not simply to enjoy it; he treats his own life as something sacred for which *he* is responsible, something *he* must not waste. He thinks it intrinsically important that he live well, and with integrity. That objective, intrinsic importance is just what the internal form of skepticism threatens; that is why it sometimes seems so irresistible.

Someone who thinks his own life would go worse if he lingered near death on a dozen machines for weeks or stayed biologically alive for years as a vegetable believes that he is showing more respect for the human contribution to the sanctity of his life if he makes arrangements in advance to avoid that, and that others show more respect for his life if they avoid it for him. We cannot sensibly argue that he must sacrifice his own interests out of respect for the inviolability of human life. That begs the question, because he thinks dying is the best way to respect that value. So the appeal to the sanctity of life raises here the same crucial political and constitutional issue that it raises about abortion. Once again the critical question is whether a decent society will choose coercion or responsibility, whether it will seek to impose a collective judgment on matters of the most profound spiritual character on everyone, or whether it will allow and ask its citizens to make the most central, personality-defining judgments about their own lives for themselves.

I have not defended any detailed legal scheme for deciding when doctors may hasten the death of patients who understandably want to die or of unconscious patients who cannot make that choice. My main concern has been to understand why people hold the apparently mysterious opinions they do about their own deaths, and to show what is really at stake in the heated public discussion of euthanasia. Part of the public discussion, as I have emphasized, centers on difficult and important administrative questions I have not considered. But much of it concerns moral and ethical issues, and that part of the debate has been seriously compromised by two misunderstandings that we have noticed but which it would be wise to mention again by way of summary.

The first is a confusion about the character of the interests people have in when and how they die. Many arguments against euthanasia presuppose that patients who are not suffering great pain, including patients who are permanently unconscious, cannot be significantly harmed by being kept alive. That assumption underlies, as we saw, the procedural claim that relatives urging that an unconscious patient would have wanted to die must meet an especially severe standard of proof, the "slippery slope" argument that the law should license no euthanasia because it may end by licensing too much, and the claim that doctors will be corrupted and their sense of humanity dulled if they are asked and allowed to kill. When we understand how and why people care about their deaths, we see that the assumption on which each of these arguments depends is fallacious and dangerous.

The second misunderstanding arises from a misapprehension about an idea we have been studying throughout this book and which we just considered again: the sanctity of life. It is widely supposed that active euthanasia—doctors killing patients who beg to die—is always offensive to that value, and should be prohibited for that reason. But the question posed by euthanasia is not whether the sanctity of life should yield to some other value, like humanity or compassion, but how life's sanctity should be understood and respected. The great moral issues of abortion and euthanasia, which bracket life in earnest, have a similar structure. Each involves decisions not just about the rights and interests of particular people, but about the intrinsic, cosmic importance of human life itself. In each case, opinions divide not because some people have contempt for values that others cherish, but, on the contrary, because the values in question are at the center of everyone's lives, and no one can treat them as trivial enough to accept other people's orders about what they mean. Making someone die in a way that others approve, but he believes a horrifying contradiction of his life, is a devastating, odious form of tyranny.

8

LIFE PAST
REASON

We turn finally to what might be the saddest of the tragedies we have been reviewing. We must consider the autonomy and best interests of people who suffer from serious and permanent dementia, and what the proper respect for the intrinsic value of *their* lives requires. The most important cause of dementia is Alzheimer's disease, a progressive disease of the brain named after a German psychiatrist and neuropathologist, Alois Alzheimer, who first identified and described it in 1906. Patients in the late stages of this disease have lost substantially all memory of their earlier lives and cannot, except periodically and in only a fragmented way, recognize or respond to other people, even those to whom they were formerly close. They may be incapable of saying more than a word or two. They are often incontinent, fall frequently, or are unable to walk at all. They are incapable of sustaining plans or projects or desires of even a very simple structure. They express wishes and desires, but these change rapidly and often show very little continuity even over periods of days or hours.

Alzheimer's is a disease of physiological deterioration. Nerve terminals of the brain degenerate into a matted plaque of fibrous material. Though researchers have expressed some hope that treatment can be developed to slow that degeneration,[1] no such treatment has yet been established, and there is apparently little prospect of dramatically reversing very advanced brain deterioration. A specialist describes the degeneration as occurring "gradually and inexorably, usually leading to death in a severely debilitated, immobile state between four and twelve years after onset."[2] But according to the U.S. Office of Technology Assessment, death may be delayed for as long as twenty-five years.[3]

Our discussion will focus only on the disease's late stages. I shall not consider, except in passing, the present structure of legal rights and other provisions for demented or mentally incapacitated people, or the present practices of doctors and other custodians or officials who are charged with their care. Nor shall I attempt any report of the recent research into genetic and other features of such diseases, or into their diagnosis, prognosis, or treatment. All these are the subjects of a full literature.[4] I will concentrate on the question of what moral rights people in the late stages of dementia have or retain, and of what is best for them. Is some minimum level of mental competence essential to having any rights at all? Do mentally incapacitated people have the same rights as normally competent people, or are their rights altered or diminished or extended in some way in virtue of their disease? Do they, for example, have the same rights to autonomy, to the care of their custodians, to dignity, and to a minimum level of resources as sick people of normal mental competence?

These are questions of great and growing importance. In 1990, the Alzheimer's Association estimated that four million Americans had the disease, and as Alzheimer's is a disease of the elderly, the number is expected to increase as the population continues to age. In 1989, a Harvard Medical School study estimated that 11.3 percent of the American population sixty-five or over probably had Alzheimer's. The estimated prevalence increased sharply with age: 16.4 percent of people between seventy-five and eighty-four were estimated to have Alzheimer's, and a stunning 47.55 percent of those over eighty-five.[5] (Other studies, using a narrower definition of the disease, suggest a significantly lesser but still alarming prevalence.[6]) The incidence of the disease is comparable in other countries. According to the Alzheimer's Disease Society in Britain, for example, 20 percent of people over eighty are afflicted, more than half a million people have the disease, and that figure will rise to three-quarters of a million in thirty years.[7] Alzheimer's cost is staggering, both for the community and for individuals. Dennis Selkoe, a leading expert on the disease, said in 1991, "The cost to American society for diagnosing and managing Alzheimer's disease, primarily for custodial care, is currently estimated at more than $80 billion annually."[8] In 1992, the annual cost of nursing home care in the United States for one individual with Alzheimer's ranged from $35,000 to $52,000.[9]

Each of the millions of Alzheimer's cases is horrible, for the victims and for those who love and care for them. A recent book dedicated "to everyone who gives a '36-hour day' to the care of a person with a dementing illness" describes the lives of some of these patients in chilling detail, not just in the final, immobile last stages, but along the way.

> Often, Mary was afraid, a nameless shapeless fear. . . . People came, memories came, and then they slipped away. She could not tell what was reality and what was memory of things past. . . . The tub was a mystery. From day to day she could not remember how to manage the water: sometimes it all ran away, sometimes it kept rising and rising so that she could not stop it. . . . Mary was glad when her family came to visit. Sometimes she remembered their names, more often she did not. . . . She liked it best when they just held her and loved her.

> Even though Miss Ramirez had told her sister over and over that today was the day to visit the doctor, her sister would not get into the car until she was dragged in, screaming, by two neighbors. All the way to the doctor's office she shouted for help and when she got there she tried to run away.

> Mr. Lewis suddenly burst into tears as he tried to tie his shoelaces. He threw the shoes in the wastebasket and locked himself, sobbing, in the bathroom.[10]

When Andrew Firlik was a medical student, he met a fifty-four-year-old Alzheimer's victim whom he called Margo, and he began to visit her daily in her apartment, where she was cared for by an attendant. The apartment had many locks to keep Margo from slipping out at night and wandering in the park in a nightgown, which she had done before. Margo said she knew who Firlik was each time he arrived, but she never used his name, and he suspected that this was just politeness. She said she was reading mysteries, but Firlik "noticed that her place in the book jumps randomly from day to day; dozens of pages are dog-eared at any given moment. . . . Maybe she feels good just sitting and humming to herself, rocking back and forth slowly, nodding off liberally, occasionally turning to a fresh page." Margo attended an art class for Alzheimer's victims—they all, including her, painted pretty much the same picture every time, except near the end, just before death, when the pictures became more primitive. Firlik was confused, he said, by the fact that "despite her illness, or maybe somehow because of it, Margo is undeniably one of the happiest people I have ever known." He reports, particularly, her pleasure at eating peanut-butter-and-jelly sandwiches. But, he asks, "When a person can no longer accumulate new memories as the old rapidly fade, what remains? Who is Margo?"[11]

I must now repeat an observation that I have made before: we are considering the rights and interests not of someone who has always been demented, but of someone who was competent in the past. We may therefore think of that person, in considering his rights and interests, in two different ways: as a *demented* person, emphasizing his present situation and capacities, or as a person who has *become* demented, having an eye to the course of his whole life. Does a competent person's right to autonomy include, for example, the power to dictate that life-prolonging treatment be denied him later, or that funds not be spent on maintaining him in great comfort, even if he, when demented, pleads for it? Should what is done for him then be in his contemporary best interests, to make the rest of his life as pleasant and comfortable as possible, or in the best interests of the person he has been? Suppose a demented patient insists on remaining at home, rather than living in an institution, though this would impose very great burdens on his family, and that we all agree that people lead critically better lives when they are not a serious burden to others. Is it really in his best interests, overall, to allow him to become such a burden?

A person's dignity is normally connected to his capacity for self-respect. Should we care about the dignity of a dementia patient if he himself has no sense of it? That seems to depend on whether his past dignity, as a competent person, is in some way still implicated. If it is, then we may take his former capacity for self-respect as requiring that he be treated with dignity now; we may say that dignity now is necessary to show respect for his life as a whole. Many prominent issues about the rights of the demented, then, depend on how their interests now relate to those of their past, competent selves.[12]

AUTONOMY

It is generally agreed that adult citizens of normal competence have a right to autonomy, that is, a right to make important decisions defining their own lives for themselves. Competent adults are free to make poor investments, provided others do not deceive or withhold information from them, and smokers are allowed to smoke in private, though cigarette advertising must warn them of the dangers of doing so. This autonomy is often at stake in medical contexts.[13] A Jehovah's Witness, for example, may refuse blood transfusions necessary to save his life because transfusions offend his religious convictions. A patient whose life can be saved only if his legs are amputated but who prefers to die soon than to live a life without legs is allowed to refuse the operation. American law generally recognizes a patient's right to autonomy in circumstances like those.[14] But when is that right lost? How far, for example, do mentally incapacitated people have a right to make decisions for themselves that others would deem not in their best interests?[15] Should Mary, the woman who couldn't recognize relatives or manage a tub, be allowed to spend or give away her money as she wishes, or to choose her own doctors, or to refuse prescribed medical treatment, or to decide which relative is appointed as her guardian? Should she be allowed to insist that she be cared for at home, in spite of her family's opinion that she would get better care in an institution?

There may, of course, be some other reason, beyond autonomy, for allowing Mary and other demented people to do as they please. For example, if they are prevented from doing as they wish, they may become so agitated that we do them more harm than good by opposing them, even though the decision they make is not itself in their interests. But do we have reason to respect their decision even when this is not so, even when we think it would be in their best interests, all things considered, to take some decision out of their hands?

We cannot answer that question without reflecting on the point of autonomy, that is, on the question of why we should ever respect the decisions people make when we believe that these are not in their interests. One popular answer might be called the *evidentiary* view: it holds that we should respect the decisions people make for themselves, even when we regard these decisions as imprudent, because each person generally knows what is in his own best interests better than anyone else.[16] Though we often think that someone has made a mistake in judging what is in his own interests, experience teaches us that in most cases we are wrong to think this. So we do better, in the long run, to recognize a general right to autonomy, which we always respect, than by reserving the right to interfere with other people's lives whenever we think they have made a mistake.

If we accepted this evidentiary account of autonomy, we would not extend the right of autonomy to decisions made by the seriously demented, who, having altogether lost the power to appreciate and engage in reasoning and argument, cannot possibly know what is in their own best interests as well as trained specialists, like doctors, can. In some cases, any presumption that demented people know their own interests best would be incoherent: when, for example, as is often the case, their wishes and decisions change radically from one bout of lucidity to another.

But in fact the evidentiary view of autonomy is very far from compelling. For autonomy requires us to allow someone to run his own life even when he behaves in a way that he himself would accept as not at all in his interests.[17] This is sometimes a matter of what philosophers call "weakness of the will." Many people who smoke know that smoking, all things considered, is not in their best interests, but they smoke anyway. If we believe, as we do, that respecting their autonomy means allowing them to act in this way, we cannot accept that the point of autonomy is to protect an agent's welfare. And there are more admirable reasons for acting against what one believes to be in one's own best interests. Some people refuse needed medical treatment because they believe that other people, who would then have to go without it, need it more. Such people act out of convictions we admire, even if we do not act the same way, and autonomy requires us to respect their decisions. Once again, the supposed explanation of the right to autonomy—that it promotes the welfare of people making apparently imprudent decisions—fails to account for our convictions about when people have that right. All this suggests that the point of autonomy must be, at least to some degree, independent of the claim that a person generally knows his own best interests better than anyone else. And then it would not follow, just because a demented person may well be mistaken about his own best interests, that others are entitled to decide for him. Perhaps the demented have a right to autonomy after all.

But we must try to find another, more plausible account of the point of autonomy, and ask whether the demented would have a right to autonomy according to it. The most plausible alternative emphasizes the integrity rather than the welfare of the choosing agent; the value of autonomy, on this view, derives from the capacity it protects: the capacity to express one's own character—values, commitments, convictions, and critical as well as experiential interests—in the life one leads. Recognizing an individual right of autonomy makes self-creation possible. It allows each of us to be responsible for shaping our lives according to our own coherent or incoherent—but, in any case, distinctive—personality. It allows us to lead our own lives rather than be led along them, so that each of us can be, to the extent a scheme of rights can make this possible, what we have made of ourselves. We allow someone to choose death over radical amputation or a blood transfusion, if that is his informed wish, because we acknowledge his right to a life structured by his own values.

The integrity view of autonomy does not assume that competent people have consistent values or always make consistent choices, or that they always lead structured, reflective lives. It recognizes that people often make choices that reflect weakness, indecision, caprice, or plain irrationality—that some people otherwise fanatical about their health continue to smoke, for example. Any plausible integrity-based theory of autonomy must distinguish between the general point or value of autonomy and its consequences for a particular person on a particular occasion. Autonomy encourages and protects people's general capacity to lead their lives out of a distinctive sense of their own character, a sense of what is important to and for them. Perhaps one principal value of that capacity is realized only when a life does in fact display a general, overall integrity and authenticity. But the right to autonomy protects and encourages the capacity in any event, by allowing people who have it to choose how far and in what form they will seek to realize that aim.

If we accept this integrity-based view of the importance of autonomy, our judgment about whether incapacitated patients have a right to autonomy will turn on the degree of their general capacity to lead a life in that sense. When a mildly demented person's choices are reasonably stable, reasonably continuous with the general character of his prior life, and inconsistent and self-defeating only to the rough degree that the choices of fully competent people are, he can be seen as still in charge of his life, and he has a right to autonomy for that reason. But if his choices and demands, no matter how firmly expressed, systematically or randomly contradict one another, reflecting no coherent sense of self and no discernable even short-term aims, then he has presumably lost the capacity that it is the point of autonomy to protect. Recognizing a continuing right to autonomy for him would be pointless. He has no right that his choices about a guardian (or the use of his property, or his medical treatment, or whether he remains at home) be respected for reasons of autonomy. He still has the right to beneficence, the right that decisions on these matters be made in his best interests; and his preferences may, for different reasons, be important in deciding what his best interests are. But he no longer has the right, as competent people do, himself to decide contrary to those interests.

"Competence" is sometimes used in a task-specific sense, to refer to the ability to grasp and manipulate information bearing on a given problem. Competence in that sense varies, sometimes greatly, even among ordinary, nondemented people; I may be more competent than you at making some decisions and less competent at others. The medical literature concerning surrogate decision making for the demented points out, properly, that competence in this task-specific sense is relative to the character and complexity of the decision in question.[18] A patient who is not competent to administer his complex business affairs may nevertheless be able to grasp and appreciate information bearing on whether he should remain at home or enter an institution, for example.

But competence in the sense in which it is presupposed by the right to autonomy is a very different matter. It means the more diffuse and general ability I described: the ability to act out of genuine preference or character or conviction or a sense of self. There will, of course, be hard cases in which we cannot know with any confidence whether a particular dementia patient is competent in that sense. But we must make that overall judgment, not some combination of judgments about specific task capability, in order to decide whether some mentally incapacitated patient has a right to autonomy.[19] Patients like Mary have no right that *any* decision be respected just out of concern for their autonomy. That may sound harsh, but it is no kindness to allow a person to take decisions against his own interests in order to protect a capacity he does not and cannot have.

So neither the evidentiary view of autonomy nor the more plausible integrity view recommends any right to autonomy for the seriously demented. But what about a patient's *precedent* autonomy? Suppose a patient is incompetent in the general, overall sense but that years ago, when perfectly competent, he executed a living will providing for what he plainly does not want now. Suppose, for example, that years ago, when fully competent, Margo had executed a formal document directing that if she should develop Alzheimer's disease, all her property should be given to a designated charity so that none of it could be spent on her own care. Or that in that event she should not receive treatment for any other serious, life-threatening disease she might contract. Or even that in that event she should be killed as soon and as painlessly as possible? If Margo had expressed any of those wishes when she was competent, would autonomy then require that they be respected now by those in charge of her care, even though she seems perfectly happy with her dog-eared mysteries, the single painting she repaints, and her peanut-butter-and-jelly sandwiches?

If we had accepted the evidentiary view of autonomy, we would find the case for respecting Margo's past directions very weak. People are not the best judges of what their own best interests would be under circumstances they have never encountered and in which their preferences and desires may drastically have changed. But if we accept the integrity view, we will be drawn to the view that Margo's past wishes must be respected. A competent person making a living will providing for his treatment if he becomes demented is making exactly the kind of judgment that autonomy, on the integrity view, most respects: a judgment about the overall shape of the kind of life he wants to have led.

This conclusion is troubling, however, even shocking, and someone might want to resist it by insisting that the right to autonomy is *necessarily* contemporary: that a person's right to autonomy is only a right that his present decisions, not past ones that he has since disowned, be respected. Certainly that is the normal force of recognizing autonomy. Suppose that a Jehovah's Witness has signed a formal document stipulating that he is not to receive blood transfusions even if out of weakness of will he requests one when he would otherwise die. He wants, like Ulysses, to be tied to the mast of his faith. But when the moment comes, and he needs a transfusion, he pleads for it. We would not think ourselves required, out of respect for his autonomy, to disregard his contemporary plea.

We can interpret that example in different ways, though, and the difference is crucial for our present problem. We might say, first, that the Witness's later plea countermanded his original decision because it expressed a more contemporary desire. That presumes that it is only right to defer to past decisions when we have reason to believe that the agent still wishes what he wanted then. On that view, precedent autonomy is an illusion: we treat a person's past decision as important only because it is normally evidence of his present wishes, and we disregard it entirely when we know that it is not. On the other hand, we might say that the Witness's later plea countermanded his original decision because it was a fresh exercise of his autonomy, and that disregarding it would be treating him as no longer in charge of his own life. The difference between these two views about the force of precedent autonomy is crucial when someone changes his mind *after* he has become incompetent—that is, when the conditions of autonomy no longer hold. Suppose that the same accident that made a transfusion medically necessary for the Witness also deranged him, and that while still plainly deranged he demands the transfusion. On the first view, we would not violate his autonomy by administering it, but on the second, we would.

Which of the two views about the force of past decisions is more persuasive? Suppose we were confident that the deranged Witness, were he to receive the transfusion and live, would become competent again and be appalled at having had a treatment he believed worse for him than dying. In those circumstances, I believe, we would violate his autonomy by giving him the transfusion. That argues for the second view about the force of past decisions, the view that endorses precedent autonomy as genuine. We refuse to give the deranged Witness a transfusion not because we think he really continues to want what he wanted before—this is not like a case in which someone who objects to a given treatment is unconscious when he needs it—but because he lacks the necessary capacity for a fresh exercise of autonomy. His former decision remains in force because no new decision by a person capable of autonomy has annulled it.

Someone might say that we are justified in withholding the transfusion only because we know that the Witness would regret the transfusion if he recovered. But that prediction would make no difference if he was fully competent when he asked for the transfusion and desperate to live at that moment, though very likely to change his mind again and be appalled tomorrow at what he has done. Surely we should accede to his request in those circumstances. What makes the difference, when we are deciding whether to honor someone's plea even though it contradicts his past deep convictions, is whether he is now competent to make a decision of that character, not whether he will regret making it later.

Our argument for the integrity view, then, supports a genuine doctrine of precedent autonomy. A competent person's right to autonomy requires that his past decisions about how he is to be treated if he becomes demented be respected even if they contradict the desires he has at that later point. If we refuse to respect Margo's precedent autonomy—if we refuse to respect her past decisions, though made when she was competent, because they do not match her present, incompetent wishes—then we are violating her autonomy on the integrity view. This conclusion has great practical importance. Competent people who are concerned about the end of their lives in the ways we noticed in chapter 7 will naturally worry about how they might be treated if they become demented. Someone anxious to ensure that his life is not then prolonged by medical treatment is worried precisely because he thinks that the character of his whole life would be compromised if it were. He is in the same position as people who sign living wills asking not to be kept alive in a hopeless medical condition or when permanently vegetative. If we respect *their* past requests, as the Supreme Court has decided American states must do, then we have the same reasons for respecting the wishes not to be kept alive of someone like Mrs. Adkins, who dreads not unconsciousness but dementia.

The argument has very troubling consequences, however. The medical student who observed Margo said that her life was the happiest he knew. Should we really deny a person like that the routine medical care needed to keep her alive? Could we ever conceivably *kill* her? We might consider it morally unforgivable not to try to save the life of someone who plainly enjoys her life, no matter how demented she is, and we might think it beyond imagining that we should actually kill her. We might hate living in a community whose officials might make or license either of those decisions. We might have other good reasons for treating Margo as she now wishes, rather than as, in my imaginary case, she once asked. But still, that violates rather than respects her autonomy.

BENEFICENCE

When one person is entrusted to the charge or care of another, the former has what I shall call a right to beneficence—a right that the latter make decisions in the former's best interests. This fiduciary right is a familiar idea in both law and morals: a trustee must act in the interests of the trust's beneficiaries; the directors of a corporation must act in the interests of its shareholders; doctors and other professionals must act in the interests of their patients or clients. The right to beneficence in such cases is not a right to have a particular person assume this fiduciary duty of care; the right takes hold only when someone does take up that responsibility. Nor is it a right that particular resources be put at the disposal of the fiduciary; the right only governs the use of whatever resources are in fact available for the beneficiary's care.

Since beneficiary and fiduciary may take a different view of the former's best interests, the right of beneficence differs from the right to autonomy we have been discussing, and may in some circumstances conflict with it. We have already noticed one potential conflict: between a demented patient's interest and his precedent autonomy when competent. Is that conflict genuine? If it is, then Margo's present right to beneficence—now, when she is demented—would be a reason to ignore her precedent autonomy, to make her happy now in spite of whatever she directed before. There is no reason to doubt that a demented person has a right to beneficence, but we face an obvious problem in considering the consequences of that right. What *are* the best interests of someone seriously and permanently demented? In the last chapter, I emphasized the distinction between what I called experiential and critical interests, and that distinction is indispensable now.[20]

Even a seriously demented person (unlike someone in a persistent vegetative state) has experiential interests. Most late-stage Alzheimer's victims still enjoy comfort and reassurance—Mary, you remember, liked most just to be held and loved. They may have fear or pleasurable anticipation about their future. But by the time the dementia has become advanced, Alzheimer's victims have lost the capacity to think about how to make their lives more successful on the whole. They are ignorant of self—not as an amnesiac is, not simply because they cannot identify their pasts—but, more fundamentally, because they have no sense of a whole life, a past joined to a future, that could be the object of any evaluation or concern as a whole.[21] They cannot have projects or plans of the kind that leading a critical life requires. They therefore have no contemporary opinion about their own critical interests.

Nevertheless, they continue to have such interests. Of course, if we think of a demented person's life in only a forward-looking way, as the life he will lead from now on, there seems very little point in speculating about his critical interests, about what would make that life more or less valuable, because he is no longer capable of the acts or attachments that can give it value. Value cannot be poured into a life from the outside; it must be generated by the person whose life it is, and this is no longer possible for him. But when we consider how the fate of a demented person can affect the character of his life, we consider the patient's whole life, not just its sad final stages, and we consider his future in terms of how it affects the character of the whole.

In many respects, the demented person is in the same position as an unconscious, persistently vegetative patient. But there is an important difference. I can think about my best interests were I to become permanently vegetative with no concern about any conflict of interests: if I am convinced that it would spoil my life to be kept alive for years as a vegetable, I can act on that conviction with no prospect of conflict—by signing a living will directing that I be allowed to die. But I know that if I become demented, I will probably want to go on living, and that I may then still be capable of primitive experiential pleasures. Some dementia victims, it is true, lead frightful, painful lives, full of fear and paranoia. Some are brutally unpleasant and ungrateful to those who care for them. But even they appear to want to continue living. And how can I know that my life will be unpleasant? Margo's life, for example, was not like that, and even after she declined further she might well have gone on enjoying her peanut-butter-and-jelly sandwiches, aimlessly turning the pages of her mystery, basking in the sun, recognizing no one, connecting to nothing, smiling and apparently content. Would it be in my best interests to go on living like that, or to die as soon as possible?

People I have asked disagree sharply about that excruciating question.

Roughly half are repelled by the idea of living demented, totally dependent lives, speaking gibberish, incapable of understanding that there is a world beyond them, let alone of following its course. They think a life ending like that is seriously marred, that the critical harm is even greater than living on as a quiescent vegetable, which is not so violent a contradiction of their reason and sense. They do not think that the possible childish pleasures of dementia would redeem its curse; some think the capacity to enjoy such pleasures would be part of that curse. They would prefer not to live on. But half take the other view. They do not think that a demented life is worse than no life at all, and for them the meager childish pleasures are better than nothing.

People in the first group may consider signing living wills stipulating that if they become permanently and seriously demented, and then develop a serious disease, they should not be given medical treatment except to avoid pain. They may consider trying to make the other arrangements I mentioned: to have their money given away, or even, if possible, to be killed. I have already argued that respect for their autonomy would be a reason for doing what they ask. But I raised the question of whether there might then be a conflict between respecting their autonomy and serving their best interests. Is there a conflict between respecting Margo's precedent autonomy, if she had signed such a living will, and doing what would later be in her best interests? Is this like the case in which we have to choose between respecting a Jehovah's Witness's autonomy and giving him a lifesaving transfusion after he falls unconscious?

Of course, there is a conflict between Margo's precedent autonomy and her contemporary experiential interests if she is still enjoying her life, but there is no conflict with her critical interests as she herself conceived them when she was competent to do so. If I decide, when I am competent, that it would be best for me not to remain alive in a seriously and permanently demented state, then a fiduciary could contradict me only by exercising an unacceptable form of moral paternalism. A doctor is no more justified in contradicting a competent adult's judgment about dementia than in contradicting his judgment about permanent unconsciousness. Once we rule out that form of paternalism—once we accept that we must judge Margo's critical interests as she did when competent to do so—then the conflict between autonomy and beneficence seems to disappear. If Margo had asked not to be given medical care for life-threatening illnesses contracted after she had become demented, neither her right to autonomy *nor* her right to beneficence would give us grounds for denying that request, even if the demented Margo is enjoying her life. We cannot say that we would be showing compassion for Margo if we refused to do what she wanted when she was competent, because that would not be compassionate toward the whole person, the person who tragically became demented. We might have other reasons for refusing to enforce Margo's living will—we might find ourselves unable to deny medical help to anyone who is conscious and does not reject it—but we cannot claim to be acting for *her* sake.

It would be a mistake to resist this conclusion on the ground that letting Margo die in these circumstances would be irrevocable. After all, both choices—to honor or not to honor her past request—are irrevocable. Just as Justice Rehnquist was wrong to assume that there is no harm in a patient's living on as a vegetable, so it would be wrong to assume that there is no harm in living on demented. But consider a different objection: that in the circumstances of dementia, critical interests become less important and experiential interests more so, so that fiduciaries may rightly ignore the former and concentrate on the latter. It is true, as I said, that demented people have no sense of their own critical interests, but before that, when they were competent, they did, and we cannot disregard this or think it no longer matters. Persistently vegetative patients have no sense of their own critical interests, but that is not a good reason for ignoring their fate, and it is not a good reason for ignoring the demented, either.

In 1991, Elizabeth Dew, a guardian appointed by a court to consider how best to care for Joseph Finelli—a fifty-six-year-old Boston father of four who was conscious but had the mental state of a six-month-old baby—recommended that he be taken off the immune-suppressing medicine necessary to prevent rejection of his transplanted heart so that he would die. Finelli did not have Alzheimer's disease; he had suffered major neurological damage during his heart-transplant operation because, his family claimed, the tube supplying him with oxygen had slipped out. The Brigham and Women's Hospital, where the operation had taken place, had cared for him for many years, at gigantic cost, and had petitioned the court to be allowed to discharge him to a specialized nursing home or his own home. The family opposed the request, and the judge appointed the guardian to consider and represent the patient's own interests. Finelli had not signed a living will, and there was no evidence of his having said that he would prefer to die than to live with an infant's mental life. He did not seem to be in pain or unhappy; he recognized familiar faces with apparent pleasure, smiled, and watched television. The guardian nevertheless said that if Finelli could decide for himself, he would prefer to be dead; that hypothetical judgment must have reflected her opinion about his best interests as well. The family was appalled at her recommendation, and the judge rejected it.[22] Finelli's family won. Did he?

DIGNITY

The phrase "right to dignity" is used in many ways and senses in moral and political philosophy. Sometimes, for example, it means the right to live in conditions in which genuine self-respect is possible or appropriate, whatever these are. But here we must consider a more limited idea: that people have a right not to suffer *indignity*, not to be treated in ways that in their culture or community are understood as showing disrespect. Every civilized society has standards and conventions defining these indignities, and these differ from place to place and time to time.

We often appeal to these standards in defining the minimum conditions of decent custodial care: we say, for example, that prisoners who have been convicted of even serious crimes are entitled to dignity in their punishment. We now think this requires that jails be clean, that prisoners not be tortured or abused, and that they be allowed at least a certain level and kind of privacy. A parallel claim is often made on behalf of the demented in the care of the community. It is said that they, too, have a right to dignity, in virtue of which they must be kept clean when they cannot or will not clean themselves, must not be herded together in crowded conditions that allow them no genuine privacy, must be shown some level of individual attention and concern, and must not be ignored or sedated to make them more tractable.

This right to dignity is usually thought to be more fundamental and urgent than the right to beneficence we have been considering, which, as I emphasized, is only a right that whatever resources are available for someone's care be used in his interests. The right to dignity is more imperative: it requires the community to deploy whatever resources are necessary to secure it. (The two rights are even more plainly contrasted in the case of prisoners. We do not require that jail conditions must be arranged in the best interests of the inmates, but we do insist that these conditions respect their dignity so far as possible.) Do the demented have a right to dignity? Some demented people, particularly in the late stages of their disease, seem to have lost the capacity to recognize or appreciate indignity, or to suffer from it. Do they have a right to dignity even then? Or is our concern for their dignity, in those circumstances, only a matter of sentimentality we cannot and should not afford? These are questions of considerable practical importance. It is expensive, tedious, and difficult to keep seriously demented patients clean, to assure them space for privacy, to give them the personal attention they often crave. Once again, we can answer these difficult questions only by reflecting further on the point of the right to dignity when we acknowledge it for the fully competent. Why do we care about indignity? Why do we care so much?

One theory treats indignity as wrong because it is so contrary to our experiential interests. This theory supposes that indignity causes its victims distinctive and especially severe mental pain, that people resent and therefore suffer more from indignity than from other forms of deprivation. People denied dignity may lose the self-respect that dignity protects, moreover, and then suffer an even more serious form of distress: self-contempt or self-loathing. If this experiential account of dignity is sound, then many mentally incapacitated people may have no right to dignity after all. Few demented people—even those who do want to be clean or to have their privacy respected—can recognize a distinctive insult to self-esteem, or have the necessary sense of self-identity to suffer a special distress from it. Self-respect, like autonomy, requires a degree of general competence and, especially, a sense of self-identity over time, which seriously demented people have lost. (Self-hatred and self-loathing presuppose an even sharper sense of identity, and though some people feel that intense distress when they realize they are becoming demented, it disappears when the dementia becomes complete.)

So on the experiential account of dignity, it seems dubious that the demented have any general right to dignity, and concern for their self-respect does seem only expensive sentimentality, like providing hairdressers for the comatose. Of course, we may still think it important to maintain the demented in circumstances of dignity out of respect for the sensibilities of their relatives or others who might otherwise suffer outrage and guilt. But if the patient himself suffers no distinctive distress of indignity, his relatives might be led to see that their own indignation and guilt are misplaced. In any case, respect for the feelings of others does not require us to recognize a right of dignity for demented patients who have no relatives or friends.

This experiential theory of indignity is unpersuasive, however, because it does not explain central features of our convictions about dignity. It cannot account for our sense that dignity has an active as well as a passive voice, and that the two are connected. We are distressed by, even disapprove of, someone who is indifferent to hygiene and lives in filth, or who neglects or sacrifices the independence we think dignity requires, or who debases himself for some immediate advantage. We say that such people have compromised their *own* dignity, and we think that someone acts worse and has more to be ashamed of when he does not recognize the indignity he has brought upon himself. We also consider unrecognized indignities to be as bad or worse than recognized ones; most of us believe, for example, that slaves live in the ultimate indignity when their subjugation is so complete that they believe it appropriate and do not resent or otherwise suffer any special distress from it. If the experiential account of indignity were right, these critical attitudes would be perverse. Someone who does not mind what others would consider an indignity might be unusual, but he would not be debased, and an unrecognized indignity would be none at all. Nor can that theory explain why the greatest indignity we can inflict on a person is to make him unconscious of other indignities, for example by sedation or brainwashing.

What other account of the right to dignity can explain all this? Why is indignity a special kind of harm, whether self-inflicted or inflicted by others, and why does it seem worse when the indignity is not recognized by its victim? I have been arguing that we not only have, in common with all sensate creatures, experiential interests in the quality of our future experiences but also critical interests in the character and value of our lives as a whole. These critical interests are connected, as I said, to our convictions about the intrinsic value—the sanctity or inviolability—of our own lives. A person worries about his critical interests because he believes it important what kind of a life he has led, important for its own sake and not simply for the experiential pleasure that leading a valuable life (or believing it valuable) might or might not have given him. A person's right to be treated with dignity, I now suggest, is the right that others acknowledge his genuine critical interests: that they acknowledge that he is the kind of creature, and has the moral standing, such that it is intrinsically, objectively important how his life goes. Dignity is a central aspect of the value we have been examining throughout this book: the intrinsic importance of human life.

Putting it this way explains how and why the right to dignity is different from the right to beneficence. We can acknowledge that it is important how someone's life goes without accepting any general positive obligation to make it go better. The distinction is necessary to explain the pervasiveness of our concern with dignity—why we insist, as I said, on the dignity even of prisoners. When we jail someone convicted of a crime in order to deter others, we do not treat him with beneficence; on the contrary, we act against his interests for the general benefit. But we insist that he be treated with dignity in accordance with our understanding of what that requires—that he not be tortured or humiliated, for example—because we continue to regard him as a full human being, as someone whose fate we continue to treat as a matter of concern.[23] Requiring his custodians to respect his dignity shows, among other things, that we appreciate the gravity of what we are doing: that we understand we are jailing a human being whose life matters, that our reasons for doing so are reasons we believe both require and justify this terrible injury, that we are not entitled to treat him as a mere object at the full disposal of our convenience, as if all that mattered was the usefulness, for the rest of us, of locking him up. (Understanding that dignity means recognizing a person's critical interests, as distinct from advancing those interests, provides a useful reading of the Kantian principle that people should be treated as ends and never merely as means. That principle, so understood, does not require that people never be put at a disadvantage for the advantage of others, but rather that people never be treated in a way that denies the distinct importance of their own lives.) It is crucially important that we make and signal this distinction. In one sense, dignity is a matter of convention, because the systems of gesture and taboo that societies use to draw the boundary between disadvantage and indignity differ. But the right that all people have—that their society recognize the importance of their lives, expressed through whatever vocabulary it has—is not itself a matter of convention.

This general account of the meaning of dignity explains what I called its active voice: our sense that people care and should care for their own dignity. Someone who compromises his own dignity denies, in whatever language his community provides, a sense of himself as someone with critical interests, the value of whose life is important for its own sake. That is self-betrayal. And our account also explains why indignity is most serious when its victim no longer suffers from the indignity. For a person who accepts indignity accepts the classification implicit in it, and accepting that one's life lacks the critical importance of other lives, that it is less intrinsically important how it goes, is a great and sad defeat.

Our present interest, however, is in the special issue of whether seriously demented people have a right to dignity in their custodial care. I argued that a person who has become demented retains his critical interests because what happens to him then affects the value or success of his life as a whole. That he remains a person, and that the overall value of his life continues to be intrinsically important, are decisive truths in favor of his right to dignity. Now we may complete the argument. We mark his continued moral standing, and we affirm the importance of the life he has lived, by insisting that nothing be done to or for him that, in our community's vocabulary of respect, denies him dignity. Though dignity is different from beneficence in the ways we have been noticing, it would be inconsistent to deny dignity while recognizing the critical interests that it confirms. So here is yet more proof of the dominating grip of the idea that human life has intrinsic as well as personal importance for human beings—the complex but inescapable idea that it is, in the sense I have been struggling to define, sacred.

CODA: FIRST THINGS AND LAST ONES

La Rochefoucauld said that death, like the sun, should not be stared at. We have not taken his advice: we have been staring at death throughout this book, though the argument has always brought us back to life, to life's dominion rather than death's, to the devastatingly important truth that what death means hinges on how and why our lives are sacred. We began with the bitter worldwide argument about abortion. That battle seems so intractable, so stuck in venom and hate, because we have been tricked, or tricked ourselves, into misunderstanding what it is really about. We have been persuaded that the central issue is a metaphysical one—whether a fetus is a person—about which no argument can be decisive and no compromise acceptable, because for one side the question is whether babies may be murdered and for the other whether women should be victimized by religious superstition. When we look more closely at what ordinary people actually feel about abortion, we can reject this fatally misleading account. Almost no one who supports anti-abortion laws really believes that a just-conceived fetus is a person, and almost no one who opposes them really believes that the argument against abortion rests only on superstition. The real argument is a very different one: we disagree so deeply because we all take so seriously a value that unites us as human beings—the sanctity or inviolability of every stage of every human life. Our sharp divisions signal the complexity of the value and the markedly different ways that different cultures, different groups, and different people, equally committed to it, interpret its meaning.

A sovereign commitment to the sanctity of life dominates our concerns about life's other edge, too: it is the fulcrum of our worries and puzzles about euthanasia. Most people's interests are not exhausted by a desire for pleasure or enjoyment, but include, as crucial to their sense of self, a desire to make a success of living, to make something valuable of their own lives. Though very few would put it in this dramatic way, most people treat living as a sacred responsibility, and this responsibility seems most intense when they contemplate death, their own or someone else's. People who want an early, peaceful death for themselves or their relatives are not rejecting or denigrating the sanctity of life; on the contrary, they believe that a quicker death shows more respect for life than a protracted one. Once again, both sides in the debate about euthanasia share a concern for life's sanctity; they are united by that value, and disagree only about how best to interpret and respect it.

Dignity—which means respecting the inherent value of our own lives—is at the heart of both arguments. We care intensely what other people do about abortion and euthanasia, and with good reason, because those decisions express a view about the intrinsic value of all life and therefore bear on our own dignity as well. We hope that everyone will make decisions about abortion that match our own sense of its gravity. We think that an unwarranted or frivolous abortion shows contempt for all human life, a diminished respect for everyone, and we want everyone to die, when they have a choice, in a way we think shows self-respect, because that bell, too, tolls for us.

But though we may feel our own dignity at stake in what others do about death, and may sometimes wish to make others act as we think right, a true appreciation of dignity argues decisively in the opposite direction—for individual freedom, not coercion, for a régime of law and attitude that encourages each of us to make mortal decisions for himself. Freedom is the cardinal, absolute requirement of self-respect: no one treats his life as having any intrinsic, objective importance unless he insists on leading that life himself, not being ushered along it by others, no matter how much he loves or respects or fears them. Decisions about life and death are the most important, the most crucial for forming and expressing personality, that anyone makes; we think it crucial to get these decisions right, but also crucial to make them in character, and for ourselves. Even people who want to impose their convictions on everyone else through the criminal law, when they and like-minded colleagues are politically powerful, would be horrified, perhaps to the point of revolution, if their political fortunes were reversed and they faced losing the freedom they are now ready to deny others.

Because we cherish dignity, we insist on freedom, and we place the right of conscience at its center, so that a government that denies that right is totalitarian no matter how free it leaves us in choices that matter less. Because we honor dignity, we demand democracy, and we define it so that a constitution that permits a majority to deny freedom of conscience is democracy's enemy, not its author. Whatever view we take about abortion and euthanasia, we want the right to decide for ourselves, and we should therefore be ready to insist that any honorable constitution, any genuine constitution of principle, will guarantee that right for everyone.

It matters as much that we live up to our freedom as that we have it. Freedom of conscience presupposes a personal responsibility of reflection, and it loses much of its meaning when that responsibility is ignored. A good life need not be an especially reflective one; most of the best lives

are just lived rather than studied. But there are moments that cry out for
self-assertion, when a passive bowing to fate or a mechanical decision
out of deference or convenience is treachery, because it forfeits dignity
for ease. We have encountered, throughout this book, a great number of
intense personal convictions about abortion and euthanasia, some of
them liberal and others conservative. They are honorable convictions,
and those who have them must live and die in their light. But it is
unforgivable to ignore the high importance of these matters altogether,
to choose or counsel abortion out of unreflective convenience, or to
leave the fate of an unconscious or demented friend to strangers in white
coats on the ground that what happens to him no longer matters. The
greatest insult to the sanctity of life is indifference or laziness in the face
of its complexity.

We have not yet begun to measure that complexity or to appreciate
its full dimensions. Doctors have recently announced new success in
using fetal tissue in treating Parkinson's disease, and some believe that
similar treatment would benefit victims of other dreadful diseases, perhaps including Alzheimer's. Women may one day be encouraged to
become pregnant just to produce lifesaving tissue through an abortion
at the right moment. In a generation or so, the great battles over abortion
and euthanasia may well have been displaced, in public imagination and
political controversy, by other, even more difficult issues about the
intrinsic value of human life. Science promises—or threatens—the
power dramatically to alter the processes of human reproduction and
embryonic development, to improve techniques for fertilization without
sex and even, perhaps, to develop new techniques for childbirth without
fertilization, to alter or create genetic codes and produce children designed after a chosen blueprint, to clone people with favored qualities
or great wealth and a passion for immortality. Science also promises—or
threatens—new medical and surgical techniques of increasing life ex-
pectancy, in some accounts to expand it to biblical magnitudes, but at
such enormous cost that developing and testing these techniques, let
alone making them available to more than a tiny minority, would drain
away the resources needed to make people's lives good as well as long.

Any of these developments, or any of dozens of others that may leap
from science fiction to medical routine, would force us to confront the
issues we have been exploring—about the relative importance of the
natural and the human contributions to the sanctity of life—in very

different terms, and it would be absurd even to speculate about how those issues would best be defined, let alone resolved, then. But if people retain the self-consciousness and self-respect that is the greatest achievement of our species, they will let neither science nor nature simply take its course, but will struggle to express, in the laws they make as citizens and the choices they make as people, the best understanding they can reach of why human life is sacred, and of the proper place of freedom in its dominion.

NOTES

1 The Edges of Life

1. B. D. Colen, "Euthanasia Issue Lives On," *Newsday,* November 10, 1992, 71. The events described in this paragraph are discussed in chapter 7.
2. See Jason Bennetta, "Irish Priests Help Women Set Up Secret Abortions," The Independent, February 23, 1992, 1.
3. See William Tuohy, "Irish Reject a Move to Allow Abortions," Los Angeles *Times,* November 28, 1992, A5. The Irish referendum is discussed in chapter 2.
4. For a recent history of the role of religion in American politics, see Gary Wills, *Under God* (New York: Simon & Schuster, 1990).
5. For one account of the development of feminist concern with abortion, see Rosalind Pollack Petchesky, *Abortion and Woman's Choice,* rev. ed. (Boston: Northeastern University Press, 1990).
6. One prominent advocate of this view is Mary Ann Glendon, who developed it in her book *Abortion and Divorce in Western Law* (Cambridge, Mass.: Harvard University Press, 1987), which I discuss in chapter 2. It has also been popular among editorialists. *The New Republic,* for example, has consistently advanced that view for many years, and George Will recently endorsed it in "Abortion: No Constitutional Right," Washington *Post,* January 26, 1992, C7.
7. *Roe* v. *Wade,* 410 U.S. 113 (1973).
8. The Supreme Court did permit states to regulate abortion in the second trimester of pregnancy in order to protect the mother's health, and that has allowed states to impose certain requirements making abortion more expensive. In *Simopoulos* v. *Virginia,* 462 U.S. 506 (1983), for example, the Court upheld a state requirement that second-trimester abortions be performed in "licensed hospital facilities"; and in *Planned Parenthood of Central Missouri* v. *Danforth,* 428 U.S. 52 (1976), the Court upheld recordkeeping requirements, applicable at any stage of pregnancy, that the state argued were necessary to protect the mother's health.
9. See David E. Rosenbaum, "The 1992 Campaign: Parties' Core Differences in Platforms," *The New York Times,* August 16, 1992, A26.
10. *Casey* is reported at 112 S. Ct. 2791 (1992).
11. *Ada* v. *Guam Society of Obstetricians and Gynecologists et al.,* 113 S. Ct. 633 (1992).
12. See, for example, Laurence H. Tribe, *Abortion: The Clash of Absolutes* (New York: W. W. Norton, 1990), and Roger Rosenblatt, *Life Itself* (New York: Random House, 1992).
13. *Cruzan* v. *Director, Missouri Department of Health,* 497 U.S. 261 (1990).
14. Rosenblatt, *Life Itself,* 183ff.
15. Yankelovich Clancy Shulman poll released September 10, 1992, Public Opinion Online, available in Westlaw, Dialog Library, poll file.

16. NBC News/*Wall Street Journal* poll released July 10, 1992, Public Opinion Online, available in Westlaw, Dialog Library, poll file.

17. Rosenblatt, *Life Itself,* 188.

18. A new battery of polls was taken following the Supreme Court's decision in the *Casey* case I mentioned earlier. See, for example, *U.S.A. Today,* June 30, 1992, 1. Once again, the polls showed that a strong majority of Americans backed the legality of abortion. But they also showed an equally strong majority in favor of certain kinds of restrictions on abortion that the Court approved in that case, including, for example, laws imposing mandatory twenty-four-hour waiting periods and laws requiring doctors to counsel on alternatives to abortion. Once again these results will seem baffling if we think that people divide in the abortion controversy only because they take different views about whether a fetus is a person. If that were the issue, then people who thought abortion was morally a serious enough matter to require waiting periods and counseling would also think, presumably, that it should be prohibited altogether. But once again, the supposed contradiction disappears when we realize that most people think abortion morally grave not because they think a fetus is a person but because they think a fetus embodies the intrinsic value of human life. On that assumption it makes great sense, as I argue in chapter 6, to think that women have a right to make the ultimate decision about abortion for themselves, but that the community may properly encourage them to take the decision seriously, as a grave moral matter. It is, of course, another question, which I also discuss there, whether a given regulation purporting only to encourage women to treat abortion as serious actually infringes a woman's right to make the ultimate decision for herself.

19. See Harold J. Morowitz and James S. Trefil, *"Roe* v. *Wade* Passes a Lab Test," *The New York Times,* November 25, 1992, A21.

20. In chapters 7 and 8, when we consider the situation of people who are permanently unconscious or demented, we will see the importance of insisting that people have interests who have had a mental life, even though they do not continue to have one. In a few paragraphs I shall consider the question of whether something—drugs taken by the mother—can be against the interests of a fetus who will in fact be born, that is, who will in fact have a conscious life. That is, of course, a different question from the one I am now discussing, which is whether abortion, which means never having a conscious life, is against a fetus's interests.

21. See Michael Flower, *Neuromaturation of the Human Fetus,* 10; *Journal of Medicine and Philosophy,* 237, 239, 245. According to F. Cunningham, P. MacDonald, and N. Gant, *Williams Obstetrics, 103* (18th ed., 1989), "local stimuli may evoke squinting, opening the mouth, incomplete finger closure, and plantar flexion of the toes" at eight weeks after conception.

22. Ibid., 245.

23. See Clifford Grobstein, *Science and the Unborn* (New York: Basic Books, 1988), 55, 130.

24. Flower, *Neuromaturation of the Human Fetus,* 246.

25. Grobstein, *Science and the Unborn,* 129. It is interesting to notice that premature infants born at twenty-eight to thirty-two weeks exhibit very different behavior from infants of longer gestational age. Grobstein quotes Arnold Gesell, in studies made forty years ago, to the effect that a fetal infant of less than thirty-two weeks "is easily roused to brief mild activity, but he is never fully roused. He neither sleeps nor wakes, but only drowses and stirs." Gesell, quoted by Grobstein, 130.

26. Ibid., 130.
27. See R. W. Apple, "Behind Bush's Mixed Abortion Signals," *The New York Times*, August 15, 1992, A1, and Andrew Rosenthal, "Bush, Asked in Personal Context, Takes a Softer Stand on Abortion," *The New York Times*, August 12, 1992, A1.
28. Rosenblatt, *Life Itself,* 185.
29. I am ignoring, in the phrase "a living organism," the remote possibility that an embryo might twin even after implantation.
30. This reading avoids perplexing philosophical questions that I believe are not relevant to my argument. These include the question of what people who say they are willing to assume that a fetus is a person for the sake of the argument are really assuming or imagining. That is a serious problem if we use "person" in the philosophical sense, because it is wholly unclear what kind of counterfactual assumption these people are making. But in the practical sense, there is no difficulty in understanding what is meant. We are asked to consider whether, even if we assign a fetus the rights persons normally have, abortion should nevertheless be permitted in certain circumstances.
31. For a discussion of the question whether infants are persons in the philosophical sense, see Michael Tooley, "Abortion and Infanticide," *Philosophy and Public Affairs* 2, no. 1 (Fall 1972).

2 *The Morality of Abortion*

1. Mario Cuomo's speech was reprinted in *The New York Review of Books,* October 25, 1984.
2. A *Time*/CNN poll conducted in June 1992 reported that 84 percent of Americans favor abortion when the mother's life is at stake. Public Opinion Online, available in Westlaw, Dialog Library, poll file.
3. The poll described in note 2 also reported that 79 percent of Americans favor abortion in cases of rape or incest.
4. See "She's Come for an Abortion. What Do You Say?" *Harper's* (November 1992): 51–2.
5. The poll described in note 2 also reported that 70 percent of the Americans interviewed favored abortion when the fetus would be born seriously deformed.
6. Though Catholics are less likely to approve of abortion than some other religious groups, they are not less likely to have abortions. According to *Facts in Brief: Abortion in the United States* (New York: The Alan Gutmacher Institute, 1991): "Catholic women are about as likely to obtain an abortion as are all women nationally, while Protestants and Jews are less likely. Catholic women are 30 percent more likely than Protestants to have abortions."
7. *McRae v. Califano,* 491 F. Supp. 630 (1980). The Supreme Court later reversed his decision, *Harris v. McRae,* 448 U.S. 297 (1980). But it did not rule on his claim that the amendment deprived some women of the free exercise of their religion because, it said, none of the plaintiffs had made arguments or alleged facts necessary to raise that issue. 448 U.S. 321.
8. 491 F. Supp. 712.
9. 491 F. Supp. 697–700.
10. 491 F. Supp. 700–702.
11. 491 F. Supp. 696–7

12. See Paul Ramsey, "The Morality of Abortion," in Robert M. Baird and Stuart E. Rosenbaum, eds., *The Ethics of Abortion* (Buffalo: Prometheus Books, 1989), 61, 66. (italics in original).

13. English translation (London: Catholic Truth Society, 1987).

14. See John Noonan, "A Nearly Absolute Value in History," in John Noonan, ed., *The Morality of Abortion* (Cambridge, Mass.: Harvard University Press, 1970).

15. Augustine, *De nuptias et concupiscentia,* quoted in Noonan, 16.

16. Epistles 121.4, *Corpus Scriptorum Ecclesiasticorum Latinorum,* 56.16.

17. See the discussion of fetal sentience in chapter 1.

18. See, for example, Stephen J. Heaney, "Aquinas and the Presence of the Human Rational Soul in the Early Embryo," *The Thomist* 56 (1992): 19.

19. See Joseph Donceel, S.J., "Immediate Animation and Delayed Hominization," *Theological Studies* 31 (1970): 76, 83.

20. Decretales 5.12.5.

21. English translation, *On Human Life: Encyclical Letter of Pope Paul VI* (London: Catholic Truth Society, 1970), 14–15.

22. *Let Me Live: Declaration by the Sacred Congregation for the Doctrine of the Faith on Procured Abortion, approved and confirmed by Pope Paul VI* (London: Catholic Truth Society, 1974), 5–6.

23. See Michael J. Coughlan, *The Vatican, the Law and the Human Embryo* (Iowa City: University of Iowa Press, 1990), 86–8.

24. *Let Me Live,* 11.

25. *On Human Life,* 16.

26. See "Catholics: 52% Support Abortion in Most Circumstances," *American Political Network* (June 18, 1992); "Catholics' Views Shift on Ordination; Poll Finds Majority Support Women Priests, Abortion Rights," Washington *Post,* June 19, 1992, A4.

27. Wills, *Under God,* 310. Wills cites George Gallup, Jr., and Jim Castelli, *The People's Religion: American Faith in the 90's* (New York: Macmillan, 1989).

28. Joseph F. Donceel, S.J., "A Liberal Catholic's View," in Joel Feinberg, ed., *The Problem of Abortion* (Belmont, Calif.: Wadsworth, 1984), 15.

29. See Joseph Cardinal Bernardin, *The Consistent Ethic of Life* (Kansas City: Sheed & Ward, 1988).

30. See Bernardin, "The Consistent Ethic of Life After *Webster,*" Address, Woodstock Theological Center, Georgetown University, March 20, 1990, 9.

31. In an address on "The Death Penalty in Our Time," reprinted in *Consistent Ethic of Life, 59,* Cardinal Bernardin makes plain that the state has the right to execute a murderer, and denies only that it should exercise that right in the circumstances of contemporary society.

32. See Sidney Callahan, "A Moral Obligation," *Sojourners: An Independent Christian Monthly* (November 1989): 18.

33. Some of these decisions, including the *Casey* decision I mentioned in the last chapter, are discussed in chapter 6.

34. See Catharine A. MacKinnon, "Reflections on Sex Equality Under Law," 100 *Yale Law Journal* 1281 (1991).

35. See *Meyer* v. *Nebraska,* 262 U.S. 390 (1923); *Pierce* v. *Society of Sisters,* 268 U.S. 510 (1925).

36. *Carey* v. *Population Services International,* 431 U.S. 678 (1977).

37. In chapter 6 I suggest that the Supreme Court made a mistake in *Harris* v. *McRae.* But its decision was hardly the result of its having previously recognized a right of

privacy in matters of procreation. After all, if women have a privacy right to terminate a pregnancy, they have a privacy right *not* to do so as well, and that fact did not prevent Congress from deciding to help women financially who make that choice. The question raised in *Harris* v. *McRae* was not whether a woman's decision to terminate is a private one, in any sense of privacy, but the very different question of whether Congress may financially support women who make one private choice about pregnancy while refusing to support women who make a different choice that they have an equal constitutional right to make.

38. MacKinnon, "Reflections on Sex Equality Under Law," 1316.
39. See Adrienne Rich, "Of Woman Born," 64 (1976), quoted in MacKinnon, "Reflections on Sex Equality Under Law," 1316 (italics in original).
40. See Robin West, "Taking Freedom Seriously," 104 *Harvard Law Review* 43 (1990): 84–5 (footnotes omitted).
41. See Carol Gilligan, *In a Different Voice* (Cambridge, Mass.: Harvard University Press, 1982).
42. Glendon, *Abortion and Divorce in Western Law,* 58.
43. Ibid., 36.
44. See Anthony Lester, "The Overseas Trade in the American Bill of Rights," 88 *Columbia Law Review* 537 (1988), and Ronald Dworkin, *A Bill of Rights for Britain* (London: Chatto & Windus, 1990).
45. Wills, *Under God.*
46. See Stanley K. Henshaw, "Induced Abortion, A World Review, 1990," *Family Planning Perspectives* 22, no. 2 (March/April 1990): 77–8.
47. Tribe, *Abortion,* 74.
48. In fact, Article 2(2) also provides that the right to life can be abridged by law, and so provides only a dubious argument that the 1974 law, even if it did abridge a right to life, was unconstitutional for that reason. The court also mentioned Article 1(1) of the 1949 constitution, which states, "The dignity of man should be inviolable. To respect and protect it shall be the duty of all state authority." That may be understood as an endorsement of the intrinsic value of human life in the detached form I have been describing, and the court apparently so construed it.
49. The Spanish Supreme Court, which does not have the powers of the Constitutional Court, had said, "Human life in formation is a good that constitutionally merits protection, is a constitutional legal good of the community and not an individual legal good." See Richard Stith, "New Constitutional and Penal Theory in Spanish Abortion Law," in J. Douglas Butler and David F. Walbert, eds., *Abortion, Medicine, and the Law,* 4th ed. (New York: Facts on File, 1992), 368, 375. But the idea that human life is intrinsically valuable, and protected by the Spanish Constitution on that ground, makes more sense, and more sense of the Constitutional Court's opinion, than the odd idea that it is a property belonging to the community as a whole rather than to any individual including itself; if the Constitution meant that odd idea, it is hard to see why the community could not, by liberal abortion legislation, waive its rights to that particular good.
50. A summary of the decision is provided in *Annual Review of Population Law* 12 (1988): 37. A translation of the amended Spanish abortion law appears on page 38.
51. *Case of Open Door and Dublin Well Woman* v. *Ireland, European Court of Human Rights* (October 29, 1992): Volume 246, Series A, Publications of the Court (Köln: Carl Heymanns, Verlag K.G.).

3   *What Is Sacred?*

1. I do not mean to take any position on a further, very abstract philosophical issue not pertinent to this discussion: whether great paintings would still be valuable if intelligent life were altogether destroyed forever so that no one could ever have the experience of regarding paintings again. There is no inconsistency in denying that they would have value then, because the value of a painting lies in the kind of experience it makes available, while still insisting that this value is intrinsic because it does not depend on any creatures' actually wanting that kind of experience.

2. Of course, we may have competing reasons for wanting something *not* to be known: how to blow up the universe, for example. But even in this sort of case, we believe that deliberately avoiding knowledge sacrifices something of intrinsic importance.

3. See John N. Wilford, "In a Publishing Coup, Books in 'Unwritten' Languages," *The New York Times,* December 31, 1991.

4. "Song of Myself," in Oscar Williams, ed., *A Little Treasury of American Poetry* (New York: Scribners, 1948), 108.

5. The idea of respect for natural processes has other dramatic consequences. When a London fertility clinic announced in 1993 that it would allow certain parents to choose the sex of their test-tube baby, for example, many British politicians quickly declared their outrage: several of them said that their objection was based not on "rational" grounds but on an instinctive distaste for interfering with the "mysteries of nature." Even if we think that their reaction was premature, or insufficiently sympathetic toward some parents, most of us understand and share the impulse behind it.

6. See Paul Edwards, ed., *The Encyclopedia of Philosophy* 6 (New York: Macmillan, 1967; New York: The Free Press, 1972), 403.

7. This distinction is emphasized in James Rachels and William Ruddick, "Lives and Liberty," in *The Inner Citadel: Essays on Individual Autonomy,* ed. John Christman (New York: The Oxford University Press, 1989), and explored in James Rachels, *The End of Life* (Oxford: The Oxford University Press, 1986), 24–7.

8. See Leo Tolstoy, *Anna Karenina,* trans. Rosemary Edmunds (New York: Penguin, 1978), 749.

9. Many people who hold that view will make exceptions: for capital punishment, for example, and for killing the enemy in war. I cannot consider, in this book, the large and important question of how far these exceptions contradict the principle. But people who believe that the natural contribution to life is paramount for a particular reason—that God has created all life—will obviously not count these as contradictions if they also believe that executing murderers or killing enemy soldiers in a just war is also God's will.

10. See "Nation's Strictest Abortion Law Enacted in Louisiana Over Veto," *The New York Times,* June 19, 1991. The Louisiana legislature overrode Governor Roemer's veto, and the strict anti-abortion law it enacted has been held unconstitutional by two federal courts. See "Court Backs Overturning of Strict Abortion Law," *The New York Times,* September 23, 1992. In 1992, the Supreme Court refused to review a lower-court decision striking down a similar Guam statute. See Linda Greenhouse, "Guam Abortion Law; High Court Reaffirms Right to Regulate, but Not to Ban," *The New York Times,* December 6, 1992, D2.

11. 491 F. Supp. 630 (1980), 696.

4   *Abortion in Court: Part I*

1. Robert Bork, *The Tempting of America* (New York: The Free Press, 1990), 112.
2. *Eisenstadt* v. *Baird,* 405 U.S. 438, 453 (1972) (italics in original).
3. In one later abortion case, for example, President Reagan's solicitor general, Charles Fried, though arguing that *Roe* should be overruled, said very firmly that it would be a serious mistake for the Court to "constitutionalize" the issue "at any point in the spectrum" by requiring constitutional scrutiny of permissive abortion legislation. Oral argument in *Webster* v. *Reproductive Health Services,* 492 U.S. 490 (1990).
4. These scholars argue that for that reason, anti-abortion laws are unconstitutional even if a fetus is considered a person, and they might reject my much stronger claim that in that event, many laws permitting abortion would be unconstitutional. The legal arguments rely on a famous and influential article about the morality of abortion by Professor Judith Jarvis Thomson of the Massachusetts Institute of Technology, "A Defense of Abortion," *Philosophy and Public Affairs* 1, no. 1 (Fall 1971), to which I referred in chapter 2. The legal arguments applying Thomson's views to constitutional law are best presented in an article by Professor Donald Regan of the Michigan Law School: "Rewriting *Roe* v. *Wade,*" 77 *Michigan Law Review* 1569 (1979). Thompson does not argue that every pregnant woman has a right to an abortion, even if a fetus is a person, but only that some do, and she recognizes that a woman who voluntarily risks pregnancy may not have such a right. In any case, as I have said, her arguments assume that a pregnant woman has no more moral obligation to a fetus she is carrying, even if that fetus is a person with rights and therefore either her son or her daughter, than anyone has to a stranger—to a famous violinist a woman might find herself connected to for nine months because he needs the use of her kidneys for that period in order to live, for example.
5. Regan questions the analogy between abortion and infanticide on the ground that parents have the option of arranging an adoption for their child. But that is not inevitably true: minority infants, in particular, may not be able to find adoptive homes, and their parents are not permitted to kill them, or abandon them in circumstances that will inevitably lead to their death, whenever they can in fact make no alternative arrangement. See Regan, "Rewriting *Roe* v. *Wade.*"
6. I discuss legal interpretation, and these two dimensions of it, throughout my book on law: *Law's Empire* (Cambridge, Mass.: Harvard University Press, 1986).
7. In chapter 6, I defend that proposition at length.
8. See "Brief of 281 American Historians as Amici Curiae Supporting Appellees" in *Webster* v. *Reproductive Health Services.* It is worth noticing that James Mohr, the historian cited in the government's brief in that case to support the claim that anti-abortion laws are traditional in America, is one of the signatories to the historians' brief.
9. Judges sometimes find such language appealing, too. In 1992, a Scottish law lord, Lord Morton of Shuna, said that a child fatally injured by medical negligence while still in the womb was a "person" for purposes of entitling its parents to sue for loss of its society. See "Baby in Womb Is Person, Judge Says," *The Independent,* July 29, 1992, 4.
10. It might be objected that states do have the power to alter national constitutional rights because some constitutional rights incorporate elements of state law by reference. The due process clause of the Fourteenth Amendment protects property, for example, and the contract clause guarantees the integrity of contracts. The legal rules

that define how someone acquires or loses property, or when a contract is formed and what it provides, are state rules defined by state laws, and states, by changing these rules, can therefore affect the details of the constitutional rights their residents have. But in these cases, the Constitution itself, just because it does incorporate by reference concepts whose dimensions are understood to be a matter of state law, grants states that limited power. It declares that states may not take away what their law establishes as property without due process, for example. The suggestion I am rejecting here—that states can affect national rights by adding new creatures to the constitutional population—is very different, because the rights that packing the population in that way would affect, including a woman's right to control her own body, are not rights whose content explicitly depends on concepts whose dimensions states alone may fix. Of course, the constitutional rights of individual citizens also depend to some degree, as I say in the text, on how many other ordinary people are or become citizens, and since the federal Congress has the right to fix immigration and naturalization policy for the nation, its decisions affect people's constitutional rights for that reason. But that power, which, once again, is explicitly provided for Congress by the Constitution, is exercised nationally. The Constitution fixes the character of the constitutional population and allows Congress, but not the individual states one by one, to decide who and how many can enter it from the outside.

11. See John Hart Ely, "The Wages of Crying Wolf: A Comment on *Roe* v. *Wade*," 82 *Yale Law Journal* 920, 926 (1973).
12. Tribe, *Abortion*, 114.
13. See the discussion of the view that fetuses have interests in chapter 1.
14. As I said in chapter 2, some opponents of abortion, like Cardinal Bernardin, have specifically linked anti-abortion to anti-death-penalty arguments, insisting that it is inconsistent to support one of these campaigns without supporting the other as well.

5   The Constitutional Drama

1. See 347 U.S. 483 (1954).
2. See 198 U.S. 45 (1905).
3. See 488 U.S. 469 (1989).
4. See *Casey*, 2804–2806.
5. It is worth noting that of the fifteen Supreme Court justices to have considered the issue since 1973, these are the only four ever to have ruled that women do not have a constitutionally protected right to an abortion. See Justice Stevens's concurring and dissenting opinion in *Casey*, 2838–2843.
6. Justice Cardozo in *Palko* v. *Connecticut*, 302 U.S. 319, 325 (1937).
7. *Bowers* v. *Hardwick*, 478 U.S. 186, 194 (1986).
8. See, for example, *Stanton* v. *Stanton*, 421 U.S. 7 (1975), and *Frontiero* v. *Richardson*, 411 U.S. 677 (1973).
9. See *United States* v. *Eichman*, 496 U.S. 310 (1990), and *Texas* v. *Johnson*, 491 U.S. 397 (1989), in which the Supreme Court upheld the right to burn an American flag in political protest.
10. It is sometimes said that the right to abortion is further from the Constitution's text than the right to burn a flag, because the latter flows directly from the right of free speech, which is specifically mentioned in the text, but the former flows from the intermediate right of privacy, which is not. This claim mistakes a highly contingent

feature of academic legal writing for an important distinction in constitutional theory. Judges and legal scholars have found it useful to develop a name—the "right of privacy"—to describe an argumentative step in the derivation of particular concrete rights from the very abstract due process clause. But that does not mean that there is a special bridge right, subsisting as a Platonic entity, that takes up space between the due process clause and a right to use contraceptives or to have an abortion. One could adopt special middling terms to use in the other two arguments as well, like "right of symbolic protest" or "right against nonracial discrimination." It is hardly a deep fact of constitutional structure that lawyers have not done so.

11. See Dworkin, "Justice for Clarence Thomas," *The New York Review of Books,* November 7, 1991.

12. In a memorable and protracted televised exchange, for example, Senator Arlen Specter of Pennsylvania repeatedly embarrassed Bork by pointing out Bork's own inconsistencies in applying originalism to particular cases, and suggesting that in Bork's hands that method, which supposedly screens out a judge's personal convictions from his judicial reasoning, usually turned out to recommend decisions that matched Bork's political preferences perfectly. Charles Fried, President Reagan's last solicitor general, dismissed originalism as obviously confused and inadequate in *his* book *Order and Law: Arguing the Reagan Revolution—A Firsthand Account* (New York: Simon & Schuster, 1991).

13. Bork, *The Tempting of America,* 5.

14. I take up, in this note, a possible reply. Suppose we are persuaded that, had the Constitution's authors ever imagined that other people might one day come to think that capital punishment, for example, was unconstitutional, or that prohibiting abortion was a denial of due process, they would have taken pains to ensure that this (as they thought) deeply mistaken opinion never took root by expressly saying that notwithstanding the general language, government was permitted to enforce capital punishment and prohibit abortion. We might say: the authors did not expressly so provide only because they could not imagine anyone holding such mistaken views, and interpreting the Constitution to forbid capital punishment or to guarantee a right to abortion is just taking advantage of an historical accident. But that argument is a weak one, in part because the counterfactual hypothesis about what the authors would have thought had they imagined the possibility of capital punishment being outlawed is incomplete. What else are we to imagine about the hypothetical conversation in which they are supposed to have considered a possibility they actually never did consider? Must we not also imagine that they had access to the experience and arguments now available to us, which they did not have? After all, the reason the possibility never occurred to them is precisely because they did not have that experience or know those arguments or live in a culture like ours now. But if we must also make those assumptions, in order to give the counterfactual sense and pertinence, then how can we speculate on what they would then have decided without first becoming clearer about what it would be right to decide? So this suggestion, too, proves unhelpful.

15. See note 6.

16. See Antonin Scalia, "Originalism, the Lesser Evil," 57 *Cincinnati Law Review* 849, 861 (1989).

17. Bork, *The Tempting of America,* 162–3.

18. *Casey,* concurring and dissenting opinion of Justice Scalia, 2874.

19. Dworkin, "Justice for Clarence Thomas."
20. Dworkin, "Pragmatism, Right Answers, and True Banality," in *Pragmatism in Law and Society*, eds. Michael Brint and William Weaver (Boulder, Col.: Westview Press, 1991).
21. I discuss integrity at considerable length in *Law's Empire*.
22. I explain why in an article, "The Reagan Revolution and the Supreme Court," in *The New York Review of Books*, July 18, 1991. See also an exchange of letters between Charles Fried and me in the same journal, August 15, 1991. Of course, it doesn't follow that the affirmative-action programs the Supreme Court has struck down were wise, or would actually have improved the position of minorities in American society. That is a different issue from the question of whether they were constitutional, or whether the Court's decisions in the affirmative-action cases lack integrity.

6   Abortion in Court: Part II

1. See 432 U.S. 464 (1977).
2. See 476 U.S. 747 (1986).
3. See 109 S. Ct. 3040 (1989).
4. *Casey*, 2821.
5. Ibid., 2818.
6. Ibid., 2818.
7. Ibid., 2820.
8. The three justices added an important observation to their argument on this point. They said that states must show more concern about the position of a pregnant woman than about that of the potential father. "It is an inescapable biological fact," they said, "that state regulation with respect to the child a woman is carrying will have a far greater impact on the mother's liberty than on the father's" *(Casey*, 2830), and they warned that though a state may acknowledge a father's interest in pregnancy as well, it "may not give to a man the kind of dominion over his wife that parents exercise over their children" (Ibid., 2831), and therefore may not give him the role that they may properly give the parents of teenage women.
9. Ibid., 2825–6.
10. Dworkin, "Foundations of Liberal Equality," in *The Tanner Lectures on Human Values*, XI (Salt Lake City: University of Utah Press, 1990).
11. *United States* v. *Seeger*, 380 U.S. 163, 166 (1965).
12. See Kent Greenawalt, "Religion as a Concept in Constitutional Law," 72 *California Law Review* 753 (1984), and George Freeman III, "The Misguided Search for the Constitutional Definition of 'Religion,'" 71 *Georgetown Law Journal* 1519 (1983).
13. John Rawls, for example, distinguishes his own and other theories of justice from what he calls comprehensive religious or ethical schemes; political theories of justice, he says, presuppose no opinion about what is objectively important. In particular, they presuppose no opinion about if or why or in what way it is intrinsically important that human life continue or prosper, though of course they are compatible with a great variety of such opinions. See his "Justice as Fairness, Political not Metaphysical," 14 *Philosophy and Public Affairs* 223 (1985).
14. Dworkin, "Foundations of Liberal Equality."
15. I do not mean that no stronger constitutional right of personal autonomy can be defended as flowing from the best interpretation of the Constitution as a whole. Indeed, I think a significantly stronger right can be. But I shall not defend any

principle broader than the more limited one just described, because that principle is strong enough to ground a right of privacy understood to include a right to procreative autonomy.

16. Greenawalt, "Religion as a Concept in Constitutional Law," and Freeman, "The Misguided Search for the Constitutional Definition of 'Religion.'"

17. We can regard the Supreme Court's decision in *Employment Division,* v. *Smith,* 494 U.S. 872 (1990), in which the Court held that regulations prohibiting Native Americans from using peyote in religious ceremonies did not violate the First Amendment, as an example of that kind of case, whether or not we agree with the decision.

18. *Seeger,* 165–6. In *Seeger,* the Court construed a statute rather than the Constitution. But since the Court's decision contradicted the evident statutory purpose, commentators have assumed that the Court meant to imply that the statute was constitutional only if so construed.

19. "Draft Declaration on the Church's Relations with Non-Christians," in *Council Daybook* 282 (Vatican II, 3d sess., 1965), quoted in *Seeger,* 181–2.

20. *Gillette* v. *United States,* 401 U.S. 437, 455 (1971) (footnote omitted). The Court also endorsed, as on a careful view supporting the distinction between universal and selective opposition, the government's claim that opposition to a particular war necessarily involves judgment that is "political and particular" and "based on the same political, sociological, and economic factors that the government necessarily considered" in deciding whether to wage war. Ibid., 458.

21. See Judge Richard A. Posner, "Legal Reasoning From the Top Down and From the Bottom Up: The Question of Unenumerated Rights," 59 *University of Chicago Law Review* 433, 444.

22. Such a law would raise other issues about intrinsic value, and in some circumstances might violate a more powerful form of the principle of privacy than the weak form I described and defended.

23. See the discussion of fetal interests in chapter 1.

24. I discuss the arguments on which the *Casey* decision relied in more detail in my article "The Center Holds!," *The New York Review of Books,* August 1992. I discussed the possibility of the Court relying on such arguments in an earlier article from which some of the material in this chapter is drawn: "Unenumerated Rights: Whether and How *Roe* v. *Wade* Should be Overruled," 59 *Chicago Law Review* 381 (1992).

25. Quotations in this paragraph are from *Casey,* 2807–8.

26. See Dworkin, *Law's Empire,* chapter 9.

27. See Linda Greenhouse, "Justices Decline to Hear Mississippi Abortion Case," *The New York Times,* December 8, 1992, A22.

28. *Harris* v. *McRae,* 315.

29. See Robin Toner, "Clinton Orders Reversal of Abortion Restrictions Left by Reagan and Bush," *The New York Times,* January 23, 1993, A1.

30. See Linda Greenhouse, "Supreme Court Says Klan Law Can't Bar Abortion Blockades," *The New York Times,* January 14, 1993, A1.

31. See Tamar Lewin, "Abortion-Rights Groups See a Rise in Attacks on Clinics," *The New York Times,* January 14, 1993, D25.

32. See "Catch-22 for RU-486," *The New York Times,* July 19, 1992, D16.

33. See Robin Toner, "Clinton Orders Reversal of Abortion Restrictions Left by Reagan and Bush," *The New York Times,* January 23, 1993, A1.

34. See Philip J. Hilts, "Abortion Pill's Sale Unlikely Soon Despite Change of Administration," *The New York Times,* November 15, 1992, A38.

7   Dying and Living

1. See KRC Communications/Research poll released in October 1991, and the ABC News/Washington *Post* poll released in January 1992, and both in Public Opinion Online, available in Westlaw, Dialog Library, poll file.

2. See Peter Steinfels, "Beliefs," *The New York Times,* November 9, 1991, A11.

3. In Britain, suicide and attempted suicide were crimes until 1961. The Suicide Act of that year decriminalized them, but assisting suicide and euthanasia remain crimes under Section 2(1) of that law. The Suicide Act does not apply in Scotland, but according to one writer, mercy killers there "may in some cases be at greater risk of finding themselves charged with murder in circumstances where the 1961 Act might have been used in England." Mary Rose Barrington, "Euthanasia: An English Perspective," in Arthur Berger and Joyce Berger, eds., *To Die or Not to Die: Cross-Disciplinary, Cultural and Legal Perspectives on the Right to Choose Death* (New York: Praeger, 1990), 85, 86. For the situation in other countries, see David W. Myers, *The Human Body and the Law* (Palo Alto, Calif.: Stanford University Press, 1990). Euthanasia is treated as "voluntary homicide" in France; see Annie Kouchner, "Mort Douce aux Pays-Bas," *L'Express* (May 1, 1992), 37. On June 24, 1991, the French National Medical Ethics Committee expressed disapproval of any reform allowing doctors to perform active euthanasia at the request of the patient. In Germany, Italy, Switzerland, Denmark, Norway, and Poland, euthanasia is classified not as willful murder but as "homicide on request" and carries a milder sanction: in Germany, for example, the penalty is imprisonment from six months to five years, and motivation is a mitigating factor. In Denmark, by contrast, the penalty is simple detention from sixty days to three years. See Lynn Tracy Nerland, "A Cry for Help: A Comparison of Voluntary, Active Euthanasia Law," 13 *Hastings International and Comparative Law Review* 115 (1989).

4. For approval rating, see Andrew Kelly, "Dutch Plan to Allow Euthanasia Under Strict Conditions," Reuters, November 8, 1991. For criticism, see, for example, Carlos F. Gomez, M.D., *Regulating Death* (New York: The Free Press, 1991).

5. See Jane E. Brody, "Doctors Admit Ignoring Patients' Wishes," *The New York Times,* January 14, 1993, A18.

6. See Lisa Belkin, "Doctors Debate Helping the Terminally Ill to Die," *The New York Times,* May 24, 1989, A1.

7. See William Claiborne, "Paralyzed Canadian Woman Wins Court Ruling on Right to Die," Washington *Post,* January 7, 1992, A9.

8. Neonatal medical decisions provide an especially horrifying example of this apparent irrationality. Some Down's syndrome babies are born with an obstructed bowel that can easily be repaired by surgery, but which will kill the infant, by starvation, if it is not. It is common for doctors, on instructions from the parents, not to operate and to let such babies die a slow and painful death, but it would be criminal for doctors to kill the infant quickly. One Dutch doctor did so, and is criticized in Gomez, *Regulating Death,* at 135, on the ground that the infant did not "want to die," and "fell prey to an act of homicide disguised as medical intervention."

9. See, for example, Kathy Marks, "Consultant Convicted of Attempted Murder," *The Independent,* September 20, 1992, 1.

10. See Lawrence Altman, "Jury Declines to Indict Doctor Who Said He Aided in a Suicide," *The New York Times,* July 27, 1991.

11. See Lisa Foderaro, "New York Will Not Discipline Doctor for His Role in Suicide," *The New York Times,* August 17, 1991, A25.

12. The case is described in David C. Thomasma and Glenn C. Graber, *Euthanasia* (New York: Continuum, 1990), 222.

13. See Ronald E. Cranford, "The Persistent Vegetative State: The Medical Reality (Getting the Facts Straight)," *Hastings Center Report* vol 18, no. 1 (February/March 1988), 27–8.

14. Raymond D. Adams, M.D., and Maurice Victor, M.D., *Principles of Neurology,* 4th ed. (New York: McGraw-Hill Information Services Company, Medical Services Division, 1989), 275–6.

15. *Airedale NHS Trust (Respondents)* v. *Bland,* House of Lords, Judgment February 4, 1993.

16. For discussions of the *Wanglie* case, see Alexander Capron, "In Re Helga Wanglie," *Hastings Center Report,* vol. 21, no. 5 (September–October 1991), 26; Marcia Angell, M.D., "Informed Demand for Non-Beneficial Medical Treatment," both in *The New England Journal of Medicine,* vol. 325, no. 7 (August 15, 1991), 511, 512.

17. The prevalence of Alzheimer's disease is discussed in chapter 8.

18. For an interesting discussion of this possibility, and of its possible impact on the desirability of legislation permitting euthanasia, see J. David Velleman, "Against the Right to Die," *The Journal of Medicine and Philosophy,* vol. 17, no. 6 (1992), 665–81.

19. See *In re Busalacchi,* No. 93799 (St. Louis County Civ. Ct., February 4, 1991) (unpublished decision reported in *The New York Times,* December 1, 1991), and Tamar Lewin, "Man Is Allowed to Let Daughter Die," *The New York Times,* January 27, 1993, A12. See also Brian McCormick, "Case looks at parental rights in medical decisions," *American Medical News,* October 21, 1991, 1.

20. See Elisabeth Rosenthal, "In Matters of Life and Death, the Dying Take Control," *The New York Times,* August 18, 1991, D1.

21. The distinction between critical and experiential interests raises a number of interesting philosophical questions, and though we do not need to consider them in this discussion I shall mention two. First, do rational people always have either a critical or an experiential reason for wanting something for themselves? Is it rational for someone to want to do something—collect stamps, succeed in business, or travel, for example—even though he does not expect to enjoy doing it, and does not think his life will be a better one for having done it, but only because it is a goal he has set himself, for instance, or for no reason at all? Second, if someone's experiential interests—what he enjoys doing—conflict with what he takes to be his critical interests, does it make sense for him to ask what he should do *all things considered,* what would be in his best interests *overall?* I have discussed these and other similar issues in my "Foundations of Liberal Equality."

22. Leo Tolstoy, *The Death of Ivan Ilyich and Other Stories,* trans. Rosemary Edmonds (New York: Penguin, 1960), 157.

23. See Bernard Williams, "A Critique of Utilitarianism," in J.J.C. Smart and Bernard Williams, *Utilitarianism, For and Against* (Cambridge, U.K.: Cambridge University Press, 1973).

24. *The Independent,* April 16, 1992.

25. J. L. Mackie, *Ethics: Inventing Right and Wrong* (New York: Penguin, 1977).
26. See Dworkin, "Pragmatism, Right Answers, and True Banality."
27. I do not mean that while internal skepticism is true, we should try to shake it off and live in delusion. We have no more reason for thinking that it does not matter how we live, if we feel that it does, than the other way around. If we believe that it does matter, then that is what we think is true, even though others disagree, and it would be silly, and contradictory, to say that it isn't really true, or that we are just pretending it is.
28. *Airedale Trust (Respondents)* v. *Bland,* 45–6.
29. *The Varieties of Reference* (Oxford: Oxford University Press, 1982) was finished and revised by his colleague John McDowell, now a professor of philosophy at the University of Pittsburgh, and it has become a classic in the philosophy of language.
30. Philip Roth, *Patrimony* (New York: Simon & Schuster, 1991), 232–3.
31. Friedrich Nietzsche, "The Twilight of the Idols," in 16 *The Complete Works of Friedrich Nietzsche* 1, 88, Oscar Levy, ed., and Anthony M. Ludovici, trans. (Russell & Russell, 1909–11, 1964 reprint).
32. Richard John Neuhaus, "The Return of Eugenics," *Commentary* (April 1988), 22.
33. Byron L. Sherwin, "Jewish Views of Euthanasia," in M. Kohl, ed., *Beneficent Euthanasia* (Buffalo: Prometheus Books, 1975), 1, 7.

8   Life Past Reason

1. Doctors are now investigating treatments that include reducing the presence in the brain of toxic substances that may play a role in neurodegeneration, enhancing the supply of trophic factors (which facilitate neuronal repair and growth) and neurotransmitters that are missing or deficient in Alzheimer's patients, and controlling diet-related factors such as blood glucose levels that appear to affect mental functioning in the elderly. See Dennis J. Selkoe, "Aging Brain, Aging Mind," *Scientific American* 135 (September 1992); Robert J. Joynt, "Neurology," 268 *Journal of the American Medical Association* 380 (1992); and Andrew A. Skolnick, "Brain Researchers Bullish on Prospects for Preserving Mental Functioning in the Elderly," 267 *Journal of the American Medical Association* 2154 (1992).
2. Selkoe, "Amyloid Protein and Alzheimer's Disease," *Scientific American* (November 1991), 68.
3. OTA document, "Losing a Million Minds," OTA-BA-323 (1987), 14.
4. Legal provision and practices of custodial care are discussed in several of the papers contained in the OTA document, "Losing a Million Minds." For discussions of clinical diagnosis and histopathology, see, for example, Guy McKhann et al., "Clinical Diagnosis of Alzheimer's Disease: Report of the NINCDS-ADRDA Work Group Under the Auspices of Department of Health and Human Services Task Force on Alzheimer's Disease," 34 *Neurology* 939 (1984); Christine M. Hulette et al., "Evaluation of Cerebral Biopsies for the Diagnosis of Dementia," 49 *Archives of Neurology* 28 (1992); Selkoe, "Amyloid Protein and Alzheimer's Disease"; and M. Farlow et al., "Low Cerebrospinal-fluid Concentrations of Soluble Amyloid β-protein Precursor in Hereditary Alzheimer's Disease," 340 *The Lancet* 453 (1992).
5. Evans et al., "Estimated Prevalence of Alzheimer's Disease in the United States," 68 *Milbank Quarterly* 267 (1990).

6. In 1992, the continuing Framingham Study determined the prevalence of dementia in its study cohort as 23.8 percent from ages eighty-five to ninety-three. See Bachman et al., "Prevalence of dementia and probable senile dementia of the Alzheimer type in the Framingham Study," 42 *Neurology* 115 (January 1992). For a discussion of the differences between the studies cited in this and the preceding note, see Selkoe, "Aging Brain, Aging Mind."

7. See "UK: Dementia Condition Alzheimer's Disease Will Hit 750,000 in 30 Years," *The Guardian*, July 6, 1992.

8. Selkoe, "Amyloid Protein and Alzheimer's Disease," 68.

9. See Abstract, 267 *Journal of the American Medical Association* 2809, May 27, 1992 (summarizing Welch et al., "The Cost of Institutional Care in Alzheimer's Disease," 40 *Journal of the American Geriatric Society* 221 [1992]).

10. Nancy L. Mace and Peter V. Rabins, *The 36-Hour Day: A Family Guide to Caring for Persons with Alzheimer's Disease, Related Dementing Illnesses, and Memory Loss in Later Life* (Baltimore: The Johns Hopkins University Press, 1981, 1991).

11. See Andrew D. Firlik, "Margo's Logo," 265 *Journal of the American Medical Association,* (1991) 201.

12. I should mention another great practical problem about the relationship between a demented person and the competent person he once was. Should the resources available to a demented patient depend on what he actually put aside when he was competent, by way of insurance for his own care in that event? Insurance schemes, both private schemes and mandated public schemes, play an important part in the way we provide resources for catastrophes of different sorts. But is the insurance approach the proper model to use in thinking about provision for the demented? That must depend on whether we believe that a competent person has the appropriate prudential concern for the incompetent person he might become, and that in turn depends on knotty philosophical problems about the concept of personal identity. I cannot discuss, in this book, either that philosophical problem or any of the other serious problems about the justice of financing the extraordinarily expensive care of demented patients in different ways. I have discussed both at some length, however, in a report, "Philosophical Problems of Senile Dementia," written for the United States Congress Office of Technology Assessment in Washington, D.C., and available from that office.

13. See discussion in Allen E. Buchanan et al., "Surrogate Decision-Making for Elderly Individuals Who Are Incompetent or of Questionable Competence," November 1985, a report prepared for the Office of Technology Assessment.

14. See George J. Annas and Leonard H. Glantz, "Withholding and Withdrawing of Life-Sustaining Treatment for Elderly Incompetent Patients: A Review of Appellate Court Decisions," September 16, 1985, a report prepared for the Office of Technology Assessment.

15. I am assuming, in this discussion, that it can be in a person's overall best interests, at least sometimes, to force him to act otherwise than as he wants—that it can be in a person's overall best interests, for example, to be made not to smoke, even if we acknowledge that his autonomy is to some degree compromised, considered in itself, as against his interests.

16. Buchanan et al., "Surrogate Decision-Making."

17. There is an important debate in the economic literature on the question whether it can be rational to act against one's own best interests. The better view is that it can.

See, for example, Amartya Sen, "Rational Fools: A Critique of the Behavioral Foundations of Economic Theory," *Philosophy and Public Affairs* 6, no. 4 (Summer 1977).

18. See Buchanan et al., "Surrogate Decision-Making." Questions of task-sensitive competence are plainly relevant to the issues considered in the Buchanan report. But when the argument against surrogate decision making relies on the autonomy of the demented person affected by these decisions, the overall, non-task-sensitive sense of competence is also relevant.

19. Problems are presented for this judgment of overall integrity capacity when a patient appears only periodically capable of organizing his life around a system of desires and wishes. He seems able to take command of his life sometimes, and then lapses into a more serious stage of dementia, becoming lucid again only after a substantial intervening period, at which time the desires and interests he expresses are very different, or even contradictory. It would be a mistake to say that such a patient has the capacity for autonomy "periodically." The capacity autonomy presupposes is of necessity a temporally extended capacity: it is the capacity to have and act out of a personality.

20. In this note I would like to explore certain aspects of the distinction between experiential and critical interests that I do not discuss in the text, but which are especially relevant to the problems of the demented. Time plays different roles in the two kinds of interest, as we saw. Experiential interests are forward looking and therefore radically time sensitive. I may care about pain I have already suffered, but not as much or in the same way about pain to come. I want not to die soon, because this will cheat me of experiences to come, but I do not want already to have lived longer, that is, to have been born earlier than I was. Critical interests, in contrast, are not temporally indexed. If I want my life to include certain kinds of achievement only because these will make my life better, I will be indifferent as to whether the achievement is in the past or future. (As Bernard Williams has pointed out, some events or achievements can take place only at certain points in a person's life—his birth and his death, for example. These time-sensitive features are, we might say, constitutive of the events. I am discussing attitudes toward events that are not constitutively time sensitive in this way.) If I want my life to be longer because I count living longer in itself an achievement, as many people do, then I will indeed be equally pleased to discover that I was born earlier than I thought or that I will die later than I feared. Even more important, how someone's experiential judgments may conflict over time differs from how his critical judgments may. People's opinions about both kinds of interest often change. I might plan a particular experience for myself—I might carefully plan and budget for a trip—that I don't enjoy, or enjoy as much, as I thought I would. Or I might make an important decision—to become a lawyer and join the bar because I approve of a lawyer's life—and then, too late, sadly conclude that it was a wasted life. In each case, my later self disagrees with the judgment my earlier self made, but the nature of the disagreement is very different.

When my two selves disagree about an experiential interest, this shows that my original judgment, which was in the character of a prediction, was wrong. My earlier self made a mistake about what my later self would in fact enjoy. In the case of critical interests, a disagreement does not necessarily mean that the earlier self made any kind of mistake, for the earlier judgment was not a predictive one, and it is possible that the second, later judgment was the wrong one.

A fiduciary, who must act in the best interests of another, must attend to this distinction. He acts in that person's experiential interests if his decisions in fact lead to that person's enjoying his life more. It is more difficult to say when a fiduciary acts in someone's critical interests; we need a further distinction. A doctor acts in his patient's *subjective* critical interest when he changes the patient's life in a way the patient regards as an improvement. (For some purposes, we need a further subdivision here: a doctor acts in his patient's *ex ante* subjective evaluative interests when he improves his patient's life judged by the patient's standards at the time the decision is made, and in his patient's *ex post* subjective evaluative interests when he improves his patient's life judged by the patient's standards after the decision has had its effect.) A doctor acts in what he takes to be the patient's *genuine* critical interest when he changes the patient's life in a way that *he*, the doctor, believes makes it better. Sometimes these two senses of critical interest are in conflict: for example, a trustee may have to decide whether to allow a beneficiary to invade the corpus of a trust to start up a business that the trustee thinks degrading or unworthy.

These various distinctions between types of interest allow an improved statement of the forms and degrees of paternalism. They allow us to distinguish between stopping someone from taking drugs because we think he is ignorant of what the experiences that will follow will actually be like, or because we think it will lead to the kind of life he now disapproves of, or because it will lead to the kind of life we but not he disapproves of. The last is genuine moral paternalism, and it is almost always objectionable in the case of adults, when it can be avoided.

21. See Israel Rosenfield, *The Strange, Familiar, and Forgotten* (New York: Alfred A. Knopf, 1992).

22. See Alexander Reid, "Report Says Patient Would Prefer Death," Boston *Globe,* July 4, 1991, 13. The court arranged a temporary settlement under which Finelli was taken home and the hospital contributed to the costs of caring for him there, pending the result of a lawsuit the family had brought against it. See Alexander Reid, "Judge Orders Hospital to Pay for Brain-injured Man's Home Care Aid," Boston *Globe,* July 18, 1991, 33.

23. Understanding the requirements of dignity in this evaluative way helps explain a feature of the institution of dignity that seems at first puzzling. Most of us would think it wrong to permit a prisoner to choose to be tortured or mutilated and then released rather than serving a long jail term, even if we thought that the deterrent effect of the torture on other potential criminals would be as great as the deterrent effect of a jail sentence. We would think it an affront to a prisoner's dignity even to offer the option to him. The experiential account of dignity would condemn this opinion as irrational fastidiousness, because that account sees the vice of indignity only in its felt consequences for its victim, and so denies that it can be wrong to treat him in a way he would prefer. The evaluative account is different in two ways. First, it sees the vice of indignity in a relation between those who show and those who are shown indignity, and gives the former as well as the latter a stake in any decision that involves its display. We have a right not to act in ways that we believe deny our sense of the moral importance of someone else, even if he would prefer that we do. Second, the evaluative account supposes that the harm done to a victim of indignity is evaluative, whether or not it is also experiential. According to the evaluative account, therefore, the harm may be genuine even when it is unrecognized, and worse than some alternative for the victim even when he thinks it better.

ACKNOWLEDGMENTS

The title *Life's Dominion* was suggested by Dylan Thomas's poem "And Death Shall Have No Dominion." Several arguments in the book were first presented, experimentally, in lectures—including an Oliver Wendell Holmes Lecture at Harvard University in the fall of 1990, a Leon Lecture at the University of Pennsylvania later in 1990, and a Melvin Nimmer Lecture at the University of California at Los Angeles in 1991—and the audience at each lecture made helpful comments. The book incorporates, in re-worked and elaborated form, certain material already published in law reviews and other articles, including the greater part of an article, "Unenumerated Rights: Whether and How *Roe* v. *Wade* Should be Overruled," in the *University of Chicago Law Review*, which was in turn based on a lecture given at the University of Chicago Law School in 1991 at a symposium celebrating the bicentennial of the American Bill of Rights. I am grateful to the editors of that review for many suggestions and citations.

Portions of the manuscript were discussed in the Colloquium on Philosophy, Law and Society at New York University, and I benefited from the comments of participants, including Lea Brilmayer, Francis Kamm, Lewis Kornhauser, Linda McClain, Nancy Morowitz, David Richards, William Ruddick, Larry Sager, and Sibyl Schwartzenbach. Thomas Nagel has discussed the themes of the book with me over a great many occasions, and his penetrating comments had great influence, as they always have. Bernard Williams taught a seminar on the manuscript with me in Oxford in 1992, and the impact of his characteristically inventive challenges and suggestions is pervasive. Susan Hurley and Joseph Raz made very useful comments in other discussions of chapters of the book, and Derek Parfit and Gerald Cohen each wrote long, generous, and searching comments on the manuscript, as did Nicos Stavropoulos and Mark Greenberg. John Finnis saved me from mistakes about the history of Catholicism and abortion, and Mary Finlay, S.C., gave me invaluable information about recent developments in Ireland. Richard Posner made several helpful comments in the course of preparing for our exchange in the symposium at Chicago. Anand Agneshwar, Alex Gendzier, and Sharon Perley, of the New York University Law School, were superb research assistants; so was Alice Hofheimer, who helped me with unfailing carefulness and imagination from the beginning to the end. Each of these gifted students made this book better and my life easier. Bobby Jindal and Sujit Choudhry, at Oxford, supplied valuable medical and health-care information. Lynn Nesbit and Lydia Wills, my incomparable agents, persuaded me to write the book, and have been helpful in a hundred ways throughout. My editor, Elisabeth Sifton, has a striking ability to see an author's thought from the inside, through his eyes, but often more clearly, and the book was sharply improved by her advice about when I should say more and when (more often) less. George Andreou of Knopf guided me patiently and cheerfully through a daunting number of publishing decisions. Stuart Proffitt, of Harper/Collins in Britain, contributed important editorial suggestions and helped to make the book more international. My secretary at New York

University, Lynn Gilbert, was efficient, warm, overworked, and inventive. Betsy Dworkin provided, as always, fierce criticism and angelic encouragement. Finally, I thank the Filomen D'Agostino and Max E. Greenberg Research Fund of New York University, and Dean John Sexton of that school, for generous support. Of course no one on this long list agrees with everything in the book; some of them disagree with a good deal.

INDEX